"In the digital economy, the relationship capital that companies develop with their customers is more valuable than traditional assets such as factories or office buildings. *The Relationship-Based Enterprise* offers comprehensive insight as to how your company can move beyond simply touting your products and sustain a dialogue with your customers that benefits both them and you."

Don Tapscott
Chair of Digital 4Sight
Author of *Digital Economy* and co-author of the recently published *Digital Capital: Harnessing the Power of Business Webs*

"A winner! Ray McKenzie captures the essence of the changes that customers and enterprises face as they navigate the emerging, high velocity world of (e)business. Fresh new perspectives on the age-old challenge of attracting and retaining customers, and yet built on rock-solid fundamentals. As the chapters unfold, the term "common sense" comes to mind. But really, it is the elegance of fundamental truths clearly articulated and integrated. Do your customers a BIG favor and read this book!"

Barry Shuler
Senior Vice-President, IR Strategy & Planning
Marriott International

"A powerful book tackling the conventional knowledge of CRM initiatives and how organizations meet the challenges. McKenzie recognizes that CRM initiatives require significant financial commitments from companies for consistent contribution to real business value. Ray provides an intriguing and compelling view of how an organization needs to define and solve the many attributes of a truly customer focused and driven company. *The Relationship-Based Enterprise* provides more than theory or vision but strikes a balance from multi-media interactions to business practices and balancing enabling technologies for engaging solutions. More of a road map than a desired state, exactly what we need today, insight to the compelling tactical challenges of CRM deployment in an easy to understand format."

Wayne H. Watson
VP of Customer Care Strategy & Planning
AT&T Broadband

"At Chase, we believe that the right relationship is everything. The value of Customer Relationship Management (CRM) to an organization and its continued success is extolled in this thought-provoking book. It will help us raise the bar on an already high client satisfaction rating."

Vincent J. Cassidy
Vice President
Chase Treasury Solutions

"Creating and maintaining a relationship with our customer is a key element of success for us. Given the changing nature of customer expectations and technology, any company that does not do this well is putting themselves at risk. This insightful and useful book can help any company develop and answer the critical questions needed to establish lasting and successful relationships, or 'conversations' with their customers."

David Hainline
Executive Vice-President and Chief Operating Officer
Chapters Online

"Someone once told me that CRM was five times more difficult to implement than ERP and 100 times more valuable. After reading this book I understand why and now know where to focus my attention so it's a success for my company."

Art Smith
Vice-President, Information Systems
TransCanada Pipelines Limited

"An excellent book, which has filled in the missing pieces in our e-business strategy."

Jos Mensink
E-Business Manager
Water Corporation
Western Australia

"This book takes the hype out of the term 'CRM' and transforms the term into a practical reality. It provides real solutions for creating a customer centric organization, and provides a roadmap for moving into the next business revolution: The Relationship Revolution."

Anita O'Hara,
Vice-President, Customer Services
UrbanMedia

"This book is bulging at the seams with clear, usable information about CRM. It takes the reader beyond the intellectual to the world of how-to-make-it-work. It is must reading for those serious about building and sustaining customer relationships that 'win mindshare, increase walletshare, and reduce churn'."

Marsha Sampson Johnson
Vice President, Customer Services
Alabama Power Company

"Must read for companies transitioning to a customer-centric, relationship-based enterprise. Offers valuable additional insight for those organizations that provide Internet-enabled care for their customers."

Brad Cunic
Vice President
Fluor Global Services

the **Relationship-Based Enterprise**

Powering Business Success
Through Customer Relationship
Management

Ray McKenzie

McGraw-Hill Ryerson

Toronto Montréal Boston Burr Ridge, IL Dubuque, IA Madison, WI New York
San Francisco St. Louis Bangkok Bogotá Caracas Kuala Lumpur Lisbon
London Madrid Mexico City Milan New Delhi Santiago Seoul
Singapore Sydney Taipei

McGraw-Hill
Ryerson Limited

A Subsidiary of The McGraw-Hill Companies

ISBN: 0-07-086081-5

234567890 TRI 0987654321
Printed and bound in Canada.

Canadian Cataloguing in Publication Data

McKenzie, Ray, 1946–

The relationship-based enterprise: powering business success through customer relationship management

Includes bibliographical references and index.

ISBN 0-07-086081-5

1. Customer relations. I. DMR Consulting. Center for Strategic Leadership. II. Title.

HF5415.5.M24   2000   658.8'12   C00-932941-2

Publisher: **Joan Homewood**
Editorial Co-ordinator: **Catherine Leek**
Production Co-ordinator: **Susanne Penny**
Developmental Editor: **Michelle Reed**
Editor: **Lynn Schellenberg**
Interior Page Design and Electronic Page Composition: **Heidy Lawrance Associates**
Cover Design: **Brian Boucher** and **Dianna Little**

Also by DMR Consulting's Center for Stategic Leadership: *The Information Paradox*, John Thorp (007-560103-6)

TABLE OF CONTENTS

For
Melissa
and
Todd

FOREWORD

Information technology offers the potential to reap huge business benefits. Customer Relationship Management (CRM) specifically offers significant opportunities for organizations to better understand and serve their customers, and, in doing so, to increase their return on existing and new business ventures. On the darker side, it also offers opportunities to squander critical resources with no resulting benefit, and in doing so to put the very survival of organizations at risk.

Generating business value from technology remains a big *management* challenge for many organizations. My earlier book, *The Information Paradox: Realizing the Business Benefits of Information Technology*, which I co-authored with DMR Consulting, focused on the dichotomy between rapid increases in IT spending and increased management questioning of the value of IT, based on less than stellar business results. One of the main causes of the information paradox is *silver-bullet thinking*, the naïve belief that technology alone can deliver business benefits. At the time, silver-bullet thinking was prevalent in technology-enabled Business Process Re-engineering (BPR) initiatives and the implementation of Enterprise Resource Planning systems (ERPs). In both cases, there was a mixed track record of success and failure—with far too many organizations disappointed in the business results of their investments.

Two years have passed since the publication of *The Information Paradox*. In that time, our discussions with hundreds of organizations across the world have shown that the information paradox remains prevalent and universal. It was certainly in evidence during the recent rush to adopt new e-business models—and the subsequent bust in the dotcom sector. Silver-bullet thinking often accompanies technological progress. In fact, the faster the pace of technological change, the richer the potential of the technology, the greater are the risks of silver-bullet thinking. Today, the telltale signs are evident in a number of e-business sectors, including customer relationship management.

With this book, Ray McKenzie and his team from DMR Consulting's Center for Strategic Leadership pick up the DMR thought leadership baton. They take an in-depth look at how to generate business value from customer relationship management —a sector of the new e-world with very high potential. They start from the platform created by *The Information Paradox*, observing that too many organizations approach CRM as a technology implementation challenge, when in fact it is about change—major organizational change and change in customer relationships. What emerges is not the story of CRM software packages and individual CRM solutions but rather the story of the Relationship-Based Enterprise.

This book confirms the central conclusion of *The Information Paradox*—that the reality in today's e-world is that managers are no longer implementing technology, they are implementing change. It presents a management *and* technology story that will stand the test of time, and that will help shape the future of Customer Relationship Management.

I encourage you to read on!

John Thorp
Author of *The Information Paradox*
Fellow, DMR Consulting

PREFACE

More than ever, technological advance appears to hold the key to sustained economic growth. Advanced computing technologies are used for everything from prospecting for new veins of gold to discovering customer preferences. The Internet can be used to open a new market on the other side of the world, to organize a global e-auction, or to have an intimate dialogue with the "consumer next door." Or all three.

The technologies of the "new economy" have immense potential. Some experts believe this potential will power a long boom, while others claim this is wishful thinking. Whatever you believe, the fact is that business decision-makers operate in an uncertain world. They must find those special links between a new technology and a new business opportunity. They know first hand that there are no "sure things" or magic success formulas. This much is clear from the boom-to-bust cycle in the development of the so-called dotcom sector of corporate North America. Both the risks and the rewards are there for all to see.

DMR Consulting is dedicated to the proposition that managers *can* bring the risks of technological innovation in line with the rewards. That technology-enabled business transformation can be actively *managed* to produce business results. That organizations *can* harness technology instead of being driven by it.

This DMR Consulting philosophy applies in spades to Customer Relationship Management (CRM)—one of the significant potential growth stories of the Internet business age. CRM holds out visions of how advanced software can be used to create 360-degree views of the customer, "lock in" customers for life, and dazzle them with "seamless branded experiences." Ambitious CRM visions have helped create boom-time values in those e-companies promising to create loyal customer bases and dominant e-brands —sometimes overnight.

In fact, there is a big gap between these CRM visions and the reality of implementation. The CRM field is still emerging and not yet mature. DMR Consulting research and consulting experience shows that the deployment is fragmented and that there are multiple definitions of CRM. As often happens, some organizations focus too heavily on silver-bullet information technology (IT) solutions, leaving out many business considerations. A bottom-line conclusion: the increasing amounts of money being spent on CRM are not being consistently translated into business value.

This gap between vision and reality creates a big management challenge, just the kind of challenge that appeals to our people. Our clients want CRM solutions. They are prepared to invest significant amounts of money in CRM—or already have done so. But the technology is not "plug and play." If there is one word that summarizes our clients' experience with CRM, it is *complexity*. The visions are simple, but the realities of implementation are complex—touching virtually every process in the enterprise.

Ray McKenzie and his team from DMR Consulting's Center for Strategic Leadership cut through the complexity of CRM, combining a fresh perspective on customer relationships with a practical management framework for handling CRM initiatives. The basic point: CRM is not about changing your software but about changing *customer relationships*. Many CRM solutions assume that relationships are things or assets that can be managed internally by the enterprise. Ray and his team take a different approach. They point out that a relationship is a process of human interaction. A relationship is defined formally as a *series of "conversations"*—meaning not just talk but many types of interactive exchange. This definition captures the true potential of CRM in the Internet era. It is a potential for *interactive exchanges* that happen not only on corporate Web sites but also in open chat rooms, not only in one-way delivery channels but also in interactive Web communities.

In the industrial world, organizations were engaged in mass marketing, delivering "messages" to undifferentiated hordes. Today, the Internet and other new technologies are enabling the market to converse. Companies must now figure out how to enter this global conversation, how to move from monologue to dialogue—and from delivering traditional services to engaging in value-adding conversations. The goal of CRM solutions is to "improve the conversation."

Looking at relationships as conversations has major implications both for the design of CRM solutions and the design of business organizations.

Most CRM solutions today focus on internal integration. Their goal is to pull together an *integrated* enterprise-wide strategy that covers all channels, lines of business, products, and customer databases. This is good—as far as it goes. This book, however, explains why internal enterprise integration is important, but not enough to retain customers and gain new ones. The bigger CRM challenge is to *connect* with customers—through conversation.

A new type of organization—the Relationship-Based Enterprise —is emerging, one that converses with customers rather than managing traditional customer relationships. The Relationship-Based Enterprise places CRM in a broader context, matching the "yin" of enterprise CRM with "yang" of how customers view the enterprise from the outside. It creates value *with* the customers rather than delivering value *to* customers. Rather than targeting customers, it becomes a target—playing the role of the hunted rather than the hunter. We believe the Relationship-Based Enterprise will be one of the major organizational forms of the 21st century, just as the assembly line and the multi-divisional corporation were in the last century.

The Relationship-Based Enterprise is a vision of the future. It points out a path for organizations to follow to reach the next level of CRM. It grows from DMR Consulting's vision of the *extended enterprise*—a model that is being used today to help our clients extend and link their information systems and business processes with those of their customers, business partners, and suppliers.

Happily, the vision of a Relationship-Based Enterprise can be translated into action, and this book shows how to proceed. It provides a management framework that defines "the 3Ds" of CRM—*discovery* of customers, *dialogue* in the relationship, and *discipline* in management. The framework is used to walk managers through ten critical questions about Customer Relationship Management. The end product is a no-nonsense practical guide to the key issues and an operational approach to implementing CRM across the enterprise. Business and technology executives gain a comprehensive view that includes all components—business, organization, technology, people, and process.

The management framework captures the practical insights of DMR Consulting clients who graciously agreed to share how they dealt with tough CRM implementation issues. We are very thankful to them. We hope that sharing this knowledge will help all of us implement CRM to become more profitable and find those sometimes-elusive links between technology and business growth.

This is the third book we have published over the last decade with McGraw-Hill Ryerson. Our last book, *The Information Paradox: Realizing the Business Benefits of Information Technology*, focused on understanding how to get value from your large IT-enabled investments. This book goes one step further. It goes to the heart of what makes CRM successful, especially if you have had difficulties integrating your CRM programs and harvesting benefits.

I would like to conclude by thanking the people in our organization who carried the torch for this book, which was truly born out of passion and determination. Bringing together so many senior, experienced people in an organization is no easy feat. Their willingness to share their knowledge with the world deserves appreciation and recognition.

Michael J. Poehner
Chief Executive Officer
DMR Consulting

ACKNOWLEDGMENTS

Much of the thinking in this book has been inspired by my association with original thinkers. Immense intellectual debts are owed to all the co-authors, who have participated under the auspices of DMR Consulting's Center for Strategic Leadership. The Center's mission is to develop processes and techniques to apply information technology (IT) intelligently in a wide range of business situations. As business becomes more and more dependent on IT, and as the Internet is used to support vital functions, the Center for Strategic Leadership is able to continuously create new applied knowledge by leveraging the expertise and experience of DMR's management consultants worldwide.

All the co-authors unselfishly contributed their experience and knowledge to make this book better, often under severe time pressures. In particular, I wish to thank the following members of our book team (in alphabetical order):

Pam Allen (Birmingham, Alabama) contributed valuable knowledge of Customer Relationship Management, particularly with regard to opening dialogues with customers, and provided important insights into the business and IT management challenges of CRM. **Linda Bulmer** (Fredericton, Canada) brought her ingenuity and her extensive experience in benefits realization, customer interaction, and measurement. Her creativity and insight from the beginning of this journey made her participation invaluable. **Ian Campbell** (London, United Kingdom) provided an astute perspective on business and IT executives' issues and a complete suite of customer discovery processes and techniques. He helped us challenge and clarify our thinking by providing us with unique experience and insights into CRM. **Ron Gardoll** (Sydney, Australia) offered his experience in electronic commerce and channel selection. We thank him for his wit and intellectual companionship and for his immense contribution. **Scott Green** (Seattle, Washington) contributed both creative ideas and a pragmatic perspective on measurement issues as well as on several of the underlying frameworks, in particular the exchange space. His thought leadership has been crucial to the development of the ideas in this book. **Cheryl White** (Denver, Colorado) brought to the team her expertise in change management and in approaches to the creation of nimble CRM environments by treating organizations as complex, adaptive systems. Her genius and wonderful ideas were greatly appreciated. **Chris Ogden** (London, United Kingdom) brought his extensive experience on how to mobilize organizations for the future and help them shift from a forecasting to a visioning stance. His concepts and contributions on the subject of the long-term evolution of CRM have added lasting value to this book. **Sean O'Shea** (Edison, New Jersey) shared his vast knowledge of and experience with CRM, the telecommunications industry, and how to give customers more control over relationships. He also guided us through key segments of the intellectual debate. **Derek Stevens** (Los Angeles, California) contributed his expertise in enterprise architecture and applied it to exploring how companies should organize to move value closer to customers. He led the way in defining the IT questions associated with business issues. **Connie Whitmore** (Edison, New Jersey) brought to the team her rigor, in-depth knowledge, and wealth of client experience related to developing CRM strategies for clients, planning customer interaction channels, and translating those plans into operational models. She provided key insights into how customers want to interact.

I am especially indebted to my visionary editorial advisors, **Lew Diggs** and **Scott Swink**, for their skillful shaping of this book, allowing its best qualities to emerge. Lew assumed a creative role in transforming the work of our practice into an integrated story, exploring key topics as well as contributing knowledge around dialogue and the potential discontinuities that may impact CRM. Scott brought a fresh perspective to the project when it was most needed and played a vital role in editing and sharpening the focus of the manuscript. Their distinctive styles and their understanding of both technology and business were critical to the presentation of the concepts, ideas, and frameworks of the Relationship-Based Enterprise.

I also want to acknowledge the work of Julie Monette, who brought her unique skills at managing projects—and consultants—and acted as the safety net for the entire project and the lighthouse in tough times.

Special thanks are due to Jacques Pigeon and Jean-Marc Nantais. Their support, guidance, and insight were invaluable from the beginning to the end of this very challenging project. They conceived the project and championed it through thick and thin. Without their commitment, this book would never have been completed.

In addition, this book captures knowledge and insight from many DMR Consulting practitioners. I would like to express gratitude to contributors who reviewed our work at various stages of development and provided valuable suggestions and insights into CRM. They include (in alphabetical order): Alan Ahrens, Manuel Alcoba, Alan Anderson, Mick Batali, William Beck, Paul Blackburn, Warren Berkan, Sharon Carroll, Jimmy Cornet, Dan DeMatteis, Don Edwards (AG Solutions), Barbara Evans, Beverly Goins, Cesar Moro Gonzalez, Coleman Hanover, Betty Hodkinson, Kenneth Hopkins, George Irwin, Mary Beth Keelty, Kerry Kirk, Gerry Kohlmeyer, Murray Kronick, Guy Lagace, Andrew Lamb, Ed Leskauskas, Tim Merriam, Kevin Mulcahy, Genevieve O'Sullivan, Kelly Pascoe, Sergey Podlazov, Darryl Salisbury, Kim Sealy,

Ted Turner, Mark Wheat. And there were many others who provided important suggestions that helped shape this book. We owe special thanks to Paul Bradish for his strategic input on managing change in a CRM environment. His ideas, insights, and experience were invaluable to Chapter 15.

This book would have been for naught if it did not reflect the practical realities of management and executive decision-making. I know that our entire team is grateful to the many organizations, including our clients, for their extraordinary generosity in freely sharing their CRM experiences, challenges, and successes. In this respect, we thank (in alphabetical order): Alabama Power, American Express Bank Ltd., AT&T, Avaya (formerly the Enterprise Networks Group of Lucent Technologies Inc.), British Gas Trading, Cadillac Jack, Clearnet, Homeside Lending Inc., Nortel Networks, Quebec Institute of Statistics, and SBC Communications Inc. Gwen Ball from Centrica deserves special mention. We are deeply indebted to her and Centrica for freely sharing their experiences, challenges and successes.

We all appreciated the genuine help and intellectual support of the team at McGraw-Hill Ryerson. To them we give special thanks for giving us the opportunity to publish another book. Their confidence in us and patience were overwhelming.

Finally, I know I speak for the entire team when I say thank you to those who provided moral support throughout this effort, and who unselfishly sacrificed weekends and vacations so that we could complete this book—our families and friends.

Ray McKenzie
November 2000

INTRODUCTION

*"A small percentage of positive growth is
expected this year."*

*"The increase marks the 31st consecutive
quarter of year-over-year earnings growth."*

*"The push for better performance
may trim projected growth."*

Growth, growth, and more growth. It's the measure of business
success. From the lowliest start-up to the world's largest corporation,
companies worldwide are trying to meet expectations for
growth held by analysts, observers, and investors. Just pick up a
newspaper, any newspaper, and turn to the business section. It's
easy to find an article with a comment on growth: "Coming off a
year of tremendous growth, the company decides to ..."; or, on
the downside, "Analysts have downgraded the company from a
strong buy to a hold, based on projections for growth in the next
quarter." Without growth there is little interest, and a natural suspicion
of impending disaster.

So how do companies achieve growth and garner business
success? Product innovation, commitment to quality, strategic
acquisitions, marketing campaigns, and advertising all contribute
to growth—but the costs are considerable. To reduce these costs
while achieving the needed growth, companies are seeking ways to
build customer loyalty. They want to win mind share, increase
wallet share, and reduce churn. These are the goals of Customer
Relationship Management (CRM).

The vision of CRM—a 360-degree view of the customer, and a seamless customer experience—is dazzling. The reality, of course, is somewhat different. In working with clients, we have found that many companies have put in place parts of a CRM program to accomplish such a vision, but few have pulled together an integrated company-wide strategy covering all channels, lines of business, and products. People issues, organizational issues, business issues, and the complexity of the needed information systems make CRM initiatives time-consuming, costly, and downright difficult. And as if that weren't enough, CRM by itself does not appear to be a complete solution for achieving customer loyalty—because CRM is still too focused on the enterprise rather than on what's really happening with its customers. As a consequence, enterprises tend to interpret customer actions as loyalty where none, in fact, exists.

For example, savvy business travelers often belong to more than one frequent-flier program. Some even stuff their wallets with frequent-flier cards from all the airlines. If they choose one airline more than the others, it's probably because that airline accepts more of their frequent-flier points, has a seat available, or maintains a convenient schedule of flights to where they want to go. But the moment this situation changes—because of competition from another airline, or because the business traveler needs to fly to a new destination—well, it's out with the old airline and in with the new. One airline thinks it has lost a loyal customer and the other thinks it has gained one. Both are wrong.

A customer may purchase products and services from a vendor several times, based on a positive sales experience and value received, and then never purchase from that vendor again. If another vendor offers a similar sales experience and more value, the customer moves on.

This is not to say that customer loyalty no longer exists. But it's getting harder and harder to lock customers into loyalty programs. Thanks to the Internet, customers are better informed, more demanding, and more in the driver's seat than ever before.

They can choose suppliers from anywhere on the globe at the click of a mouse. In this highly competitive environment, targeting customer lock-in to achieve lifetime loyalty—and profits—is probably an illusion.

So if customers won't lock in, where does that leave CRM? Integration of CRM initiatives end-to-end will certainly not yield the anticipated results, and enterprise-wide integration is probably not achievable, anyway. The fact is, the fundamental nature of business relationships is changing. Companies slow to grasp this fact, and who focus too strongly on integration of the CRM solution within their enterprise, will find themselves unable to build and sustain the levels of growth required for business success. They will have only half of the answer. They need a more balanced vision to find the full answer.

An emerging organizational model for the 21st century, the Relationship-Based Enterprise, provides that vision. The Relationship-Based Enterprise places CRM in a broader context, matching the "yin" of enterprise CRM with the "yang" of how customers view the enterprise from the outside. It offers a model for establishing long-term relationships with customers who can find alternative suppliers in a minute. This model structures the "white spaces" that exist between the enterprise and its customers, as well as the economic exchanges or "conversations" that occur in these spaces so that relationships can be sustained. It is aimed at those organizations that have tried to leverage one or more of the components of CRM, but have yet to get the benefits expected from those investments.

A Relationship-Based Enterprise builds customer relationships—and sustained business growth—in a world where loyalty programs no longer lock customers in for a lifetime.

A New View of Relationships

Relationship-Based Enterprises take a new and different view of relationships. A relationship—with a customer, a business partner, or between organizations—is not a thing. It is not an asset that, once established, automatically lasts a lifetime. Instead, it is a process of human interaction—and a constant work in progress. It involves far more than just the simple exchange of money for products or services.

For the Relationship-Based Enterprise, a relationship is a series of "conversations." These conversations consist of (1) a set of economic exchanges, (2) the offering that is the subject of the exchange, (3) the space in which the exchange occurs, and (4) the context of the exchange—all that is known about the customer. Given this definition, it is easy to see that relationships do not just "happen." Rather, they are the result of management decisions—decisions about the best way to design and execute conversations. And a successful Relationship-Based Enterprise treats all relationships as conversations.

The Internet and other communication technologies have opened the door to many types of interactive conversations, business-to-business (B2B), business-to-consumer (B2C), and intra-organizational. These conversations include talking, buying, selling, serving, and trading. They can start and end quickly, or they may be carried out over an extended period of time. And one conversation may lead to another. This means that some relationships may be relatively short-lived, while others may last a lifetime.

Thinking about relationships in this way allows organizations to design, build, and sustain relationships, conversation by conversation.

The Importance of Conversations

In the past, many enterprises operated successfully by securing relationships with their suppliers and those that they supplied (their customers), through ownership, agreement, contract, or partnership. Such relationships often necessitated the integration of the enterprise's business processes and information systems with those same suppliers and customers. This kind of integration created exit barriers—locking enterprise to enterprise. But all of this has changed. The Internet provides a way for organizations to more easily connect, disconnect, and reconnect. This freedom and independence from customized and special interfaces means that something more than integration is required to sustain a relationship. Conversations are that something more.

The Relationship-Based Enterprise ensures that conversations are taking place, and that the enterprise remembers everything about individual customers and its conversations with those customers. The Relationship-Based Enterprise has the ability to recognize and create conversations with different types of customers because it understands the kind of conversation that each wants. It also uses those conversations to continually discover its customers and to make decisions concerning how it will organize itself to serve those customers. It can have a conversation with buyers or users, or simply with shoppers; with those who want to be involved in the creation of the product or service; or with those who want control over the delivery of the solutions being sought. The Relationship-Based Enterprise is a vision of what companies can become when they treat relationships as conversations.

A Relationship Management Framework

Relationship-Based Enterprises are starting to emerge as one of the major organizational forms of the 21st century, just as the mass production assembly line and the multi-divisional corporation were in the last century. Companies moving to embrace this new organizational form are seeking ways to apply the understanding that relationships are conversations, so that they can make the necessary management decisions and take the appropriate actions. Figure 1 provides a framework for these decisions and actions.

Figure 1: *The Relationship Management Framework*

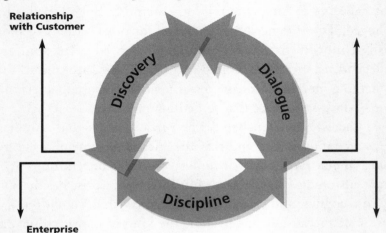

As illustrated, the Relationship-Based Enterprise requires special competencies in discovery, dialogue, and discipline. This is because the value a Relationship-Based Enterprise provides to its customers is not in any specific product or service, but is created through the conversations that it has with its customers.

Discovery focuses on the customer. It is centered on learning. And it is the basis for recognizing, remembering and understanding customers. Since "perfect information" about customers is not possible, discovery is the only realistic and practical alternative. Discovery also balances any internal bias toward cost by focusing the energies of the enterprise on both costs and revenue.

Dialogue focuses on the relationship. It is centered on conversation and ensuring that value is created in every conversation with a customer. Since the "perfect product or service" is not possible, dialogue is the only realistic and practical alternative. Dialogue balances any internal bias toward products and services, by focusing the energies of the enterprise both internally (on products and services) and externally (on customers).

Discipline focuses on the management decisions that must be taken concerning the organizational and management mechanisms that enable continued discovery and dialogue. Since the "perfect organization" is not possible, discipline is the only realistic and practical alternative. Discipline balances any internal bias toward integration, by focusing the energies of the enterprise on both internal integration and external connections.

Discovery, dialogue, and discipline are not just "to do" lists for managers. In particular, they are not a sequence of tasks or steps. Rather, they are a management focus, the day-to-day preoccupations, that create a Relationship-Based Enterprise.

Ten Critical Questions

To help companies move towards the new organizational form, the Relationship-Based Enterprise, and to improve the effectiveness of CRM initiatives, there are ten critical questions to answer. These have been identified as the most critical from amongst the literally hundreds associated with CRM initiatives. The questions have been grouped under discovery, dialogue, and discipline, and are discussed at length in Parts II, III, and IV of this book.

The ten critical questions are:

Discovery
1. "Who are our customers?"
2. "What do our customers want and expect?"
3. "What is the value potential of our customers?"

Dialogue
4. "What kind of relationship do we want to build with our customers?"
5. "How do we foster exchange?"
6. "How do we work together and share control?"

Discipline
7. "Who are we?"
8. "How do we organize to move value closer to our customers?"
9. "How do we measure and manage our performance?"
10. "How do we increase our capacity for change?"

By examining these questions within the context of the Relationship Management Framework, as illustrated in Figure 2, executives will be able to guide: (1) the evolution of their relationships with customers; (2) the creation of a company-wide relationship management game plan; and (3) the selection of solutions with the most appropriate combination of technology.

Figure 2: *Ten Critical Questions for Relationship Management*

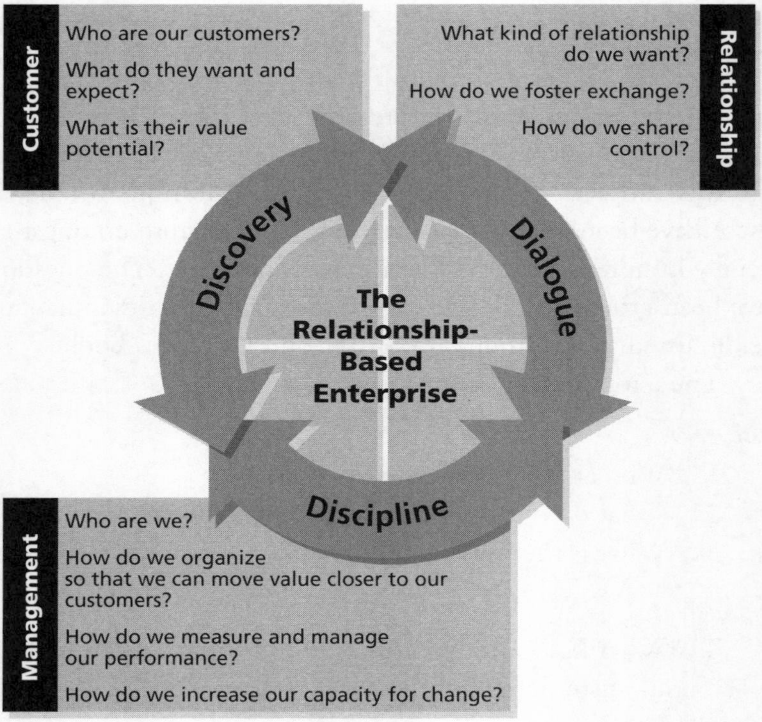

Finally, Another Paradigm Shift?

In the new economy, business managers seem to wake up every day to the news of some new paradigm. Each threatens to destroy the enterprise as it is known. But even with the constant waves of change hitting organizations, the sky is not falling. Building strong relationships with customers is a business strategy that has been employed for a very long time to sustain growth and to increase the profitability of a business. The Relationship-Based Enterprise, which includes CRM, is merely a logical extension of what has gone before.

The intent of this book is to describe the Relationship-Based Enterprise and CRM in simple, clear, hype-free language. The text cuts through the confusion and jargon that is a part of the new economy to provide business and technology executives with a no-nonsense and practical guide. It defines issues, presents options, and provides examples of the choices made by others.

Paradigm shifts ebb and flow. But good relationships—with customers, suppliers, and other businesses—have been the keystone of business for thousands of years. *The Relationship-Based Enterprise —Powering Business Success through Customer Relationship Management* offers a simple and straightforward set of frameworks for building and sustaining relationships based on conversations. It helps you ask, and answer, the right set of questions. In sum, it enables organizations to understand how current CRM initiatives can be made to sustain growth and power business success.

The Relationship-Based Enterprise and Customer Relationship Management

1

CHAPTER

The Relationship-Based Enterprise

Ah, but a man's reach should exceed his grasp,
Or what's a heaven for?
—Robert Browning,
"Andrea Del Sarto," 1855

Companies, like people, strive for perfection. And companies involved in Customer Relationship Management (CRM) initiatives are no different. But what if the perfect CRM initiative lies forever beyond their grasp? What if CRM "heaven" doesn't exist?

Perfect information about customers is a major tenet of CRM. To obtain this information, companies invest in computer and information systems that are specifically aimed at assembling, refining, and honing large, integrated customer databases. This investment, involving millions of dollars, is supposed to enable dramatic improvements in marketing, such as the targeting of individual customers and the tailoring of products and services to meet these customers' specific needs, thereby turning them into long-term loyal customers. And a complete, 360-degree view of customers is supposed to deliver the capability to cross-sell and up-sell, giving companies an increased share of their customers' wallets, minimizing the cost of acquiring new customers, reducing churn, and thus fueling growth.

A new breed of companies, moving toward an emerging organizational model—the Relationship-Based Enterprise—has begun to question whether CRM by itself can deliver these benefits.

Characteristics of the Relationship-Based Enterprise

Imagine an organization unconcerned about whether or not it has perfect information about its customers. An organization that doesn't focus on customer loyalty and that is not concerned about accurately targeting a particular market segment. That accepts it will never have the perfect product or service. That is just not interested in the perfect process for dealing with each customer.

Such an organization might seem disconnected from reality and bound for failure.

But the truth is things change. For example, five years ago, who knew that new companies without profits—the dotcommers—would be worth billions? Or, that a corporate giant with nearly a century of experience, such as the *Encyclopaedia Britannica*, would be brought to the brink of bankruptcy? While the owners of *Encyclopaedia Britannica* spent time and energy improving an already excellent product, their customers were buying computers that not only came with free encyclopedia software, such as Microsoft Encarta, but that also provided access to a whole new world of on-line information. The *Encyclopaedia Britannica*, one of the best paper-based references in the world, suddenly seemed old-fashioned—and very expensive.

The new economy is dominated by incredible competition, where customers can choose from a wide variety of suppliers, products, and channels. The Internet allows individual consumers, and not just large multinational companies, to shop the world over for a supplier that meets their needs. And when consumers change the way they choose products and services, institutions like *Encyclopaedia Britannica* suffer. Out of touch with what their customers really wanted, and perhaps lulled into complacency by the brand loyalty of days gone by, they were slow to recognize a new reality—that customers today are playing a much stronger role in business relationships.

The most successful new companies—the Amazons, the eBays, the Yahoos, and many others—deeply understand this new reality. They are not just "enabled" by the Internet; they "get" it. And in aggregate, they exhibit characteristics of an emerging organizational model—the Relationship-Based Enterprise. Its characteristics are not yet fully formed, so a rigorous and formal definition of this model would be premature. However, certain characteristics already stand out clearly.

The Relationship-Based Enterprise is Conversation-Centered

Rather than striving to acquire perfect information about customers, or to produce perfect goods and services, or to build perfect processes, the Relationship-Based Enterprise engages its customers in *conversations*, as detailed in Chapter 3, "The New Language of Relationships."

This concern with conversations, as opposed to transactions, distinguishes the Relationship-Based Enterprise from the traditional enterprise. Unlike a transaction-centered enterprise, the Relationship-Based Enterprise knows that it must do more than focus on each "moment of truth" or each individual transaction. It knows that its customers are constantly changing. And it knows that conversation is the only way that it will be able to discover who its customers are, what they want, and what they expect. Instead of delivering a monologue to its customers, it engages its customers in conversations that are true dialogues.

All Relationships are Handled as Conversations

The Relationship-Based Enterprise also recognizes that to provide products and services that meet the demands of its customers, it must engage its suppliers and partners in this same kind of conversation. And so it treats all relationships as if they were conversations. The Relationship-Based Enterprise deals with every relationship —whether it is with a customer, supplier, regulator, stakeholder, partner, or employee—in the same way. And this approach entails changing the very nature of all communications.

Conversation has always been a part of a business relationship. But for many years, customers could only converse with sales people or assistants in stores. Now, fueled by the technologies of the communications revolution, interactive exchange is both technically feasible and affordable. Customers can converse with agents in call centers, with each other in Web-based user groups, with e-mail partners, with chat room participants, with affinity-group members, with Web masters, and with "intelligent" software agents that operate on portals and Web sites. Given customers' new capabilities, it is even more important that organizations treat their relationships with customers as conversations.

Customer Interactions Can Occur Anytime, Anywhere, and Anyhow

The most widely recognized benefit of Internet usage and e-commerce has been to provide businesses with the ability to deliver information and service anytime and anywhere. It has allowed organizations to overcome the traditional barriers of time and geography. But another major benefit is the ability to interact with customers in ways that better serve the needs of those customers. For the Relationship-Based Enterprise, this means adding "anyhow" capabilities to "anytime and anywhere."

Today's demanding customers decide where, when, and how they deal with their suppliers, reversing the control that organizations had over delivery channels and business hours. Static relationships, in which customers primarily act as buyers with limited conversation at a few points in time, are being replaced by dynamic relationships, in which customers play many different roles, including buyer, user, self-server, and co-designer of a product or process.

The overall trend is from monologue to dialogue, from the one-way communication used in the mass market to two-way communications between individual customers and business. The new standard is interactive and conversational.

The Value is in the Conversation

The Relationship-Based Enterprise recognizes that it is conversations with customers that create value. It takes responsibility for ensuring that these conversations are occurring and that value is created in each and every exchange that is a part of the conversation. As a result, the enterprise has the mechanisms it needs to remember and recall conversations with customers.

How did this shift come about?

Commerce used to be simple. Companies produced, distributed, sold, and delivered products and services to customers. Customers played the role of buyer. They were the last link in a sequential supply chain. Value was "delivered" to the buyer along with the product or service. The market determined the price and it measured the value of the product. The buyer bought. End of story.

Many approaches toward customer relationships are based on this simple model. The role played by the customer in value creation is minimized. This model can be called *value delivery*.

Now, as customers begin to converse more freely with enterprises, the roles of both parties in the creation of value are starting to change. Customers are even becoming involved in the design, development, production, and delivery of products and services. In such cases, they act more like employees, business partners, or suppliers rather than traditional customers.

Under this emerging model, especially in markets such as software where technological change is rapid, there are major impacts for both suppliers and customers. Some customers may prefer to act only as buyers. But others may be early adopters of a new product who want to participate in prototyping and testing. Still others may be experts who are opinion leaders in the field. Or there can be customers whose opinions help evolve a product and improve its quality. When customers play these roles, the boundaries between enterprise and customer become blurred. They become co-designers and co-producers of products and services. Are they buyers or are they partners in a supply chain? They are both. If the prior model was about *value delivery*, the emerging model is about *value creation*.

Perfection is Not the Focus

The Relationship-Based Enterprise knows that value no longer comes in a box. The old value-*delivery* model, in which the enterprise offers products and services for consumption by customers, links value exclusively to the quality of products and services. The more perfect the products and services are, the greater the value delivered.

In contrast, the new value-*creating* model employed by the Relationship-Based Enterprise is about both parties *exchanging* value through conversations, as well as products and services. The Relationship-Based Enterprise engages its customers in working with the enterprise to produce value. The more customers it can involve in its processes, and the more that it can move that involvement upstream toward design, the greater the value that is created—for both parties. Consider, for example, the customers of Dell. They are more than prepared to work with Dell to define the configuration of a computer. Value is not in the computer itself, a standard commodity, but instead is in the conversation that creates the configuration of the precise computer that they will purchase.

For the Relationship-Based Enterprise, even the best information in the world about any particular customer or group of customers has a shelf life. Customer information is perishable. The only reasonable and practical approach to knowing who customers are and what they want and expect is an ongoing conversation—a conversation that will allow the enterprise to continue to discover its customers. Through conversation, it can learn the exact nature of its customers' needs, and it can learn how to adjust and adapt its business processes to support those needs. The Relationship-Based Enterprise is not only open to a dialogue with its customers but is also prepared to allow them to have access to its processes and to share control over those processes, sharing information, knowledge, and expertise.

The Relationship-Based Enterprise is not interested in perfect information about its customers. It knows that its customers are constantly changing in response to their own needs, as well as the pressures and opportunities of their environment.

The Hunted Become the Hunters

Like a traditional company, the Relationship-Based Enterprise recognizes the importance of defining market segments and targeting those customers with messages, products, and services. But it also knows that in the new economy, the rules of the game have changed. In the old economy, the company was the hunter. It developed programs to segment and target its customers.

Traditionally, companies broadcast messages and delivered products for sale to market segments (usually demographic and geographic). The key to success was accurate targeting in a relatively stable marketplace, where the segments were big enough to hit and did not move very often or very quickly. In the emerging model, companies want to become conversation partners with individual customers or small groups of customers (often groupings such as affinity groups, clubs, or professional groups). The challenge is not to target them but to engage them in a dialogue and then exchange the information (or personalized messages, as defined in Chapter 13) that they want to hear. The most effective solution is not to target these customers, but to become their target. Web sites, stores, even call centers, must line themselves up in the cross-hairs of their customer's sights: becoming targets that can start conversations. The customer hunts for the best deals and information from a sea of suppliers and Web sites, some owned by companies, others by consumer groups, and still others by special interest groups. The hunted have become the hunters.

Conversations are Conducted in Real Time or Near Real Time

The Relationship-Based Enterprise is passionate about response time. Where possible, it conducts all conversations in either real time or near real time. The immediacy of dialogue is what matters, in part because the customer is only a click away from going somewhere else and partly because information is such a significant part of every product or service. Immediacy is a key factor in the quality of the conversation, as well as the value obtained from that conversation.

Playing chess long-distance by snail-mail was fun—but a lot more long-distance chess gets played in real-time over the Internet.

Near-instantaneous communication with anyone, anywhere in the world, characterizes the current communications revolution. Interestingly, this communications revolution can be viewed as being less about technology evolution than about human pursuit of communication. Companies obsessed with real-time communications are leaders of the communications revolution and are the staging ground for the Relationship-Based Enterprise.

Figure 1-1 illustrates the characteristics that have been identified so far.

Figure 1-1: *The Relationship-Based Enterprise*

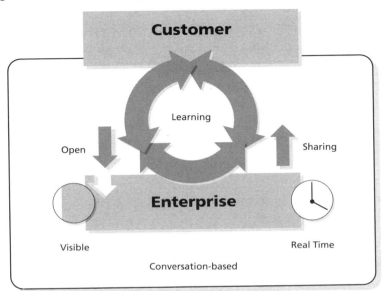

Child of the New Economy

To reiterate, the Relationship-Based Enterprise, a child of the new economy, recognizes that it is not possible to have perfect information about customers, a perfect product, or a perfect organizational structure. Instead, it focuses its efforts on continuous learning, which is only possible when it engages its customers in conversations. Being conversation-based and externally focused are the principle characteristics of this emerging organizational model. It is very easy for an enterprise to consider spending time and energy trying to get the "perfect information" about its customers, in the hope that this information will allow it to anticipate its customers' every need, to provide just the right product at just the right time and place. It is also easy for any organization to become focused on spending time and energy to get the "perfect offering" in the hope that this perfect offering will take the market by storm and launch the enterprise on a path of unparalleled growth and prosperity. And it is easy for an organization to consider spending time and energy trying to get the "perfect organizational structure" and management processes so that it may continually respond to the changes in the environment.

In the new economy, these are elusive—and dangerous—illusions, disconnected from the new reality of business relationships. To fully understand this new reality, the Relationship-Based Enterprise, and where this is all going, it is worth looking back in time to trace how companies began to evolve beyond the Integrated Enterprise model.

A Step Back in Time—Evolving Beyond the Integrated Enterprise

For more than a decade, through re-engineering, downsizing, and rightsizing, organizations have spent enormous amounts of time and money improving every aspect of their internal operations. Lower operating costs and higher quality were seen as the path to providing customers with increased value, and as the keys to profitability and growth. The focus of much of this effort was at the boundaries between functions, processes, departments, divisions, and workgroups. These boundaries were seen as barriers that lessened the effectiveness and efficiency of business operations.

Integration of all aspects of the business was a central theme of such programs. As illustrated in Figure 1-2, business processes and information systems were integrated horizontally, from supplier to customer. Management and planning processes were integrated vertically, from the corporate level down to the task or job level, in some cases including measurement systems for each division, department, work group, or individual. Such initiatives ensured that:

■ all aspects of a business were synchronized with strategic plans

- the cycle time from "concept to cash" was reduced
- employees had the opportunity to make improvements to the process before the quality of the products and services could decline
- costs were reduced
- value was added to the products and services at every step along the way.

Figure 1-2: *The Integrated Enterprise*

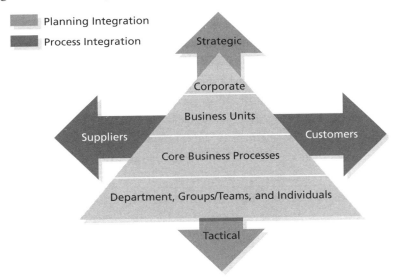

Over the years, attention shifted from the "white spaces" within organizations to the "white spaces" between organizations. The white space between an organization and its customer is the "place" where business exchanges occur. Initial efforts to address these new white spaces followed the same pattern that was employed to address the internal white spaces—the integration of information systems and business processes.

Then came the re-engineering boom, which changed many investors' and employees' views of a successful business organization. The models of success were the product and service "factories" that were engineered and integrated to be lean and mean. These factories featured a streamlined hierarchy that often included the outsourcing of non-core functions. And they interfaced with both customers and suppliers using private information networks, such as those associated with electronic data interchange (EDI). Re-engineering solidified integration as the approach toward the white spaces that exist between the enterprise and its customers.

The next step was to extend the concept of the networked company much further. The first dot-com companies used the power of the Internet to create business networks—completely flat networks—of agile, entrepreneurial enterprises that form, dissolve, and re-form to meet changing customer needs. The non-hierarchical, loosely coupled partnerships established by Amazon.com early on are an example of these networks. They were designed for rapid growth.

The introduction of the Internet as a vehicle for conducting business profoundly affected the very nature of the white spaces between an enterprise and its customers (see Figure 1-3). This is because the Internet is vastly different from any other technology. Its single most distinguishing characteristic is the ability to support an interactive dialogue. As a result, these white spaces become more than just another place to conduct business-as-usual.

Enterprises that have led in this area are those in the e-commerce space, and e-tailers in particular. They focused much of their energy on the conversations that occur in the white space between themselves and their customers and, as a result, engaged and captivated their customers. This type of customer focus in the new economy marks the emergence of the Relationship-Based Enterprise, which is more than a "customer-centered" enterprise, more than an "integrated" enterprise, more than an "extended" enterprise, and more than a learning organization. Unlike these traditional enterprise models, many of which did well in the external white spaces but not so well in their internal white spaces, the Relationship-Based Enterprise is about balance.

Another way of thinking about a Relationship-Based Enterprise is as a "recombinant" enterprise, like a strand of recombinant DNA, produced when segments of DNA from different sources are

Figure 1-3: *The White Spaces*

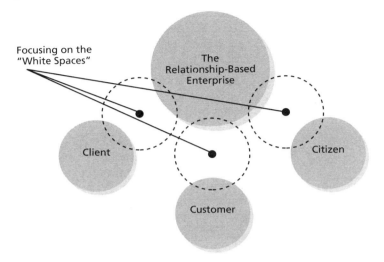

joined to produce new genetic material. A Relationship-Based Enterprise has the ability to attach and detach as the needs demand, creating new business forms. Such connections are not necessarily aimed at integrating the processes of production and delivery, but at all of the other kinds of support required to facilitate the relationship. The Internet provides a standard platform to give the enterprise the freedom to attach to any other enterprise.

While CRM depends on the integrated environment, it alone is simply not enough. To be successful in its relationships with customers, today's enterprise must become both fully integrated and fully connected. Being fully integrated and being fully connected are not the same. Integration is done from the point of view of the products, services, and processes of the enterprise. Connection is from the point of view of the customer. Full connection implies that every aspect of the business of an enterprise is accessible to a customer. Figure 1-4 illustrates this distinction. The arrows labeled "connections" illustrate how deeply these customer connections must penetrate the enterprise, providing access not just to departments, groups, and individuals but to the core processes of the business.

Figure 1-4: *Integration and Connectivity*

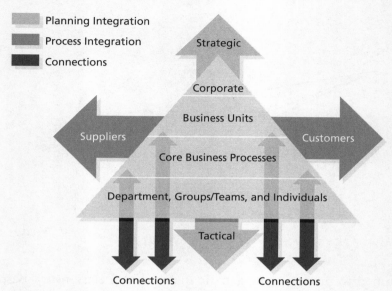

These connections traverse the "white spaces," as was seen in Figure 1-3. The white spaces are where both connections and conversations occur. As shown in Figure 1-5, both the customer and the enterprise have their own value-creating processes. The customer's value-creating process is represented as Search, Acquire, Use, Maintain, and Dispose. The enterprise's value-creating process is represented as Research, Design, Build, Sell, and Service.

The challenge faced by the emerging Relationship-Based Enterprise and its customers is to dynamically connect their processes so that each may realize the value they seek. Some have suggested that the best way to connect these separate value-creating processes is to recast one or the other so that both are identical. For example, if the enterprise were to recast its processes as attract, transact, fulfill, service and retire, then their processes would more closely resemble the processes of their customers. This approach is not the approach taken by the Relationship-Based Enterprise. First, it would be relatively expensive. And secondly, it would limit its flexibility—each customer may have a different set of value-creating processes.

Figure 1-5: *Value-Creating Processes*

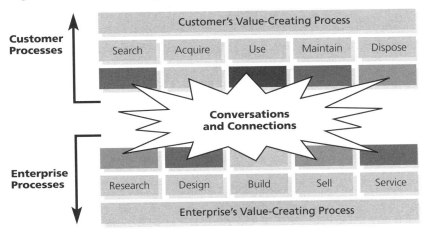

In the new model, Relationship-Based Enterprise uses conversation to dynamically join its processes with those of its customers. As a result, it can create just the right process for the right customer and the right situation. For example, when one customer approaches a lender for a mortgage, the conversation may involve a dozen exchanges, while a different customer may only require one or two exchanges to complete a similar conversation. It may be pointless and tiresome to force the second customer through the same dozen exchanges. At the same time, it may be too risky to allow the first to secure a mortgage with only one or two exchanges. Dynamically connecting business processes when and where required provides the greatest degree of freedom, and the vehicle for this dynamic alignment is "conversation."

Finding the Right Balance

The fact that the enterprise must now become the hunted affects management's choice of not only the e-commerce and CRM technologies they employ, but also their choice of business and organizational designs.

Figure 1-6: *From Push to Pull: Changing Customer Roles*

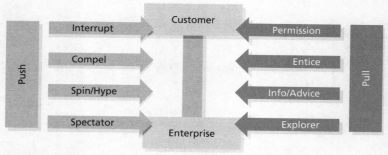

Associated with this new perspective is a move from monologue to dialogue. This move changes the nature of marketing. The traditional "push" methods are being replaced by "pull" methods more appropriate to a marketplace where customers take the initiative—in searching for information, in shopping around, and in negotiating personalized prices and services. Figure 1-6 contrasts the characteristics of a relationship that is dominated by a push approach versus one that is dominated by pull. The shift from push to pull is evidenced by the following changes:

- marketing by interrupting the customer is giving way to permission-based marketing
- compelling the customer to listen to advertising is giving way to enticing the customer to listen to messages
- spin and hype are giving way to information and advice.

Going forward, both enterprise and customers have new roles to play. The balance is shifting, from "push" to "push *and* pull." As organizations engage their customers in more and more conversation, the goal is not to do away with push advertising. Mass marketing is still an effective method of creating a target, and building traffic on a company's Web site. At the same time, there is no substitute for a sticky, conversational site that keeps surfers clicking their way back, or an enterprise that engages its customer in a dialogue.

Window on the Real World:

Centrica

No one understands changing customer expectations better than companies like Centrica, a new holding company for British Gas in the U.K.'s deregulated energy industry. With the Centrica Group, British Gas is responding to a completely new situation: suddenly, their customers have a choice. Instead of being captive "spectators" they are now explorers with their own energy agenda. The customer role—and the role of British Gas—changed dramatically.

British Gas looked at their assets, and decided that customer information and customer ownership was probably their true "competitive advantage" for success in the deregulated environment. To leverage this advantage, British Gas identified a diversification strategy articulated around its customer base—in effect, a Customer Relationship Strategy. In a bold move, management decided to go from simply selling gas to selling household services—including electricity, maintenance of gas central heating, financial services (including credit card), automobile roadside assistance, and home security systems. Its new business vision was solving household-related problems, i.e., taking the inconveniences out of running a home.

The bold move into electricity and other household services worked. Centrica enabled a business (the old British Gas), whose assets were 19 million gas consumers in 1996, to evolve within three years into a completely new business with 15 million customers purchasing gas, appliance servicing, plumbing services, insurance services, credit card services, and vehicle repair and recovery services. In addition, Centrica entered the electricity market and acquired over two million customers and nearly 15 percent of the market within its first year. Centrica now has over 3 million electricity consumers and over a million credit card customers. Centrica has also entered the telecommunications market, offering a fixed line, mobile and Internet services on one bill.

Thanks to management's clear perception of changing customer/enterprise dynamics, British Gas has evolved into Centrica —a new kind of company whose share price has trebled in the two and a half years since its de-merger.

In 2000, Centrica acquired Direct Energy Marketing Limited, the Canadian natural gas retailer, and Avalanche Energy, a Canadian gas and oil producer. These are the first steps in Centrica's plans to build a North American energy business with at least five million customers using the now well-established Centrica business model.

Summing Up the Zeitgeist—Patterns of Change

New technologies have enabled organizations to change the way that they communicate with customers, as illustrated in Figure 1-7. The result is a shift in the focus of major improvement programs. Internally focused improvement programs absorbed billions of investment dollars over the last decade. Total Quality Management focused on getting better quality products into the hands of customers. Service Quality Programs focused on increasing customer satisfaction through a variety of measures—not just better products. Customer Loyalty Programs used discounts and points in an attempt to buy customer loyalty. Business Process Redesign focused on improving the products and services to everyone in the value chain, including the customers within the organization itself. And finally, Customer Care Programs took an integrated approach to improved service, often through the use of call centers. Business managers invested because they expected to improve their company's competitive position, and because they assumed programs would contribute toward the growth of a loyal customer base.

Figure 1-7: *Patterns of Change*

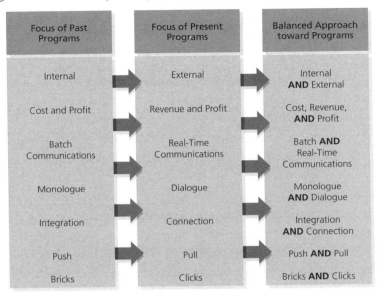

Focus of Past Programs	Focus of Present Programs	Balanced Approach toward Programs
Internal	External	Internal **AND** External
Cost and Profit	Revenue and Profit	Cost, Revenue, **AND** Profit
Batch Communications	Real-Time Communications	Batch **AND** Real-Time Communications
Monologue	Dialogue	Monologue **AND** Dialogue
Integration	Connection	Integration **AND** Connection
Push	Pull	Push **AND** Pull
Bricks	Clicks	Bricks **AND** Clicks

Each of these programs yielded its share of successes and disappointments. The success rate, as presented in *The Information Paradox*, hovered between 40 and 60 percent. This was a typical—but unacceptably low—success rate. "Implementation problems" were blamed for the disappointments. Nearly all the stories follow a similar pattern. The improvement programs were:

- often fragmented and not adequately sponsored by senior management
- not linked to the organization's overall business strategy
- not tied to specific financial and business objectives, leading to inadequate performance management and measurement
- stymied by requirements for major organizational changes to which management may not have been fully committed
- not properly enabled by information technology, which was sometimes poorly applied or not fully integrated with the business

■ subject to everyone raising the bar at the same time
when, in some industries and markets, everyone
improved service across the board, giving no single
company the expected competitive advantage.

Seeking to avoid these problems, and driven by the Internet,
enterprise improvement programs changed focus: from internal to
external. Organizations moved beyond the narrow internal focus
that was a fixture for a decade and shifted their efforts toward an
external focus—from the enterprise itself to the connections it has
with its environment. But, as dramatically exemplified by the dot-
com phenomenon in late 1999 and early 2000, some organizations overshot the mark. They became overly focused on what was
"external" to the enterprise.

Most recently, a new pattern of change is unfolding, driven
by intense competition, increased customer choice, new business
models, greater customer expectations, and the availability of new
technology. As a function of the Relationship-Based Enterprise
organizational model, improvement programs are focusing on
both the external and the internal. Marketing programs, as illustrated earlier in Figure 1-6, are moving from a "push" strategy
toward one that includes both "pull and push." Rather than creating an integrated enterprise, they are moving toward creating the
"connected and integrated" enterprise. They are moving from a
focus on "costs and profit" toward a focus on "revenue, costs, and
profit." In the Relationship-Based Enterprise, improvement programs seem to be striking a balance between business strategies
and change programs. They are leaving behind the "or" mindset
of paradigm shifts because there are just too many such shifts to
count. They are replacing this mindset with "and" thinking.

2 CHAPTER

What is Customer Relationship Management, Anyway?

Everything that is hard to attain is easily attempted by the generality of men.
—Ptolemy, c. 100–178 AD, "Tetrabiblos"

In baseball, you don't know nothing.
—Yogi (Lawrence Peter) Berra, 1925–

CRM, it turns out, is easy to attempt and hard to attain—as discovered by many clients of DMR Consulting. Looking back, with much experience and hindsight, they might paraphrase Yogi Berra: "In CRM, you don't know nothing." Looking ahead, they definitely want better answers.

The following scenario typifies their experience.

Undertaking a Major CRM Initiative

Daytimer Entry—April 1, First Quarter:
"Executive committee votes to invest in CRM software
package. Package appears to support most operational
details. Predicted benefits compelling. Stronger customer
relationships, customer loyalty, better customer information,
and a stickier Web site. Should see an increase in profits by
fourth quarter."

The decision for CRM is cut and dried. Only the brave would
have stood up at this point and seriously questioned the wisdom
of proceeding.

Daytimer Entry—July 1, Second Quarter:
"Need to realign CRM objectives. Call center, sales force,
and Web master on different tracks. Call center wants to
generate simple customer profiles that provide up-to-date
records covering services provided and complaints received.
Sales force wants sophisticated household profiles that provide
key demographic, psychographic and family budget information. Web master only wants to analyze 'trail of clicks'
left by browsers."

Each group wants to shape this new system to meet its own
objectives. Coordination is becoming difficult. At times over the
last few months, voices have been raised.

Daytimer Entry—October 1, Third Quarter:
"Executive Committee meeting to review CRM progress.
Realignment of CRM objectives still underway. Many
issues, big and small. A lot of overlaps and confusion
between organizations. Responsibilities for issues hard to
pin down. What's going on here?"

More than one CRM solution is being developed, and the
scope of the entire program is now a lot less clear than it seemed
in the original presentation.

Daytimer Entry December 31, just prior to close of
Fourth Quarter:
"Executive Committee meeting to review increase to CRM
budget. Question: What do we mean by CRM anyway?
Silence all around the table."

This pattern of events seems typical for CRM programs. The difficulties can be characterized as vision versus reality, simplicity versus complexity, and unclear language.

Vision versus Reality

Many in the industry present CRM as a competitive weapon, the next silver bullet, the priority solution, the thing that must be implemented today. If all of the promises were to materialize, one would expect every organization to have:

- Wal-Mart's product selection
- Priceline's prices
- DeBeer's quality
- Domino's speed
- FedEx's information
- 7-Eleven's convenience
- Nordstrom's customer service
- Amazon's anticipation.

It is only a slight exaggeration to claim that "the perfect company" is the vision for CRM. But to realists, particularly those who have attempted major CRM initiatives, the perfect company sounds like the punch line to an old joke. A huge credibility gap exists between vision and reality.

Where does this gap come from, especially when the basic premise of CRM sounds so right and true? Even the three words—Customer Relationship Management—have a compelling ring. After all, there is nothing more important to any organization than its relationships with customers. And everyone wants loyal customers, customers who through their purchases vote again and again for the same company. In the chaotic, ever-changing business environment of the new economy, product and technological innovation no longer provide sustainable competitive advantage. And so CRM seems like an obvious way to achieve customer loyalty, business stability, and growth.

To deliver these loyal customers, CRM initiatives promise customer information systems that provide a 360-degree view of the customer. This means that the company can determine the product and service preferences of any customer and remember all interactions. Building on this all-encompassing customer profile, a company will organize all of its interactions with a customer into a "seamless experience." This seamless experience will allow customers to buy, get service, negotiate a contract, and inquire about delivery without being aware that they are dealing with a large and complex organization. And certainly without being shuffled from one department to the next, which in the past seemed almost to be expected in dealing with large organizations. Customers become dazzled by the experience and locked into a relationship for a long time, ideally a lifetime. The benefits are stated dramatically—"owning the customer," "erecting exit barriers," "surrounding the customer," "increasing share of mind," and "increasing share of wallet."

The expected financial results of this 360-degree view are alluring. They are described as long-term revenue and profit streams from customers locked into a relationship. In many cases, that revenue is to be generated with minimal costs for conventional marketing and advertising because lock-in would drive repeat purchases, related purchases, and referrals.

Now here's the reality.

Without exception, managers in the telecommunications, financial services, and energy sectors have found that the promises of CRM are compelling. But none of those who participated in the interviews for this book had come close to making all these promises pay off. The vision of building a "perfect company" with CRM initiatives is still a long way off. What these managers said, in no uncertain terms, was that CRM is hard to achieve because of its unanticipated complexity.

Expecting simplicity and finding complexity is what creates the credibility gap for CRM.

Simplicity versus Complexity

The basic concepts of CRM really are simple, and it's easy to see the benefits. After all, who wouldn't want a 360-degree view of customers or a seamless set of interactions across all channels and product lines? This is part of CRM's appeal. And for a small business, where everybody knows everybody, seamless interactions and a 360-degree view are fairly simple to implement. It's CRM on a small scale.

But in a large-scale enterprise, integrating customer information across many business units creates a long list of "things to do." How many databases are involved? How easy it is to change their design? How many channels, processes, employees, and profit centers are involved? How many bosses must lend their support?

Managers of large organizations find it hard to develop an integrated perspective on customers that can be shared by all employees. It is hard to "redefine a business" and customer groups without using a product or service lens. It is also difficult to implement the organizational and cultural changes required by CRM. And while many experience technology integration problems, these problems are seen as secondary when compared to the hurdles of business transformation.

In many cases, managers had to deal with a complex brew of inter-related problems. Front office functions—marketing, sales, product management, and customer service—have traditionally operated as separate departments with distinct goals, budgets, business processes, and work cultures. They are often supported by separate software or technology "islands." Integrating the processes and software applications of these units is not easy. In some cases, these processes and applications need to be completely replaced to make an enterprise-wide CRM solution profitable. In addition, there is the challenge of integrating front office with back office processes, ordering, delivery tracking, and production scheduling.

Finally, CRM is not the only initiative that is being undertaken; it is a part of a larger pattern of change in most organizations.

It must be integrated with existing customer-focused systems. This adds yet more levels of complexity to any CRM program. In large-scale organizations, the simplicity of the vision quickly collides with the complexity of the management issues involved. Herein lies the contradiction. The idea of lifetime customer loyalty, or of conversing with customers, is simple. But how do you design the program and the organization to make it happen?

The complexity of CRM contributes to a variety of management problems that are often associated with CRM initiatives. These problems formed the context for the daytimer entry described at the beginning of this chapter:

- *Lack of clear program scope:* The basic problem is to identify the business units participating in a shared CRM program (as distinct from individual initiatives). Does the program or software implementation project apply to call centers, the sales force, stores, and branches? Does it apply to the entire enterprise? What about suppliers and business partners?

- *Lack of clear objectives:* CRM solutions can be designed to achieve many different objectives, both soft and quantifiable. Soft operational objectives include increases in loyalty and customer satisfaction. Quantifiable operational objectives include increases in customer-retention rates, product cross-sold per customer, or revenues per customer. Financial goals might be to increase sales of a specific unit, or to help meet revenue and profit goals for a division or the whole enterprise. What are the objectives? Are they competing or complementary? Are there too many objectives?

- *Lack of shared understanding:* Lack of clear scope and objectives does not help to promote shared understanding of the program. Do the business units involved in the programs share an understanding of the program's scope and objectives? How about CRM? And what about the linkages to other change programs?

These kinds of management problems are not new. They have been encountered in past change programs. Just think back to the rush to build Web sites, or the move toward e-commerce, or the implementation of an Enterprise Resource Planning (ERP) package. These change programs seemed simple when they began but they became complex—and risky—and more costly—faster than anyone could have anticipated. The same is true of CRM. And so even before organizations can begin to test how loyal their customers are, they begin to struggle with these kinds of problems. And after a period of months, the complexity of CRM and of customer relationships becomes visible. Managers then ask: "What are we really trying to achieve? How fast can we really go? What do we mean by Customer Relationship Management?"

Window on the Real World:

AT&T

AT&T by any measure is large-scale. In fact, with 120 million customers, AT&T is the largest telecommunications company in the United States and a worldwide leader in communications services. It has five different lines of service—each with its own CRM strategy, channels, and touch points. Talk about complexity. What AT&T needed was an enterprise-wide CRM strategy based on integrated customer systems that ensured "the left hand knew what the right hand was doing" and supported cross-selling. Their goals were to:

- Increase customer loyalty
- Increase profitability
- Decrease time-to-market for new services
- Reach customers with targeted offers in the most cost-effective way
- Reduce costs per transaction, customer service costs, and customer service time.

Amazingly, AT&T has made excellent progress in meeting these goals. How did they do it? Well, one thing they didn't do was build an enterprise-wide customer information database across all five service lines. That would have been a huge undertaking, costing far too much, and taking too much time. Instead, they opted for a more gradual approach. They decided to build a software layer on top of two key customer information systems, one from marketing and the other from billing. This approach enabled AT&T to move fast and make excellent progress toward their CRM goals. Today, AT&T agents get a single view of key customer information across all service lines from a single window, as opposed to retrieving information from five different information systems.

But it wasn't easy, and there are still many outstanding issues.

According to Maryann Collyer, Director of Customer Service Systems at AT&T and a member of the CRM integration team, CRM is powerful in theory but troubled in practice. It can take a long time to implement and quickly become very expensive. It requires strong executive support and requires considerable downstream administration. And although a central owner for CRM is desirable, it requires significant re-engineering of business processes, roles, responsibilities, and measurements as it affects several functions within an organization. Information technology (IT) is secondary as a critical success factor. The key is getting departments to sit down together—and work differently. There is no easy resolution to this key issue.

Both field experience and client interviews confirm that CRM initiatives are sweeping in scope and business impact. They can become mired in complexity, touching every process in the enterprise. Managers end up with the impression that CRM is not a single, unified solution, but rather a complex puzzle. It is not surprising that managers and the literature report that approaches to CRM implementation are often fragmented—reducing the "bang for the buck."

Unclear Language

One of the contributors to the management problems experienced by large-scale organizations is unclear language. This is as true of Business Process Re-engineering (BPR) and ERP as it is of CRM. Too often these acronyms substitute for clear language. In the process, they add to the complexity of CRM.

The terminology of CRM is rich and it has evolved quickly. Because of this, neither business managers nor experts seem to agree on a common definition of CRM. The lack of a universally agreed definition is not just a theoretical problem for marketing experts, it is a practical problem for business and technology managers who are involved in financing, designing, implementing, or managing complex business solutions that are focused on customer relationships.

One sign of the problem is that the experts offer very different definitions of Customer Relationship Management. In his book, *Loyalty.com: Customer Relationship Management in the New Era of Internet Marketing*, Frederick Newell defines it as:

> A process of modifying customer behavior over time by strengthening the bond between the customer and the company.

Martha Rogers and Don Peppers, in *Enterprise One to One: Tools for Competing in the Interactive Age,* say the idea behind CRM is to:

> Establish relationships with customers on an individual basis, and then use the information you gather to treat different customers differently. The exchange between a customer and a company becomes mutually beneficial, as customers give information in return for personalized service that meets their individual needs.

Other experts give more sweeping definitions of CRM, describing it as a business and technology discipline that helps companies acquire and retain their most profitable customers. Or they describe it as the implementation of customer-centric business strategies that drive re-engineering of work processes. In this case, CRM is seen as supported, not driven, by CRM technology. And of course many vendors still present CRM primarily as a software tool.

These experts are not fighting or even disagreeing; they are merely emphasizing different aspects of a multi-faceted phenomenon. This adds to the complexity confronting managers—instead of cutting through it. It adds to the confusion.

There's more. Besides expert definitions, there are rich descriptions of CRM in the industry that identify a host of CRM applications and functions (see Figure 2-1) that may need to be addressed as part of a CRM program. There are also a wide variety of models available that describe the data and information platforms that are required for full implementation (see Figure 2-2).

Figure 2-1: *CRM Applications*

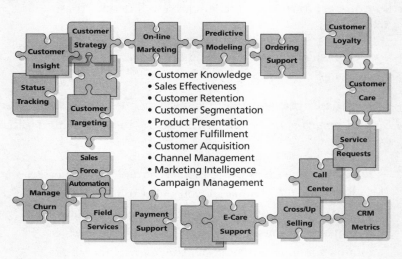

Shared vocabulary may be less important in small organizations doing simple things, but it is important in large-scale organizations. Clear language helps people develop a shared conceptual framework for getting the job done, especially when that job is complex.

The term Customer Relationship Management also overlaps with terms used to describe other programs. Figure 2-3 illustrates just a few of these overlapping terms and the potential for ambiguity. For example, how is Customer Relationship Management different from Relationship Marketing? Or Relationship Management? And what about Value Chain Management or Demand Management? What are the linkages between Customer Relationship Management, Partner Relationship Management, and Supplier Relationship Management? Like the Ancient Mariner surrounded by saltwater, managers are more likely to be frustrated than sustained by all these terms and definitions.

Figure 2-2: *CRM Data Platforms*

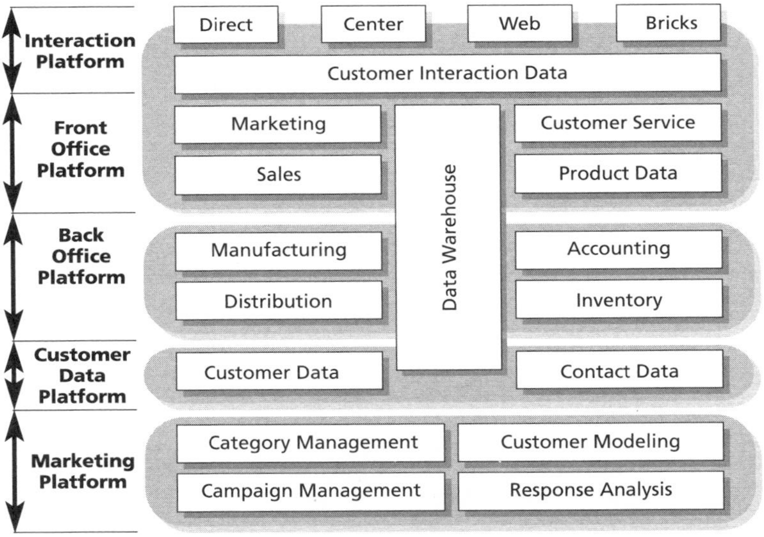

Interaction Platform	Direct	Center	Web	Bricks
	Customer Interaction Data			

Front Office Platform	Marketing		Customer Service
	Sales	Data Warehouse	Product Data

Back Office Platform	Manufacturing		Accounting
	Distribution		Inventory

Customer Data Platform	Customer Data	Contact Data

Marketing Platform	Category Management	Customer Modeling
	Campaign Management	Response Analysis

All these terms are in current usage and describe real programs in many organizations. Mapping this ocean of terms drives home the need to define the boundaries of Customer Relationship Management and the linkages that connect it to all these other programs—past, present, and future.

As CRM initiatives begin to reach critical mass, emerging from individual business units and getting applied across the entire enterprise, or merging with broader programs such as e-commerce, then clear language—and a clear conceptual framework—become increasingly important. Large groups of people need to share an understanding of terms and how they may contribute to the solutions described by those terms.

And the Answer is...

The "Relationship" part of CRM consists of conversations, which are made up of economic exchanges and everything that goes with them. CRM is easily defined as a way of handling these conversations. This simple idea, which forms the underlying theme of this book, leads to fresh perspectives, clear language, and actionable frameworks. It reduces all definitions of CRM to their basic essence, enabling managers to build a shared understanding of the broad objectives for CRM and guide the details of CRM initiatives. Managers need only ask, "What is this investment of resources doing to improve our conversations with customers?"

Viewing relationships as conversations—and CRM as a way to build those conversations—cuts through the complexity of CRM program management. It helps improve CRM program design and achieve the ultimate objective of the Relationship-Based Enterprise—bridging the white space between itself and its customers with strong, dynamic relationships.

Figure 2-3: *The Ocean of Terms*

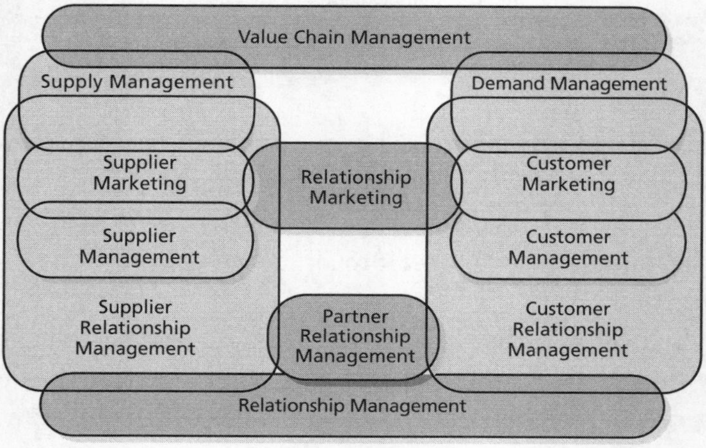

3

CHAPTER

The New Language of Relationships

*Nothing astonishes men so much as
common sense and plain dealing.*
Ralph Waldo Emerson
Essays: First Series, 1841

The more that organizations are confronted with the contradiction of simplicity versus complexity, the more important it becomes to "get back to the basics." In the case of CRM, the basics do not relate to technology, but instead revolve around two simple questions: "What is a customer relationship?" and "How does a relationship work?"

The new language of relationships offers a way to answer these questions and, in doing so, to structure lasting business relationships. This new language is a formal, complete, and pragmatic taxonomy where:

■ a relationship is defined as a series of conversations
   ■ a conversation is defined as a series of economic exchanges
      ■ an exchange is a discrete interaction between an enterprise and a customer
         ■ an offer is the object (defining feature) of an exchange.

This taxonomy provides a complete definition of customer relationships and a common language for understanding, structuring, building and managing those relationships.

The Basics

The foundation of any relationship is, of course, mutual trust and respect. This is a given. The new language of relationships provides a common sense way to build on this foundation by enabling enterprises to better understand the actions that must be taken to design, measure, manage, and sustain a business relationship—and, more specifically, a customer relationship. As illustrated in Figure 3-1, in the new language of relationships:

■ A **relationship** is a series of conversations. For example, the relationship between a bank and a customer grows from a series of conversations about mortgages, credit cards, investments in mutual funds, and other offers of the bank. It is only when these conversations extend over a significant period of time that it is safe to conclude that a relationship exists between the bank and the customer. An effective conversation is one that provides the shortest possible route to obtain the value sought by the bank and its customer. In this case, an effective conversation would lead to quick selection, and approval, of the right mortgage option for the customer.

■ A **conversation** is a series of exchanges or, more specifically, a series of economic exchanges. If the conversation, as in the example above, is about securing a new mortgage, then each of the exchanges or interactions that the customer has with the lender concerning that mortgage

—whether in-person, over the telephone, or over the Internet—is a part of the conversation. The conversation includes exchanges such as an interview with the loans officer, filing a mortgage application, and getting information on interest rates. A conversation may be carried out over an extended period of time.

- An **exchange** is a discrete interaction between a customer and an enterprise, an interaction that happens all at once or at one point in time. Once an exchange has begun, it continues until it is complete. Time may elapse before the next exchange in the same conversation. Each exchange includes an offer. The offer defines the key characteristics of an exchange. For example, the exchanges involving the approval of a mortgage, from browsing the bank's Web site to shaking the loan officer's hand, are basic elements of the conversation. The offer that is part of the exchange may include a product, a service, information, or simple advice. Exchanges occur within the context of a particular customer and are shaped by the business decisions that have been made by the enterprise.

Figure 3-1: *Relationship—Defined*

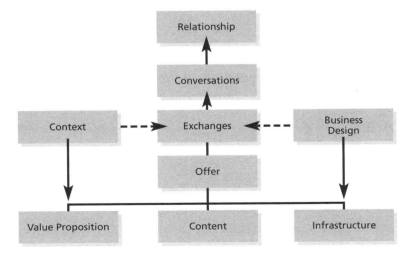

■ **An offer** is more than a product or service. It can include
anything—a product, service, solution, knowledge, information, data, tools, processes, or any other resource that
provides value. Any of these can be the *content* of the
offer. In the example of a bank, the content may be
information on mortgage rates, advice on the housing
market, or solutions to a home financing problem. Each
offer carries either an implied or explicitly stated *value
proposition*. The value proposition in the case of a bank
might be, "convenient home financing at the lowest possible rate." The *content* of an offer is conveyed through
some predefined or accepted *infrastructure* or channel,
whether person-to-person, via e-mail, telephone, over the
Internet or through some other medium or forum. The
offer brings together the value proposition, its associated
content, and an enabling infrastructure.

As further illustrated in Figure 3-1, there are two other important elements to the new language of relationships: context and
business design. While they are not part of an exchange per se,
they play a major role in shaping the exchanges.

■ **Context** includes all that is known about the customer
and the situation surrounding the conversation with that
customer. It includes the role that the customer plays in
an exchange, information concerning prior conversations, as well as any interpretations that can be made
from a combination of the knowledge of the customer
and the knowledge of past and present conversations. In
the example of the conversation about a mortgage, the
context includes information on the financial situation of
the household, the customer's history with the bank, as
well as the lender's knowledge of the goals, objectives,
and dreams of that customer. The context has a strong
influence over the value proposition that is a part of
every offer. For example, if the bank has a long-standing

relationship with the customer then the value proposition may be "services provided with no additional fees" or "same-day approval of any mortgage application."

- **Business design** includes all of the decisions taken by the bank with regard to its mission, goals, objectives, policies, procedures, processes, and infrastructure—decisions that it must make to conduct its business successfully. These decisions have an effect on all aspects of the conversation with a customer, one of the more concrete implications being the nature of the infrastructure that enables each exchange. In the case of the bank, will it offer services to its customers through "bricks alone" or through a combination of "bricks and clicks," or will it rely on other parties to provide the infrastructure?

Building on the Basics: Value Creation

The definitions and taxonomy of the new language of relationship presented above offer a common language for understanding relationships—and a guide for how to structure conversations that create value.

The need for a common language is well understood. For example, six sigma quality programs have been described by chief executive officers such as Jack Welsh of General Electric and Scott McNealy of Sun Microsystems as creating a "common language" for understanding and meeting customer requirements for products and services (*Fortune*, May 1, 2000, p. 126).

But a common language is equally important for understanding the relationship with customers. Enterprises can no longer rest on the "value delivery" model, where the adoption of a common language is only internally focused. They must move toward the "value creation" model, where the common language is also focused outward—on the customer. Enterprises must deliver a relationship that creates value for both them and their customer.

Applying the new language of relationships, it is easy to see that conversations can be adjusted and modified to provide different kinds of value for customers—even customers who may be buying the same product. To see how this can happen, consider the following three-act "play" that presents three different ways to shop for groceries.

Getting the Groceries or ... Conversations

The Players

Bob is a busy professional with sole responsibility for doing his family's grocery shopping. *The Supermarket* is an enterprise exactly like the supermarket near you, featuring a meat aisle, produce section, frozen food aisle, and so on, with long lines at the checkout counters. *The Home Delivery Service* is an enterprise, such as Streamline of Boston, that offers shopping and delivery services. Its employees drive to the Supermarket, shop and wait in line on Bob's behalf, and deliver groceries to his home. *The On-line Supermarket* is a Web-based supermarket and home delivery service like Grocerycart.com.

Background

Bob's grocery list is identical from shopping trip to shopping trip. Within his usual three bags of groceries are the same items each week; there is no difference in the product that changes hands between the various grocery enterprises and their customer. To Bob, how he gets the groceries is more important than what he gets. What changes are the methods of shopping, selection, and delivery: three very different "conversations" built from the many small exchanges that are a part of getting groceries.

Act I: The Supermarket Conversation

Bob goes to the supermarket most weeks late on Sunday night with his standard list, makes his selection, and pays for the goods with cash. The supermarket does not really care what he buys, how fast he consumes what he has purchased, or how often he comes back for more. He goes to the store because of its location and because the wheels of all carts are well lubricated. The conversation is short and simple, with the key exchange being money and personal time for product.

The supermarket does have a loyalty scheme, which uses CRM to track purchases via a loyalty card. The supermarket offers a 10-percent rebate on certain frequently purchased items. The conversation is routine and Bob remains fairly anonymous, but gains a price advantage based on the supermarket's limited knowledge of his family's usage patterns. An additional set of exchanges —computerized information-gathering and analysis, building a simple purchase profile, the discounting of purchases—is added to the simple exchange of money for product. These added exchanges make the conversation slightly more complex, but Bob does not really notice.

Act II: The Home Delivery Conversation

Bob hates shopping on Sunday night. Can he get someone else to do the shopping for him? He calls up the home delivery service. They ask him to sit down with an agent and create a shopping list, which he does, and the agent shops for him. His three bags are delivered to a secure cabinet in his garage. He pays the service for the groceries plus a monthly "subscription fee" of $30, and a one-time set-up charge of $50.

The agent likes grocery shopping, and tries to get Bob more engaged in the process, even suggesting he purchase specials and consider new menus. But Bob doesn't really want to be engaged in the process; his main concern is making sure he still gets the store discount for frequently purchased items. The conversation he wants to have and the conversation structured by the home delivery service really don't match up that well. Plus, he finds the fees quite high. After a few weeks, he "fires" them.

Needless to say, the home delivery conversation adds a new set of exchanges to the simple money-for-product exchanges with the supermarket. The conversation is more complex, now involving the multi-dimensional exchanges of information, money, services, products, and discounts.

Act III: The On-line Supermarket Conversation

Bob really, really hates having to go back to the supermarket on Sunday night. He's beginning to rethink his decision to fire the home delivery service. Then he hears about the on-line supermarket, a new dot-com company. Their shopping list is held on a Web site where Bob can modify it by clicking through a fairly simple menu—from his PC at work or home! He can also just click once on his standard list to get the same basic set of groceries each week.

In many respects, the on-line supermarket is similar to the home delivery service, except Bob has the option of taking home delivery or, for a slightly reduced weekly fee, he can pick up the three bags himself. Of course, the on-line supermarket ensures that he still gets that good old store discount. This conversation is richer than that of home delivery, since the Internet link makes it easier to handle the multi-directional exchanges of information, money, services, products and discounts that are a part of the conversation. Bob likes this conversation with the on-line supermarket, which he continues week after week.

The Point of the Story

Bob has some real choices about how to get his groceries, and none of them are about changing the product. The differences among the three choices lie in how the exchanges are combined to create completely different conversations. Yet Bob finds differences in the "value" offered by each type of conversation. This value goes deeper than "convenience," "better information," "good advice" or just plain "quality service"—it arises from a richer, more focused conversation. Of course, Bob doesn't recognize that this is what is happening. From his perspective, shopping is just "easier."

Business conversation is not chat or socializing. It is a series of exchanges (talk, purchases, hits on Web sites) that combine into meaningful patterns that create value.

The business models of companies like Streamline and Grocerycart.com are based on the creative design of conversations. Such conversations can provide so much value to both parties that they choose to continually enter into such conversations over an extended period of time. And as defined by the new language of relationships, a series of conversations is a relationship—and it may be a long-term relationship. Whether consciously or not, both Streamline and Grocerycart.com are focusing on the conversations they have with their customers as they make key business decisions, and as they choose how to apply CRM software to meet the challenge of relationship management.

The Complications of Real Situations

While the new language of relationships contains relatively simple and straightforward definitions, this does not mean that the business situations that they describe are just as simple and straightforward. In fact they are not. Enterprises have many conversations occurring simultaneously with many different customers. And, because organizations very often have multiple business lines and multiple offerings, they will be engaged in many, many conversations. In some situations, organizations will even become involved in a number of conversations with the same customer. Other complications are illustrated in Figure 3-2.

By themselves these complications are not a problem. However, they do become a problem when an enterprise does not realize that two different departments are conversing with the same customer; or does not recognize that the customer standing at the counter is the same one who recently made a significant purchase over the Internet; or does not track the pattern of its conversations with customers; or is unable to recall a prior conversation. The opportunity for cross-selling is lost. The opportunity for up-selling is lost. The opportunity for multi-channel branding is lost. And the opportunity to build a relationship with the customer is lost forever.

Figure 3-2: *Complications of Real Situations*

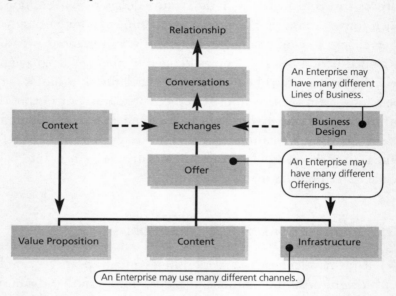

The story of Bob does not illustrate the many challenges that will be faced by most organizations in their efforts to create engaging conversations with their customers. These challenges revolve around the way that an organization chooses to segment its customers, the number of channels that an organizations uses to deliver its offerings, the way the organization has chosen to structure its business, and the variety of products and services that it offers its customers.

Each of these has the potential to create hurdles for the effectiveness of CRM.

How Conversations Create Value and Competitive Advantage

How exactly do conversations in business create value? As seen above, exchanges carry offers that customers value. When Bob chose the on-line supermarket he signaled that the company's combination of Web ordering, telephone service, and home delivery matched his shopping and purchasing processes to create the most value among the alternatives. For other customers, the physical supermarket or the home delivery service might provide a better conversation.

Figure 3-3: *Conversations Connect Value-Creating Processes*

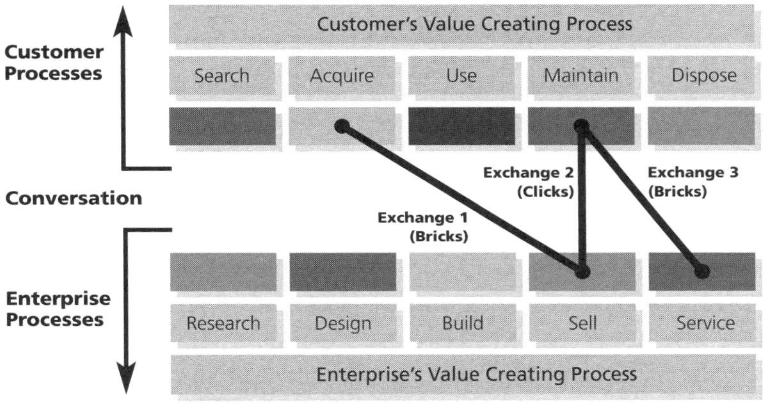

Conversations also link value-creation processes of the enterprise and the customer. The simplest example is that the buying and shopping processes of customers must be linked to the marketing and selling processes of the enterprise: this is the only way a sale will be made. Figure 3-3 illustrates an example, more complex than the one presented between Bob and the on-line supermarket, of the connections between the value-creating processes of two separate organizations.

The exchanges shown could link the product design and manufacturing processes of a computer producer like Dell with the purchasing and usage processes of a business customer. The exchanges might occur via a personalized corporate Web page used to configure computers as well as at other places where Dell and the customer deal with each other.

In common sense terms, conversations help to ensure that products and services meet customer needs. Some of those conversations might, for example, involve customizing an order of Dell PCs for a certain user community—say, sales—in the purchasing company. Or it might involve personalizing the corporate Web page that links the purchasing department to Dell. Or it might just involve two people talking about delivery schedules on a regular basis.

In Figure 3-3, both the customer and the enterprise have their own value-creating processes. The customer acquires the benefit and value of owning a computer through the processes of searching, acquiring, using, maintaining, and disposing. Dell obtains the enterprise value of manufacturing and supporting its products through the processes of research, design, building, selling, and servicing. When these processes are connected with conversation, value is created for both Dell and its customers. And the more that the exchanges in these conversations move toward the beginning of their respective value-creating processes, the greater the value created for both. In the case of Dell, and many other hardware manufacturers, the servicing process may be de-emphasized because emphasis is placed instead on the design and building of high-quality products that require a minimum of after-sales support.

Value Creation and the Relationship-Based Enterprise

The Relationship-Based Enterprise speaks the new language of relationships and understands how value is created. It knows that value is in the conversation, not the product or service, as was pointed out in Chapter 1. This is in contrast to the more inwardly focused approaches of the CRM world, where it is often suggested that the value-creation processes of the enterprise should be "locked in" as in a traditional supply chain. These inwardly focused approaches suggest that if an enterprise achieves an integrated, 360-degree view of the customer, customers will only shop on certain sites because the browsing experience is so complete, personal, or agreeable. Such "lock in" certainly happens in some cases, but it is not a realistic assumption upon which to build a growing business.

In contrast, conversations do not "lock" processes together. They adjust, like telephone switchboards, to route the traffic between enterprise and customer processes, to make the right connection between senders and receivers of messages on both ends of the conversation. Value-creating processes need to adjust to the customer and the situation. For example, when a new customer approaches a lender for a mortgage, the conversation may involve a dozen exchanges. A known and loyal customer, on the other hand, may only require one or two exchanges to complete the conversation. It would be pointless and tiresome to force the second customer through the 12 exchanges—and risky to allow the novice debtor to secure a mortgage with only one or two exchanges.

The new language of relationships provides a common sense way for Relationship-Based Enterprises to think about structuring and building conversations—conversations that provide value.

Window on the Real World:

American Express Bank

American Express Bank is a global bank with total assets of US$13 billion in 38 countries. Its core business is private banking, personal financial services, correspondent banking, corporate banking and global trading. As a subsidiary of American Express, it operates under one of the most respected service brands in the world.

Because of their many complex products, and the extensive support these products require, American Express Bank found creating a unified CRM strategy very difficult. Nevertheless, they recognized that developing an integrated, enterprise-wide CRM strategy was crucial to improve customer service, productivity, and cross-selling. For American Express Bank, that meant a sensitive blend of vision, customer-centric business process redesign, and intensified dialogue with customers. It also involved an enterprise-wide integration that was both functional and geographical. One of the critical success factors was to designate the sales organization as "relationship manager" for CRM.

At American Express Bank, the sales function currently owns the "relationship" with all customers. Therefore, it is a natural fit for them to own CRM. According to John Ruane, senior director of sales, "the relationship manager—the sales organization—is essentially a quarterback: it calls the plays and positions all the players. A central leader is needed; otherwise the left hand will not know what the right hand is doing."

According to Ruane, the relationship manager function is to know the customer's business, understand its industry and needs—and then call the plays across all the other functions. A central customer information system then becomes a safety net to ensure that all players know what they are doing in terms of customer care and cross-selling.

"CRM cannot work effectively unless there is centralized relationship management," adds Farhad Subjally, senior director of product management. "Ideally, a central relationship organization should own part of the budget from all functions involved across the enterprise so CRM re-engineering efforts and adjustments can be implemented faster. However, a cross-functional CRM team involved in deciding on new directions can be as efficient, especially with a strong product management function as an influencer."

The goal of the relationship management function is to ensure that customers get the same branding experience every time and across all channels.

4

CHAPTER

The Exchange Space

New technologies that evolved from the cumulative innovations of the past half-century have now begun to bring about dramatic changes in the way goods and services are produced and in the way they are distributed to final users.
—Alan Greenspan,
U.S. Federal Reserve Board Chairman,
"Economic Challenges in the New Century"
(speech), March 22, 2000

People have exchanged goods and services in the same way for thousands of years. They went to the town market—the first exchange space. At the market, producers sold the things they had produced or provided a service, and, after the requisite haggling, the buyers bought and then used them. These exchanges took place in a physical space, the marketplace, and at set times, on market days. It was how business got conducted. But it was also something more.

The marketplace was the place where things happened. Minstrels sang, jugglers juggled, and fire-breathers breathed fire. People talked. News was exchanged. Buying and selling occurred in a rich context of human interchange. Modern shopping malls continue this tradition.

Now new technology—everything "e"—has created a new marketplace, the World Wide Web. This new marketplace has many advantages over the old marketplace but at the same time it is inherently impersonal, global, fragmented, and does not exist in a single place. The challenge faced by companies doing business on the Web is to overcome these inherent limitations—by creating personal connections, local presence, wholeness, and a sense of belonging to a community. In essence, the task is to reinvent the traditional marketplace.

Reinventing the Marketplace

Many separate elements of the traditional marketplace exist on the Web. People get entertained, meet one another, form communities with common interests and, of course, exchange goods and services. But, as some of the most successful dot-com companies have intuitively discovered, the way that these are combined makes a huge difference.

Companies like Amazon.com and Furniture.com were among the first to perceive that their job was not just to sell things. Their primary innovation was not to do business on the Web. Their primary innovation was to use the Internet, along with other technologies (including overnight package delivery), to redesign traditional marketplace conversations and create new and surprising ways for these conversations to occur.

For example, Amazon enables Web-literate book buyers to become involved in conversations where they can shop for books, read book reviews, share opinions with other readers, keep abreast of the bestseller lists, and find related audio and video entertainment. Amazon created new, friendly exchanges as an integral part of these conversations, including personalized recommendations based on the individual's exchange history. They also enabled time-pressured professionals and businesses to get fast delivery. Exchanges that were formerly separate, one with sales and one with delivery—each with its own potential problems and potential delays—were brought together into a single conversation. The result: strong growth in the number of customers and surprising loyalty among those customers.

Similarly, Furniture.com is transforming the experience of shopping for furniture into a series of more agreeable exchanges and conversations through its Web site—allowing its customers to review "rooms" of different styles. Or check prices and merchants by clicking on a chair, instead of calling stores and waiting for answers. Or get information and advice from trained call-center agents rather than booking appointments with interior decorators. It would seem to be part of Furniture.com's business strategy to redesign the entire experience of furniture shopping "exchange by exchange."

Companies like Amazon.com and Furniture.com are succeeding because they have been able to design a series of exchanges that accumulate into a dialogue-rich conversation. These conversations are central to their relationship with their customers. And "conversation design" is central to their success.

How Exchanges Occur

The exchange space illustrated in Figure 4-1 is the new marketplace, the place where conversations take place in the connected economy. The exchange space identifies the types of exchanges that occur between the enterprise and the customer and the roles that are involved in those exchanges—exchanges that create a conversation. This new marketplace is a natural extension of the traditional patterns of economic exchange that people have engaged in for thousands of years. It is a simple model that can be used to design new and interesting conversations that enable organizations to meet business objectives.

Figure 4-1: *The Exchange Space*

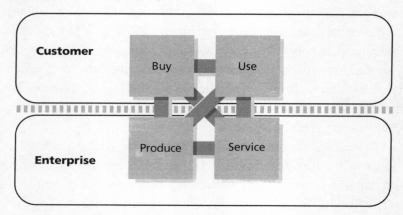

No company went magically from packaged CRM software to a better relationship. Consciously or not, the software was applied to improve the conversation between the enterprise and its customers, and to redesign the exchanges among four key roles into more interesting, more valuable, more rewarding conversations.

To better understand how an enterprise and its customers can work together to design exchanges and conversations, it is first necessary to review the four roles in the exchange space.

Customer Roles

There are two ways customers participate in exchanges in the exchange space, the *buy* role and the *use* role, as illustrated in Figure 4-2. (Customer roles are depicted above the horizontal line, enterprise roles below.) These roles are the same as those in the traditional marketplace. Obviously, the customer filling the buy role buys, and the customer filling the use role uses the products and services acquired by the buyer. The customer in the buy role is responsible for the decision to acquire the products and services, and the approval of contracts and payment arrangements.

In some situations, one person could perform both the buy and use roles; in other cases, groups of individuals who work in separate parts of the organization fill these roles.

Figure 4-2: *Exchange Space and Roles*

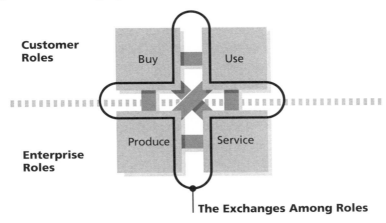

Customer Roles

Buy   Use

Enterprise Roles

Produce   Service

The Exchanges Among Roles

The buy and use roles included in the exchange space are clearly an over-simplification of reality. For example, marketing literature has distinguished roles such as the technical and economic buyer, and others that may influence purchasing decisions. The reason for focusing on these two core roles is to keep this model as simple and practical as possible. The focus is not on the details of each role, but the design of the exchanges among roles that create the conversations that link an enterprise with its customers.

Enterprise Roles

There are two ways enterprises participate in exchanges in the exchange space of Figure 4-2: the *produce* role and the *service* role. These roles are also the same as those in the traditional marketplace. The enterprise department filling the produce role produces, and the department filling the service role provides a service. The produce role is undertaken by the department responsible for the design, production, and delivery of whatever it is that the enterprise has to offer. This department is also responsible for maintaining links with customers in the buy role, delivering products to customers in the use role, and providing the necessary service infrastructure to the enterprise's own service role.

The service role is fulfilled by that part of the enterprise that provides the services required to support ongoing relationships with customers. The primary focus of the service role is providing services to customers in the use role. In addition, the service role often facilitates the relationship between the user and the producer by providing the producer with information concerning possible improvements to the offering. Again, each of these roles could be played by an individual, or by groups of individuals from different parts of the enterprise.

Just as it is easy to define additional roles on the customer side, it is easy to identify other roles for the enterprise, such as those included in various published definitions of the value chain. In particular, the sell role is explicitly excluded from the exchange space because there is now a strong shift from "push" to "pull and push." Organizations have for a long time targeted customers, but now they are trying to become targets themselves with "sticky" Web sites and other devices. The hunted have become the hunters. And therefore a stronger representation is given to the buy role on the customer side than to the sell role on the enterprise side of this model.

Understanding Roles

It is easiest to visualize different people or companies playing the buy, use, produce, and service roles. However, people or companies and their roles are separate. The same person or company can play more than one role. The exchange space is about roles and how they are played, not about people or companies with certain job descriptions. Jobs may be aligned with or cut across roles. People or companies from the customer side may play produce and service roles, and vice versa. In fact, one way of enriching and improving conversations and exchanges is to cross over and play roles "on the other side." For example, when a parts supplier moves people into an auto plant, or when computer buyers are given customized Web pages by Dell, enabling them to "move into" Dell's PC configuration system, then these customers are taking part in the produce role. Bringing the customer closer to the source of value creation creates a richer conversation between enterprise and customer, and also makes the enterprise more competitive.

One final twist on roles. Traditionally, humans play roles. But increasingly, electronic systems are also playing roles—automatically ordering (buy), dispensing cash (service), delivering customized newspapers and portfolio analyses (produce). The exchange space can be used to design conversations that involve human-to-human exchanges, human-to-system exchanges, as well as system-to-system exchanges.

Window on the Real World:

SBC Communications

SBC Communications is a global telecommunications company offering a wide range of innovative services and solutions to meet customers' needs. SBC currently provides local service in 20 of the top US markets located in Arkansas, California, Connecticut, Illinois, Indiana, Kansas, Michigan, Missouri, Nevada, Ohio, Oklahoma, Texas, and Wisconsin. SBC has launched an historic initiative to expand nationally into 30 top markets outside of its traditional service region. Under a new brand, SBC Telecom, the company will provide local and long-distance voice and data services in these 30 markets—the first time a former Bell operating company will compete for business and residential local phone customers on a national scale.

"Ironically," says Ron Devincenzi, director of billing and customer care at SBC, "CRM appears to be suffering from an outbreak in technology." According to Devincenzi, the goal for many systems development managers has become one of adapting off-the-shelf products rather than funding in-house development of new systems. Companies are now seeking to take advantage of technologies that will drive superior service without becoming bogged down by internal development. However, notes Devincenzi, "It is necessary to actively and continuously involve the user population in systems development in order to achieve the gains in productivity that management anticipates when funding the project."

At SBC, Devincenzi found that systems developed through incremental refinements and high-profile user involvement are destined for success. Those developed externally and representing radical change run the risk of being rejected by the user population.

The problem for most companies is that incrementally developed, user-friendly systems are likely to take so long to evolve that what might have been perceived as state-of-the-art three years ago has now become a technological dinosaur. The key to resolving this enigma lies in a combination of senior management commitment to innovation tempered with the identification of user needs, as well as the ability of internal system development groups to integrate outstanding off-the-shelf software with existing systems in order to consistently ensure that the CRM environment maintains a competitive edge.

Using the Exchange Space to Build Conversations

The roles and exchanges identified in the exchange space match the experience of veteran sales and service professionals working with business customers—selling them office supplies, integrating their information systems, providing them with complex financing solutions. These professionals do not think of their relationship with customers in broad terms. Rather, they understand and deal directly with those that play "buy" and "use" roles. Veteran sales and service professionals network with a variety of buyers (purchasing department) and users (marketing, treasury, chief information officer, and so on) to build coalitions of support for their company. Similarly, a skillful financial advisor knows that she is often selling not only to the buyer, usually the head of the household, but indirectly to the entire family. These other family members can be viewed as users of the various services and, in this role, influence household financial decisions: a home purchase or sale, a choice of university, or a date of retirement.

The practical application of the exchange space is to understand and design the exchanges that link roles. Exchanges are the basic elements, or building blocks, of a conversation. The right combination of exchanges creates a conversation that delivers value to both the customer and the enterprise. And conversations that continue over a period of time create what we commonly call "a relationship."

There is literally an infinite number of possible ways to structure and sequence the exchanges that make up a conversation. Because of these possibilities, organizations have an opportunity to use conversation design for competitive purposes.

Figure 4-3 provides an illustration of a very simple conversation. In this simple conversation there are five interdependent exchanges:

- Exchange 1—A customer decides to acquire services from an ISP.
- Exchange 2—After a survey of available service providers, the customer negotiates the terms of the service with a particular ISP.
- Exchange 3—An employee from the ISP then spends time with the customer to establish the access procedure.
- Exchange 4—That same employee notifies his service department that the customer has been given access and will start to use the service.
- Exchange 5—Finally, the customer starts to use the service.

Traditionally, organizations have used their products and services as the focus for providing value. Value was originally delivered with handcrafted products, then by mass production, then through quality programs, then by bundling services with products or by productizing services, and more recently through mass

Figure 4-3: *A Simple Conversation*

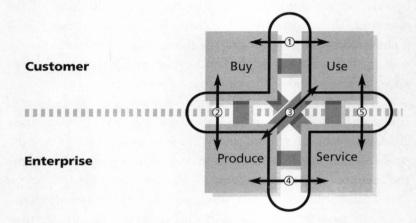

① A Customer (Use Role) decides that Internet access is required
   to support the business, and communicates this need to the
   Purchasing Department (Buy Role).

② Purchasing Department (Buy Role) contacts a number of suppliers
   (Produce Role), and commits to getting the service from a local
   ISP (Enterprise).

③ The Sales Rep (Produce Role) for the ISP and Customer (Use Role)
   set up an access procedure.

④ The Sales Rep (Produce Role) for the ISP notifies its service
   organization (Service Role) of the agreement with the customer.

⑤ Customer (Use Role) uses the service.

customization. Now organizations are moving to the next level.
They are personalizing conversations with their customers. And
personalization requires a deep understanding of who these customers are and what role they are playing.

In the exchange space, exchanges can take many forms and
generally include the exchange of useful information, advice, and
resources, as well as cooperation, coordination, and collaboration.
All of these forms of exchange produce value. However, the value
does not always consist of money or products. Consider, for example the pooling of resources, executive time, and knowledge
involved in setting up a secure Web site shared by airlines and
their business travelers. The site is used for designing new services

and features for frequent fliers. Many hours of paid time are spent exchanging suggestions—without any cash changing hands. Similarly, on a larger scale, airlines and jet manufacturers create joint aircraft design teams staffed by cross-disciplinary marketing, service, and engineering groups from both companies. All these people are paid by their respective employers. Value is created without any exchange of money between enterprise and customer.

The exchange space can also be used to help develop an overall strategy with respect to exchanges. For example, an organization may decide that it does not want to resource the "produce" role, and that it wishes to partner with other organizations to fulfill this role. Or the organization may decide that its primary purpose is the production of quality software, and that it will not provide any services associated with that software. Their business strategy is to fix software problems in the next release. In this case, they have chosen to emphasize the produce role and minimize the service role. Clearly there are many possibilities. The exchange space focuses attention on the need for decisive choices about what role to emphasize, and in what situation.

Designing exchanges and conversations has also been applied in business-to-business settings, with success recorded in industries where buyers and users traditionally experience costly, time-consuming exchanges: ordering expensive lab chemicals, booking airline tickets, or ordering parts for a fast-moving auto assembly line. Streamlining the conversations—whether the conversation involves exchanges that check a catalog for information, process a routine payment, or negotiate a legal contract—can save a business customer more money than a 10-percent price reduction. And, at the same time, enhance the value provided to customers.

These examples point to an important fact: value-creating exchanges and conversations come in many forms. It is far harder to generalize about exchanges than about roles, but here are several examples of the important types of exchanges that business managers might design and influence:

- **Information exchanges and scanning:** conversations, reading ads, browsing Web sites, talking to friends, consulting independent brokers or "infomediaries"
- **Shopping and purchasing:** comparing prices, bargaining, buying, negotiating agreements for contracts and service levels
- **Financing and paying:** monthly payments and installment plans, leasing, and financing
- **Collaboration and resource pooling:** joint product-design teams, joint solutions-development teams, and quality-improvement teams
- **Realizing value:** returning defective products, realizing product warranties, and obtaining service under leasing contracts.

From Exchange Spaces to Value Chains

The exchange space is a very simple representation of the exchanges that occur at the boundary or in the white space between an organization and its customer. It can also represent the exchanges that occur at the boundaries of a business-to-business relationship. And it can be extended to illustrate the series of relationships that are part of a value chain.

Figure 4-4 illustrates this extension of the exchange space into a series of exchanges between three separate organizations—a supplier, an enterprise, and a customer. In this simple example, E*Trade acquires both products and services (news, quotes, and charts) from its suppliers, Reuters *et al*, so that it may package, price, and distribute products for its customers. At the same time, it may use some of the products and services that it acquires from its suppliers to provide in-house services, such as trade executions.

In this extension of the exchange space, one organization is connected to another, which is connected to another, and so on and so on. When this is done, the produce and use roles overlap as the exchange space is extended into a value chain. The reason

Figure 4-4: *The Exchange Space—Extended*

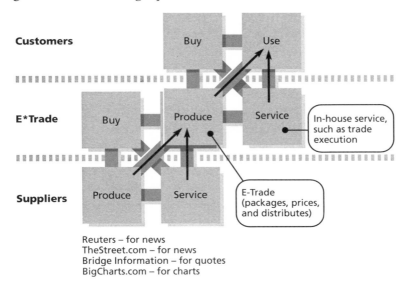

Reuters – for news
TheStreet.com – for news
Bridge Information – for quotes
BigCharts.com – for charts

for this overlap is that "use" and "produce" are the same thing. In the above example, E*Trade "uses" a particular product or service so that it may "produce" some new product or service.

Extending the exchange space into a value chain illustrates some of the more subtle aspects of a value chain. Every organization that participates in the kind of value chain illustrated in Figure 4-4 must add value. In fact, each enterprise must provide value that is over and above that which its customers could get by going directly to the enterprise's supplier. Should a customer determine that its supplier (the enterprise) is not adding value, the customer will attempt to "tunnel" under the enterprise and go directly to the enterprise's supplier to meet its needs. The Internet has made this kind of tunneling possible through the real-time or near real-time communications that can take place between any two organizations, anywhere in the world.

The example illustrated in Figure 4-4 is actually incomplete. A more complete example of the exchanges and conversations that take place in a value chain is illustrated in Figure 4-5 and Figure 4-6. Without getting into the detail of the conversations that are illustrated in Figure 4-5 and Figure 4-6, it should be instantly obvious to the reader that exchanges and conversations are without question complex. In fact, even Figures 4-5 and 4-6 are reasonably simple compared to what actually happens in a normal business situation. This means only one thing—that any discussion about what happens in the "white space" between an enterprise and its customer requires serious attention. The design of exchanges and conversations is critical to the success of any enterprise.

The series of exchanges that make up a conversation between an enterprise and its customers can very quickly become complex. Dealing with this complexity is essential. The success of the relationship with any customer is based on the degree to which that conversation provides value to both the enterprise and the customer. What happens in the "white space" between the enterprise and its customer is as important if not more important than what happens inside the enterprise. Over the last decade organizations have spent incredible amounts of money designing and redesigning their internal operations. The focus now is moving to the white spaces between organizations.

Figure 4-5: *Realistic Conversations: Part 1*

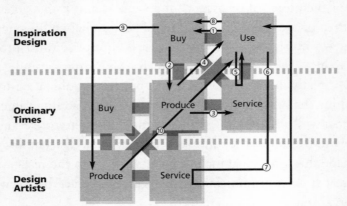

① Inspiration Design (User) needs an Internet Service. One of the features of the service offered by Ordinary Times is access to a wide variety of services offered by independent design artists.

② Inspiration Design (Buy) acquires the service from Ordinary Times.

③ Ordinary Times (Produce) notifies its Service Department (Serve) about the new agreement with Inspiration Design.

④ Ordinary Times (Produce) notifies Inspiration Design (Use) that the service is now available.

⑤ Inspiration Design (Use) starts to use the service.

Figure 4-6: *Realistic Conversations: Part 2*

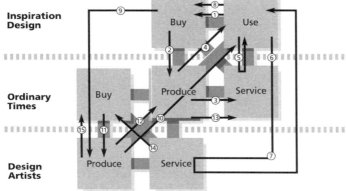

⑥ In some cases when Inspiration Design
⑦ makes a request for service they are
permitted direct access to the Web sites
of Design Artists.

⑧ In other cases where custom work is
⑨ required, Inspiration Design goes directly
⑩ to the Design Artist for service.

Prior Conversations:

⑪ Ordinary Times acquired the right to place
the Web address of certain Design Artists
on its, Ordinary Times, Web site.

⑫ Several Design Artists deliver Ordinary Times
the right to access their Web sites.

⑬ Ordinary Times places the addresses of these
Design Artists on their own Web site.

⑭ The Design Artist pay Ordinary Times
⑮ a commission each time that Ordinary Times
refers a customer to a Design Artist.

And there are still other factors that complicate the design of exchanges and conversations, and that make careful design imperative. As illustrated in Figure 4-7, in those cases where the enterprise has a number of product lines, the customer who buys products from one product line may also buy products from a second product line. In some cases it may be of vital importance for the enterprise to know, while negotiating a contract, that the customer purchases product from both product lines.

Finally, it is important to understand the two sides of the value chain, as illustrated in Figure 4-8. When an enterprise looks toward its customer, and captures information about that customer and the conversations that it has with that customer, it engages in CRM. In a business-to-business situation, for exactly the same conversation and at exactly the same time, the customer will be capturing information about its supplier—the enterprise. And so, when the customer looks at its conversation with the enterprise, what it sees are the exchanges with a supplier. As such, the customer is essentially involved in Supplier Relationship

Figure 4-7: *Many Combinations*

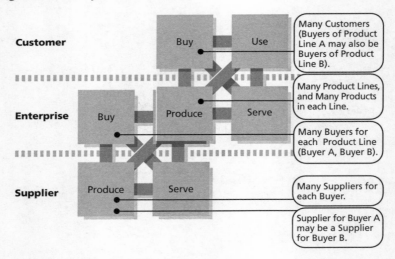

Management (SRM). This means that there are two totally different perspectives on exactly the same conversation. The enterprise sees a customer through its CRM and at the same time the customer sees a supplier through its SRM. CRM and SRM are the two faces of the value chain.

In a business-to-business situation, it is highly likely that one of the customers of an enterprise will also be a supplier to that enterprise. This means that when an enterprise engages in a conversation with one of its customers, it may become important to know whether or not that customer is one of its suppliers. In fact, the success of the conversation may depend on knowing whether or not a customer is also a supplier. Turning back to the definition of the term "relationship" in Chapter 3, the context of an exchange should include not only information about the conversation with a customer, but also information about the supply-side conversations that have occurred with that customer.

The extension of the exchange space into a value chain, and identifying the two faces of the value chain, reveals a number of the issues that must be addressed by both the business and tech-

Figure 4-8: *The Two Sides of the Value Chain*

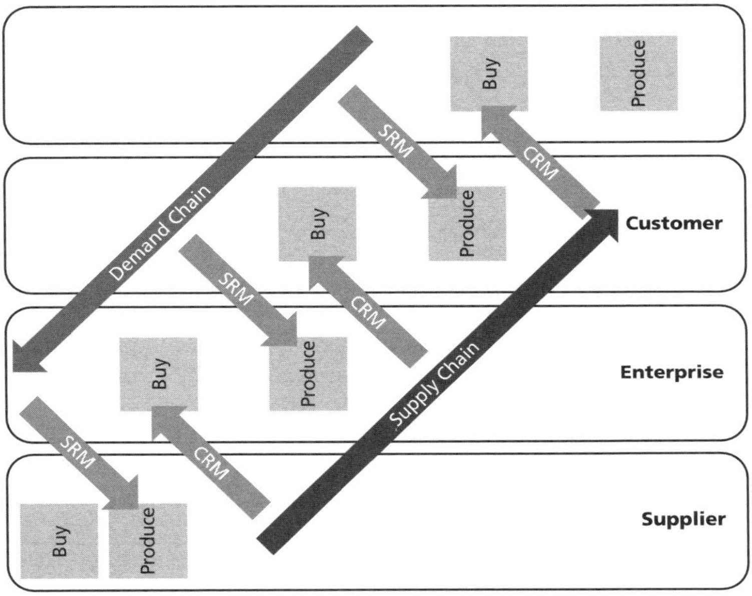

nology systems that are required to support CRM. These issues are further explored in Parts II through IV, which deal with the ten most critical questions associated with CRM initiatives.

Keeping it Real

In real life, simple ideas become complicated fast. And although this book focuses on trying to make life simpler, it is still grounded in reality. For example, Chapter 2 contrasts the simple appeal of CRM with the complex reality of its implementation. In this chapter, the exchange space started out as a simple representation of how conversations occur, and quickly grew more complex as it was applied to realistic situations. But this does not detract from its usefulness. It enables managers to work in more predictable ways as they consider the conversations that they have with their customers. Conversations are complex. Relationships are complex.

Designing conversations is and will remain hard work, but it is important hard work.

New e-technologies and innovations haven't changed human nature. The rich interaction people enjoyed in the old, traditional community marketplaces is not easy to recreate in the new cyber-marketplace, the World Wide Web. Many of the companies that have succeeded are doing so by designing better conversations. But so far they have worked intuitively, based on their instinctive knowledge of customers. The exchange space adds structure to that intuition.

5

CHAPTER

The Relationship Management Framework

"What is the use of a book," thought Alice,
"without pictures or conversations?"
—Lewis Carroll,
Alice in Wonderland, 1865

One might also ask, what's the use of a book without action? Or, to be more precise, a business book without actionable advice? Chapter 3, "The New Language of Relationships" and Chapter 4, "The Exchange Space" paint, in a practical, no-nonsense way, a vivid picture of the conversations and exchanges that are central to every relationship. But a picture does not actually create a conversation. Nor does it help an organization sustain a relationship, and especially a relationship with today's demanding customer. Something more is required.

Why a Management Framework?

Like the Mad Hatter's tea party, relationships are constantly in motion. The guests connect, disconnect, and reconnect, as customers do with enterprises. The party runs on the Internet 24 hours a day, seven days a week, worldwide. It all looks spontaneous. But as any host or hostess knows, throwing a good party depends on attention to detail—the right combination of food, drink, ambience and, of course, the right guests. Attention to detail requires a structured approach. Similarly, sustaining conversations with customers requires structure—a Relationship Management Framework.

A Relationship Management Framework enables the Relationship-Based Enterprise to converse fluently, at many levels, over an extended period of time, with many different customers. It is a comprehensive management framework for handling the continuous and varied set of management activities that are required to organize conversations. It is a way to take action, repeatedly and successfully.

The Relationship Management Framework translates pictures of what conversations should be into practical designs that work for real customers, customers who may not all want the same style of relationship. It helps cut through the complexity so often associated with CRM initiatives and builds a shared understanding of any CRM program. And finally, it enables organizations to focus on only the most critical of the hundreds of possible questions associated with CRM. When used in a disciplined way for all these purposes, the Relationship Management Framework becomes the soul of the Relationship-Based Enterprise.

Discovery, Dialogue, and Discipline

Successful organizations become obsessive about certain actions to the point where these actions become preoccupations. These preoccupations drive strategic thinking and day-to-day management decisions, and shape the enterprise culture. They are not sequential steps to be completed one after another, like the activities required to build a house; they are the essence of the house itself.

The Relationship Management Framework (Figure 5-1) focuses actions around three preoccupations: discovery, dialogue, and discipline. *Discovery* is about customers, *dialogue* is about relationships, and *discipline* is about management. Together, discovery, dialogue, and discipline are the preoccupations that create, sustain, and manage customer relationships.

Figure 5-1: *The Relationship Management Framework*

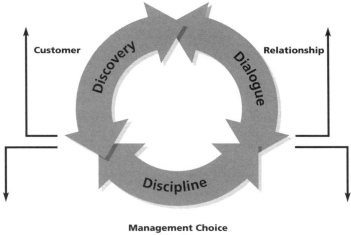

Discovery

Being preoccupied with discovery means seeking ways to build ongoing knowledge about customers. Consequently, discovery is centered on learning. It can be supported by a variety of technologies such as data warehousing, customer information systems, data mining, and analytical software.

Discovery provides the basis for recognizing, remembering, and understanding customers. It enables the enterprise—in a world where the customer is constantly changing—to identify and define their customers, customer preferences, and the customers' potential value to the enterprise. This knowledge provides the context for the exchanges that grow into ongoing conversations that build and sustain relationships with customers.

Discovery is also the practical response to the desire for "perfect" information about customers. As pointed out in Chapter 1, perfect information about customers is not a realistic option in a dynamic, changing business environment. And if building up perfect information as though it were a static business asset is not possible, then the traditional search for perfect loyalty must give way to the more realistic alternative—engaging in conversations with customers. Of course, conversations are not always predictable, at least not in the same way as mass-marketing and distribution systems have been for decades. Sometimes, conversations with today's customers are downright surprising. And leveraging the surprise factor of conversations means leaving aside the traditional search for "perfect information" about customers, "perfect products and services," and a "perfect organization." The realistic, practical alternative is to continually discover customers. Engaging in conversations where information and value is exchanged—dialogues, not monologues—is how discovery occurs.

Dialogue

Being preoccupied with dialogue means creating relationships with customers based on conversations. The preoccupation is centered on ensuring that value is created in every conversation with a customer. The objective of dialogue is to create the value that both the customer and the enterprise seek. Dialogue means working together, it means sharing resources, and it involves an offer. Dialogue is where "conversation design" becomes an operational reality.

Dialogue enables the enterprise to define the relationship style that customers desire, the type of conversations and exchanges that will support that relationship, and how the enterprise can foster continual exchange and share control of the relationship.

Like discovery, dialogue is a practical response to the dynamic, changing business environment—in this case, where perfect products or services are no longer possible due to rapidly changing customer needs, customer expectations, competitive actions, and evolving technology.

Discipline

Becoming preoccupied with discipline means making management decisions about the operational mechanisms necessary to enable continuous discovery and dialogue. The objective of discipline is to design the business in a way that supports conversations with customers and therefore the desired relationship.

Discipline enables the enterprise to develop its identity and branding, its organizational structures and infrastructures, its methods of measuring and managing performance, and its ability to change and to manage change.

Like discovery and dialogue, discipline is a practical response to the dynamic, changing business environment—in this case, where perfect organizational designs are no longer possible because of the dynamic nature of the new economy. In the flat, fluid organizational structures of e-commerce and e-business, an organization can be, at various times, a customer, a partner, a supplier, a contractor, an integrator, a distributor, a portal—and more.

A Linked and Balanced System

Discovery, dialogue, and discipline are actually linked together to form a system of preoccupations (Figure 5-2) for dealing with constant change. The Relationship-Based Enterprise constantly discovers its customers, replenishing its customer knowledge through conversations and its understanding of the context of those conversations and adjusting value propositions as necessary. Engaging customers in dialogue enables discovery by building and sustaining relationships, created by conversations that consist of value exchanges, with the content of these conversations adjusted as necessary to sustain the relationships. And discovery and dialogue are enabled through management discipline, which focuses on achieving specific business outcomes for customers by ensuring the business is properly designed to facilitate the right conversations and relationships. Market research gives way to conversation and knowledge sharing, which enables customers to help design products, channels, and value-creating conversations. Discovery, dialogue, and discipline are the 3Ds of the Relationship-Based Enterprise.

Figure 5-2: *Preoccupations*

	Domain	Goal	Means	Variable
Discovery	Customer	Customer Knowledge	Context	Value Proposition
Dialogue	Relationship	Value	Conversation	Content
Discipline	Management	Business Outcomes	Business Design	Infrastructure

The 3Ds also help balance the internal and external focus of an enterprise. This dual focus differentiates the Relationship-Based Enterprise, and it counterbalances the characteristically inward-looking focus of enterprises engaged in current CRM initiatives. As illustrated in Figure 5-3, the tension between internal and external is characterized by cost versus revenue, products and services versus customers, and integration versus connections.

Discovery balances the enterprise's internal bias toward cost by focusing the energies of the enterprise on both costs and revenue. Dialogue balances the enterprise's internal bias toward products and services by focusing the energies of the enterprise both internally (on products and services) and externally (on customers). And discipline balances any internal bias toward integration of business processes and information systems by focusing the energies of the enterprise on both internal integration and external connections.

Figure 5-3: *A Balanced Focus*

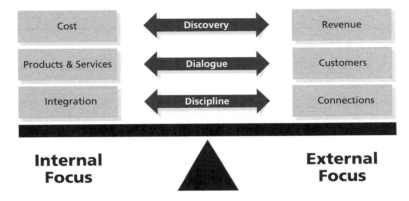

The focus of each "D" is action. Discovery, dialogue, and discipline provide managers with perspectives, processes, and guidelines to create and sustain a Relationship-Based Enterprise. They are the actionable part of the definition of CRM.

The Framework in Action: Delivering Groceries … and Relationships

In Chapter 3, the new language of relationships revealed why Bob and his family chose the Web-enabled grocery shopping service offered by the on-line supermarket. From the perspective of Bob and his family, home delivery of a standard grocery order is not a major part of their lives. In fact, groceries take far less time and thought than ever before. The on-line supermarket, however, has a different story to tell. On one level, its business mission is to "deliver the groceries." But on another, it must also "deliver relationships" and build an organization to support those relationships. This is the perspective from the enterprise side of the relationship.

To win the business of the Bobs of the world, real-life on-line supermarkets have undergone a process similar to the one Grocerycart.com experienced.

First, Grocerycart.com developed a broad vision for its business: it would create virtual grocery stores on-line rather than in the "real" world. A fleet of vans and personal delivery agents would distribute the groceries the last mile from warehouse to home. Customers would be drawn to Grocerycart by the convenience of shopping from any PC, with prompt delivery of just the right groceries, plus laundry and household consumables.

In essence, Grocerycart's business vision defined the type of relationship it wished to have with customers. To translate this vision into reality, the company had to plunge into the details of management—determining how to inventory household needs, arrange pick-up and delivery times, get the shopping lists right, revise the menus, and do reminders. It turned out that the largest part of Grocerycart's effort was associated with sustaining the relationship and the organizational mechanisms needed to support that relationship. Their CRM program quickly became complex and multi-faceted. There were hundreds of things to do, and hundreds of questions that needed to be answered.

To simplify and answer these questions, Grocerycart could have used the Relationship Management Framework. First, it is a useful instrument for organizing Grocerycart's management activity under broad headings that can be widely understood within the organization. Beyond that, discovery, dialogue, and discipline form a linked system that enables managers to trace—and more effectively manage—linkages among all the issues and questions. For example, engaging customers in conversations on nutrition under *dialogue* can lead to new *discoveries* about the customer and at the same time identify the management decisions—"Should we carry this line?"—required under *discipline*.

Consider the examples in Figure 5-4 of how Grocerycart managers did, in fact, apply their preoccupations with discovery, dialogue, and discipline—although certainly not by these names—to turn Grocerycart's relationship vision into real conversations with customers.

Figure 5-4: *Applying the 3Ds*

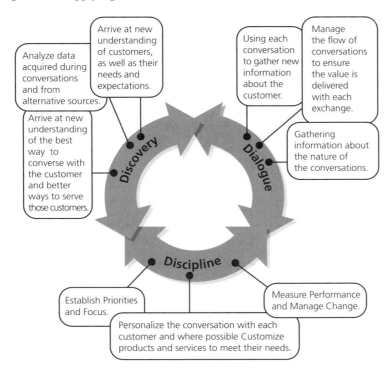

In Figure 5-4, dialogue provided the raw material for discovery, discovery provided the insight and understanding that powered discipline, and discipline provided the choices that modified both the approach and methods of both discovery and dialogue. The knowledge gained through discovery enabled the enterprise to recognize and remember customers, as well as to personalize further conversations with those customers. The results appeared simple to Bob. Behind the scenes at Grocerycart, however, the process was complex. And complexity will continue to grow as new, more convenient communications channels are added to the mix—set-top boxes on cable TV, hand-held terminals, and Internet-linked appliances, such as the refrigerator.

The learning process of discovery was tightly linked with the conversations that were a part of dialogue and provided valuable input to discipline. Management took action concerning a long list of issues—the design of customer information systems, intelligent Web sites, call centers, and other channels. And of course, not only did the decisions taken by management affect the approach taken to discover and converse with customers, but discovery and dialogue provide direct input to management decision-making.

As further illustrated in Figure 5-5, each "D" is linked to the elements that define a relationship. Without this kind of linkage, translating conversation designs—pictures of conversations—into "conversation parties" with real customers would be much more difficult.

Clearly, Grocerycart is not just managing the delivery of groceries, it is managing in a very real way "the delivery of a relationship" and the organization to support that relationship. This need to manage relationships is just as important when the customer is another enterprise as it is when the customer is Bob. Sustaining a relationship with a customer, whether in a business-to-consumer

Figure 5-5: *Linkages of the 3Ds to the Definition of a Relationship*

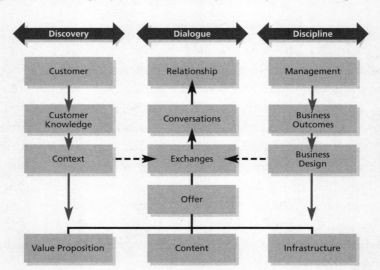

context as with Grocerycart, or in a business-to-business situation, requires a focus on the conversations that create the relationship. An enterprise must actively address the things that are required on its side of the conversation. And these things involve the 3Ds–discovery, dialogue, and discipline.

The Relationship Space

The concepts of discovery and dialogue can also be used to find solutions to a central problem of every enterprise, that of customer segmentation. They enable the enterprise to complement traditional demographic and psychographic segmentation with true relationship-based segmentation: the precise identification of customer groups according to the relationship style, and type of conversation, they want with the enterprise. To take a basic example, two upper-income professional households—next-door neighbors—may want two completely different types of conversations with their grocery supplier. One may see the task as a chore and want the basics supplied on a regular basis with little effort on their part. And so identifying exceptions through a Web page or via a call center could be very attractive. The other may see the task as a pleasurable escape and a chance to try new brands or sample alternatives. This second customer may enjoy extending the conversation over the counter of the delicatessen.

Relationships, conversations, and exchanges can be designed and managed to meet the needs of specific customers and customer groups, even down to segments of one. The relationship space (Figure 5-6) provides a map of the main types of relationships that can be designed and built with customers. This framework maps relationship styles along two dimensions: the amount known about the customer along the discovery axis; and the richness of the conversations with those customers along the other axis.

Located on these axes are four quadrants that highlight four possible relationship styles. At the outer corners of the quadrants, at the most extreme limits of the axes, the styles are as follows:

- **Price-centered relationship**—no knowledge of customer and little or no dialogue. This type of relationship is associated with sales of commodity products at the lowest price. Here the enterprise exhibits operational leadership.
- **Product-centered relationship**—a great deal of knowledge about types of customers, most likely in the form of customer segmentation, with little or no dialogue with specific customers. Products and services are customized to meet the needs of finely defined customer segments. Here the enterprise exhibits product/service leadership.
- **Need-centered relationship**—little knowledge about customers en masse, but a great deal of dialogue concerning the requirements, needs, and problems of specific customers. In this type of relationship the process for delivering products and services is personalized to meet the needs of each individual customer. Here the enterprise exhibits exchange leadership.
- **Value-centered relationship**—a great deal is known about individual customers, and significant dialogue with those customers. This type of relationship is associated

Figure 5-6: *Relationship Styles and Customer Groups*

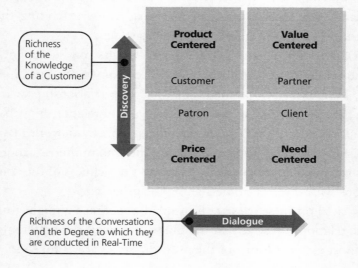

with organizations that work together with their customers to create the needed products and services.

Here the enterprise exhibits conversation leadership.
The Relationship-Based Enterprise has the flexibility to use any and all of these relationship styles depending on the nature of the conversations required by its customers.

To find out where customers and customer groups are positioned in the relationship space, managers need to answer two common sense management questions: "How well do we know and understand the customer?" and, "How dynamic are our conversations and exchanges with that customer?"

The extreme corners of the relationship space highlight the four possible relationship styles and types of conversation. To label these styles, the typical customer groups are named as follows: patron, customer, client, and partner. The relationship style that corresponds to each of these groups is price-centered, product-centered, need-centered, and value-centered.

The Patron Group

Members of the patron group have a relationship with the enterprise characterized by very simple conversations. They buy products or standard services anonymously, trading money for what is on offer, and move on. A patron limits the information exchanged to "my credit card number" or a similar bit of data. Exchanges of money for product are conducted impersonally "over the counter." Organizations that serve patrons well offer them high-quality commodities at the lowest price and an efficient purchasing experience. The enterprise has only very limited knowledge of patrons.

The Customer Group

Members of the customer group also have relationships with the enterprise that can be characterized by very simple conversations. However, the enterprise has intimate knowledge about customers, most likely in the form of precise segmentation by type. Organizations that serve the customer group well focus on customizing their products and services to meet the needs of a specific type of customer. They typically track buying patterns and offer rich product lines matched to specific segments. Enterprises focused on the customer group invest more in products and services than in relationships with individual customers. Their efforts are driven by their understanding of a finely segmented marketplace.

The Client Group

Members of the client group have a relationship with the enterprise characterized by rich conversations concerning specific requirements, services, or problems. The enterprise has a great deal of knowledge about specific customers; however, it has relatively limited knowledge about the client group as a whole. The clients it does converse with are engaged in far-reaching, complex conversations and they attach value to a lively interactive exchange. Enterprises that serve the client group well personalize their conversations. They are prepared to personalize channels, electronic interfaces, and the processes they use for interacting with their clients. But they are not prepared to track buying patterns or offer rich product lines matched to specific client segments. The relationship itself is far more important than the product or service.

The Partner Group

Members of the partner group, like those in the client group, have a relationship with the enterprise characterized by rich conversations and cooperation. The enterprise maintains a great deal of knowledge about individual partners, as well as about them as a whole (their industry, their needs in general, the issues they face, business trends, and so on). Partners cooperate closely with the enterprise to co-create value, entering into a rich exchange of information and other resources. Effective partnering with this group of customers creates value through multi-faceted conversation. This type of relationship may involve a joint venture or the kind of sharing that is common among the members of a community.

How it all Works Together

The Relationship-Based Enterprise combines elements of discovery and dialogue, supported by the appropriate discipline, to foster any, and all, of these relationship styles, depending on the nature of the conversation required by its customers. Most large-scale enterprises serve a mix of patrons, clients, customers, and partners.

Consider the different relationships styles of the customers who have selected Grocerycart as their preferred grocery supplier.

- **Patrons:** The clickstreams on Grocerycart's Web site reveal frequent visits by a group of customers known among the staffers who field e-mail queries as "price scavengers." As defined in this chapter, these are patrons. They visit often, scan the specials, and send e-mails asking whether Grocerycart will match weekly specials on local supermarkets. They order for pick-up—but only once every ten visits or so. Grocerycart.com keeps a "specials" section posted on its Web site to attract these patron group "eyeballs," but only in hopes of recruiting some into the customer or client groups.

- **Customers:** Just next door to Bob, Carol and her son have different requirements. Carol is a busy professional and her son is a graduate student at university. They want to order groceries on the Web and get home delivery, but executed in a very different way than Bob's arrangement. They prefer to select their menu once and then let Grocerycart track their buying patterns and deliver "just what we need" each Thursday morning at 7:00 a.m., with a minimum of dialogue. Grocerycart can meet their requirements by building a simple customer profile based on this household's fixed schedules, predictable shopping menus, and consumption patterns. Once Carol and her son decide what they want, they don't change their minds often. And they don't want to repeat themselves!

- **Clients:** Tom and his family are clients. They are Web-literate, like to converse with others, and are hungry for information as well as groceries. Lively conversation and dialogue have value for them. Tom's household wants flexible channels and interfaces (Web site, phone, Palmtops, and so on) that enable them to change their preferred grocery menus frequently, order at irregular intervals, change from home delivery to pick-up, cancel the service for two weeks while traveling, and save time. For Tom and his family variety is the spice of life, and this is how they see the groceries that they buy. The Grocerycart Web and home delivery service is designed to withstand the stress of such intensive dialogue.

■ **Partners:** Grocerycart currently has no partners, but it is considering the potential. For example, the marketing group is looking at the possibility of recruiting people like Bob's nutrition-conscious wife, Jane, into a chat room co-sponsored by Grocerycart and a virtual community of health, fitness, and medical sites. They are hoping people like Jane will join and perhaps even become a discussion moderator and eventual community leader.

The case of Grocerycart reflects the realities faced by many organizations—most notably large-scale companies and rapidly growing companies—companies with a diversified customer base. There are obviously many relationship styles and many different "conversation parties" that can be organized, as well as many possible CRM strategies.

The relationship space helps visualize how relationships can evolve and support decisions concerning everything from corporate strategy down to the design of infrastructures and the selection of technology. It helps organizations manage CRM by cutting through the complexity that so often seems to characterize CRM initiatives.

Answering the Ten Critical Questions

The hard facts of life are that managers involved in CRM initiatives will not have time to start by "designing a conversation" on paper and then putting in place the technology and organizational structures to support that conversation. Rather, they will be dealing with two challenges simultaneously. First, they will be conversing with customers and trying to adjust the "exchanges" in real time as they talk, or interact over phone lines and Web links. Secondly, they will be implementing a specific part of a CRM initiative or software package. And they will be confronting one of the hundreds of specific questions that are raised by CRM. Questions such as, "How do we train call center agents in CRM methods?" or "When do we ask for help from the CEO?" and many, many more. CRM touches every business process of an enterprise.

The rest of this book considers the ten questions considered to be the most critical. These critical questions provide a common sense framework that organizations can use to get to the heart of Customer Relationship Management. Or, rather, the specific facet of a CRM program that they are dealing with this week or this month.

The ten critical questions are integrated into the Relationship Management Framework, as shown in Figure 5-7. They provide a concrete way of managing the processes of discovery, dialogue, and discipline. By answering the questions, organizations develop their approach to CRM with the balanced perspective of a Relationship-Based Enterprise.

Discovery: The first three critical questions, grouped under discovery, are aimed at the continual profiling of customers:
1. "Who are our customers?"
2. "What do our customers want and expect?"
3. "What is the value potential of our customers?"

Dialogue: The questions under dialogue focus on the evolution of the relationship between the enterprise and its customers:
4. "What kind of relationship do we want to build with our customers?"
5. "How do we foster exchange?"
6. "How do we work together and share control?"

Discipline: The questions under discipline focus on the management decisions and choices that must be made concerning those mechanisms that will enable continual discovery and dialogue.

7. "Who are we?"
8. "How do we organize to move value closer to our customers?"
9. "How do we measure and manage our performance?"
10. "How do we increase our capacity for change?"

These ten critical questions have been developed through a review of client experiences, our insights, and best practices in the field of CRM. Answering them systematically will help organizations clarify the focus and objectives of their CRM initiatives. They also help clarify the scope of those initiatives—whether they include call centers, Web sites, sales forces, the entire enterprise and perhaps its value chain. With the Relationship Management Framework and its associated ten questions, executives will be able to guide:

- the evolution of their relationships with customer
- the creation of a company-wide CRM game plan and
- the selection of solutions with the most appropriate combination of technology. In fact, the successful and profitable use of technology for CRM in large measure depends on how well these simple questions are addressed.

Answers to these questions build an important part of an organization's approach to Customer Relationship Management —and are the basis of the Relationship-Based Enterprise.

Figure 5-7: *The Relationship Management Framework*

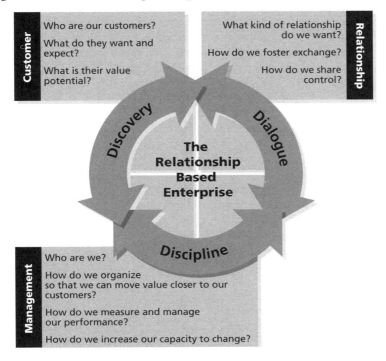

Discovery — A Process of Learning

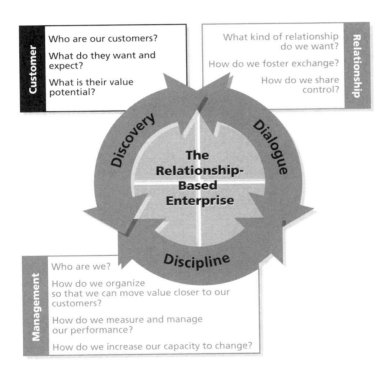

"Discovery is an information-gathering and sense-making process that serves as the basis for making a choice."

—Ralph D. Stacey, **Complexity and Creativity in Organizations**, 1996

6

CHAPTER

Who Are Our Customers?

Elements of an Answer

- **Define customers** —What the term "customer" means
- **Identify customers** —How to discover the ideal customer
- **Anticipate customers** —How to forecast customer characteristics
- **Recognize customers** —How to identify customers on contact
- **Remember customers** —What information is needed

Many organizations assume they know their customers. They point to demographics, psychographics, analyst reports, loyalty programs, price-competitiveness, and so on, and say, "We've done our homework; we know exactly who our customers are." In many cases, customers are seen as fixed assets that are somehow "owned" by the enterprise. Some organizations can't imagine losing customers en masse for any reason, short of a disaster. The very idea that they may not know who their customers are is simply inconceivable.

The Relationship-Based Enterprise makes a contrary assumption —that it does *not* know its customers. There is no guilt, fear, or shame associated with this assumption. It's just a different starting point. For the Relationship-Based Enterprise, customers are a fluid, ever-changing element of a business equation. They are not measured and documented, like stock in a warehouse. Rather, they are conversed with, and their processes are connected with those of the enterprise. Such conversations and connections reveal who customers are today, which is different from who they were yesterday and, most likely, different from who they will be tomorrow.

The Relationship-Based Enterprise's preoccupation with discovery, dialogue, and discipline means that it can continually discover and re-discover its customers—constantly adjusting its understanding of who they are—as its customers grow, evolve, and change. The preoccupation with dialogue keeps the conversation going, and the preoccupation with discipline manages how conversations take place. Discovery focuses the enterprise's attention on customers—and three critical questions: "Who are our customers?" "What do our customers want and expect?" and "What is the value potential of our customers?" Answering all three of these questions results in a constantly current profile of customers.

Figure 6-1 Discovery: *The Customer Profile*

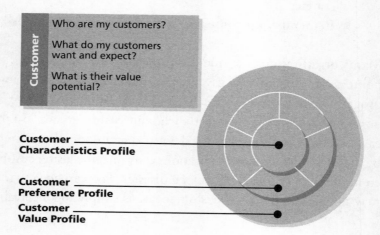

This profile consists of their characteristics, their preferences, and their value potential, as illustrated in Figure 6-1.

The first of these questions, "Who are your customers?" and the resulting customer characteristics profile, is the subject of this chapter. Chapters 7 and 8 describe how to add the other elements needed to maintain a constantly current profile of customers—a customer preference profile and a customer value profile.

The place to start is with a clear understanding of the term "customer."

What the Term "Customer" Means

Organizations need to understand exactly what is meant by the term "customer" if they are going to start conversations or design conversations with their customers. Without a clear understanding of the term, those conversations will simply not work.

One way to understand the term "customer" is to define the customer role. A customer is simply the recipient of the products or services resulting from a conversation. However, because people and companies are separate from the roles that either plays, it is rather limiting to define what a customer is or is not in this way.

Another way to define the term "customer" is through context. For example, a customer can be both an individual and a member of a group. In a typical household, a child might never be seen by a utility company, or if seen, only viewed as a part of the energy-consuming unit, not a distinct customer. However, a cereal company may see the same child as an individual consumer and a decision-influencer, and a video-game provider may see him as a member of an on-line user group. The child is seen by three separate enterprises. Each sees the child in only one way. However, there are situations where this child could interact with the same enterprise as either an individual or as a member of a group. If the on-line video provider sees the child only as a member of a group, then its conversations would be directed toward the group, and the enterprise might miss the opportunity to establish a relationship with the child. Understanding the multiple dimensions of customers, depending on context, allows the Relationship-Based Enterprise to create appropriate conversations.

Still another way to define the term "customer" is through the enterprise's products and services. Every time a business develops a new product or enters a new market, it should ask: "What is a customer?" Without this simple question the results may be unexpected. In 1984, for example, when Apple Computer introduced the Macintosh, in doing so it redefined what it meant by the term customer. As it turned out, the term customer described writers and graphic artists who were interested in desktop publishing. According to Guy Kawasaki, former chief evangelist of Apple Computer, Inc., this wasn't intentional. But, says Guy, "desktop publishing saved Apple Computer" (*Rules for Revolutionaries*, p. 87).

Defining and redefining what the term "customer" means can be a critical success factor in business, particularly when the marketplace is undergoing rapid and significant change. Consider, for example, the following story of HiVolt Energy, and its efforts to redefine its customers.

HiVolt Announces a New Strategy

Not many years ago, HiVolt Energy was a proud monopoly. But then legislation stripped away its major assets—hydroelectric dams, long-distance power lines, and even regional switching stations. By law, HiVolt was obliged to compete with other energy retailers. It didn't take HiVolt long to realize that its market share was about to shrink.

Upon reviewing its strategic alternatives, HiVolt decided to leverage its long-standing relationships with customers and the reputation of its brand. It would enter the emerging home-management services market. The new services to be provided—along with electricity—included home maintenance, energy efficiency, shopping, babysitting, car-pooling, environmental compliance, mortgages, and insurance.

"Rather than establishing alliances or acquiring, we will diversify by partnering with our customers," the CEO told financial analysts during a recent conference call. The vision, she explained, is to "help working parents manage work and family."

"Our strategy is to transform HiVolt Energy, a single-product monopoly, into an integrator of home services, to be known as E-Hearth. It will not build from the ground up; instead, it will establish partnerships with other service providers and with community groups."

The E-Hearth Home Services announcement generated a good "story" among analysts, investors, and the media-consuming public. Behind the scenes, however, HiVolt managers struggled with the assumptions underpinning their new strategy. In one meeting, HiVolt operational managers outlined a plan to speed up call-center service—assuming that basic service quality was key to retaining energy consumers in a competitive market. But the marketing team for the new E-Hearth organization saw faster call-center service as a secondary concern. They wanted an immediate telemarketing campaign to push energy-related home maintenance and energy efficiency services—assuming that *these* were the keys to retaining energy consumers. As the discussion wore on, both parties began to realize that their knowledge of customers and what they want was far from perfect.

The question, "What do we mean when we say customer?" began to pop up frequently in the meetings.

The process of finding an answer to this question is central to the relationship-based approach that HiVolt has chosen. The answer is strategic, both in scope and intent. It is a question of business design, and closely linked to the many decisions that management must make concerning the discipline that will be needed to make the strategy successful.

In redefining the term customer, HiVolt needed to find customer groups that would enter into the types of conversations that would aggregate into long-term relationships. They needed more than a finely segmented description of the energy market, something that current systems already delivered. They needed to challenge many long-held assumptions, as shown in Figure 6-2.

Challenging their assumptions led HiVolt managers to abandon the long-standing and comfortable meaning of the term customer: rate-paying households. With its E-Hearth home-management services strategy, HiVolt entered a less certain world where the term customer would mean more than it did in the past. They would have to define and redefine what they meant by customer in an attempt to identify their ideal customers. Home-management services were not the same as delivering electricity through a meter on the wall.

How to Discover the Ideal Customer

To discover the ideal customer for their E-Hearth initiative, HiVolt started by collecting data through exhaustive market research. Their marketing team reviewed the current HiVolt geographic

Figure 6-2: *Management Assumptions and Challenges*

Management Assumption	Challenge
"We own the customer."	This was true when we held a monopoly, and may remain true for the short term. But it is not true in a competitive environment where customers have choices. Now the tables have turned, we want customers to "own" us instead!
"We can build on established customer relationships."	The relationships were established in monopolistic markets where customers faced high switching costs. There is no guarantee that these relationships will last in a more competitive market.
"Our large customer base is a major asset."	This is true only if we can in fact build on established customer relationships.
"Our customer database is a gold mine of information."	It may be a gold mine of electricity-related information. It remains to be seen whether this is true for our new services.
"CRM software and the Web will enable new levels of information and service integration."	This will happen only if our assumptions about our customer relationships prove correct.

and demographic segmentation schemes, which were based on consumption volumes. They conducted open-ended discussions with customer and employee focus groups. They spent a lot of time in call centers, listening to calls and talking to the agents about customer concerns. They even rode with service crews, who actually had more direct contact with customers than any other group in HiVolt.

Predictably, they discovered that the majority of HiVolt electricity consumers took the meter on the wall for granted. They simply did not contact HiVolt very often for any reason, so there was very little marketing information to be gleaned from their account files. But the marketing team did discover that some consumers had previously relied on heating oil or gas, and had switched to electricity as an energy source. Most of the dialogue between HiVolt and its customers was generated by a small group of consumers, professionals with families, who tended to contact the company quite often concerning payments and credit, inaccurate bills, advice on home insulation, and repair of electrical heaters. There were also a number of small businesses that had special energy requirements, such as small shops, family businesses, and restaurants.

To segment customers into groups, the marketing team mapped all of their customer data into the relationship space, introduced in Chapter 5. As illustrated in Figure 6-3, it classified customers as patrons, customers, clients, and partners. The consumers who took electricity for granted and rarely contacted HiVolt were grouped as patrons. Those who showed signs that they had responded to promotions concerning the advantages of electricity and the messages of HiVolt were grouped as customers. Those households and commercial customers who used standard services but who often required special attention were grouped as clients. The small percentage of customers who had worked closely with HiVolt to develop unique solutions to their energy problems were grouped as partners.

Figure 6-3: *Relationship Styles of Major Customer Groups*

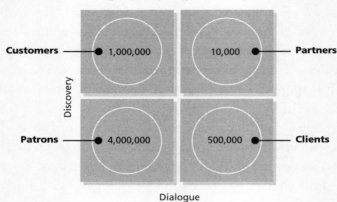

The marketing team then posed the question: "What is the potential of each of these customer groups to become customers of the full services of E-Hearth?" Here's what they decided:

- **Patrons**—A large number of households classified as patrons would be price-sensitive. This group could easily be tempted to switch to competing energy sources, and HiVolt determined that they had little interest in the types of services to be offered by E-Hearth. HiVolt would need to focus on standard marketing and pricing strategies to retain these customers in a free market.
- **Customers**—Consumers classified as customers were deemed more loyal to electricity as an energy source. The marketing research team concluded that this group might be interested in two or three of the new E-Hearth services, the most likely being energy efficiency and environmental compliance.
- **Clients**—Consumers classified as clients were found to be satisfied with HiVolt services, as demonstrated by the high satisfaction ratings they gave to HiVolt call centers and service crews. They were characterized as professionals with families for whom E-Hearth services would save time.
- **Partners**—Consumers classified as partners were estimated to be willing to pay for truly "integrated solutions"…

and willing to work with HiVolt to help design those solutions. The marketing team thought partners would eventually be more profitable than any of the other groups, but would require a number of specialty services that would take time to develop.

The final, most important question for the marketing team was, "Which groups are ideal customers, and how do we evolve those relationships?"

Use of the relationship space to frame an answer enabled HiVolt management to see, at a glance, the magnitude of the challenge for its E-Hearth initiative. Most of its energy users were patrons. But the ideal group of customers for E-Hearth is a combination of customers, clients, and partners. New conversations would have to be developed, initially with customers and clients and then with partners. The marketing team determined that customers and clients were open to new conversations, centered around customized solutions and personalized service channels aimed at "helping households manage work and family." Partners, though more profitable, would need additional customized services, which would be offered later.

There was also an opportunity to develop patrons into either customers or clients, which would require targeted marketing campaigns. For example, a campaign to develop patrons into customers might focus on raising patrons' awareness of the advantages of electricity as opposed to natural gas. Getting patrons to think about energy consequences and adopt electricity as their energy choice would open the door to E-Hearth services for energy efficiency and environmental compliance.

How to Forecast Customer Characteristics

In developing the preliminary customer definitions and overview of characteristics, HiVolt gathered much basic information. However, in the process, judgment calls were made. Necessarily, these judgments were based on the proposed strategy of E-Hearth.

But more information, based on real data from E-Hearth customers, was needed as the basis for marketing strategy development, information systems planning, and action. To move in step
with customers, E-Hearth would need to forecast the major characteristics of ideal customers (and less than ideal customers)—
forecasts based on continual data collection and assessment.

Note that gathering and assessing customer information is
the first step towards customer segmentation, which has the
potential to produce high returns in a relationship-based strategy.
In large-scale organizations like HiVolt, customer segmentation is
a job that never ends; this is, in fact, why discovery is a preoccupation of the Relationship-Based Enterprise. It involves a long,
complex learning cycle through the 3Ds—especially when the aim
is to understand customers, in both the buy and use roles and as
individuals and members of a group. There are many possibilities.
As a result, customer segmentation should generally be kept distinct from the basic steps of customer definition and customer
identification. Segmentation is dealt with extensively in Chapter 7,
which examines the second discovery question: "What do customers want and expect?" Assessing customer characteristics is a
first small step in the overall process.

At this early stage, without actually delivering E-Hearth services, the HiVolt market research team was able to make only preliminary forecasts about the future potential of the four customer
groups. As illustrated in Figure 6-4, "Customer Characteristics
Profile," the team compared current customer characteristics with
potential characteristics. The profile would be updated regularly as
new information became available.

Developing an overview of current and future customer characteristics and listing them in a characteristics profile provided HiVolt
with a simple platform for three linked management processes:

- articulating the business design and marketing strategy
  as it evolved
- building the customer knowledge needed to support
  expanded conversations and relationships

■ building the information systems required to support customer definitions and more continually current profiles.

Figure 6-4: *Customer Characteristics Profile*

Group	Current Characteristics	Future Potential
Patron	- Bought house with electric heating installed. Has not had time to consider switching - Wants to avoid the expense of buying gas appliances - Price is OK, not thrilled - Electricity User – Buying is not a decision	- May switch to gas when prices are deregulated - May consider investing in multi-source equipment - No evidence of trust in HiVolt - Impossible to determine cross-sell potential
Customer	- Switched from oil or gas to electric heating - Invested in electric appliances and home insulation - Thinks in terms of "heating cost" not price/BTU - Expresses brand loyalty in focus group - Views HiVolt as heating company	- Likely to stay with electricity when prices are deregulated - Will not switch for small price difference - Likely to buy 2 or 3 E-Hearth home services
Client	- Similar to brand-loyal customer today - Complains a lot about service, but usually satisfied - Higher than average number of service calls - 2-3 kids - Time pressured Professional - Environmentally aware - Active in community, youth groups, sports	- Potential of using 5-10 services, such as babysitting, tutoring, shopping, family transportation - Wants help with emission control and energy use - Wants integrated approach to home services - Will want to design the service package and control details
Partner	- Runs a small shop or restaurant - Requires special assistance in addressing the energy problems - Helped to design the solution	- Likely to stay with electricity because of solutions developed - Brand loyal and good candidate for insurance and plumbing support

These management processes would become more effective as current and future customer characteristics continued to evolve. In addition, there were many other, more general customer characteristics that could be used to improve the organization's understanding of their needs and to broaden and deepen their conversations, such as home ownership, financial status, lifestyle, and household maturity. The important thing for HiVolt was to establish the type of data that needed to be collected and validated.

How to Identify Customers on Contact

Customer definitions and overviews provide vital information for marketing, operations, and strategic planners. The most immediate problem in a changing business, however, is more basic: "How do we recognize all these different types of customers?" If call-center agents can't tell a customer from a patron, or a client from a partner, they can't have the right conversations, thereby putting the relationship at risk.

For HiVolt, a large organization with 6 million customers, the problem was huge. HiVolt was used to dealing with customers semi-anonymously. More precisely, it dealt with their energy meters and checking accounts, identifying households only by name, address, and payment status. Many that had been grouped under the label patron actually preferred this type of relationship. Implicitly, they preferred the recognition standards they had experienced as participants in the mass market: they remained faceless, free to end a relationship without any need for explanation or discussion; yet their name and address were usually enough for an employee to access their files and answer basic questions if a service or payment problem arose.

These recognition standards would not be acceptable to customers and clients of the emerging E-Hearth organization. To expand relationships with customers and clients, HiVolt/E-Hearth agents needed to recognize them instantly, on contact—whether by phone or via the Web. Instant recognition was viewed as an opportunity to impress both customers and clients, and to help retain patrons.

To achieve instant recognition, HiVolt/E-Hearth decided to employ data markers. As shown in Figure 6-5, data markers vary depending on the nature of the business and the employee actions that must be taken once customers are "recognized" as belonging to some group or category. The key to identifying data markers lay in the conversations that HiVolt/E-Hearth wished its agents to have with customers. Each conversation would be a response to some "condition" or opportunity.

Figure 6-5: *Data Markers*

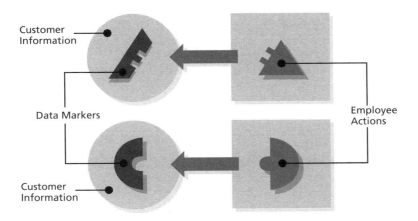

Following are some of the conditions and associated data markers in the customer information that HiVolt/E-Hearth identified:

- **Value proposition**—identifying the value proposition to be made to a customer. An example data marker is "purchases more than $5,000 per quarter."
- **Timeline considerations**—allowing the employee to take appropriate actions based on time considerations. An example data marker is "long-term customer."
- **Sales cycle considerations**—signaling the employee to take very specific sales actions. An example data marker is "sale of home."
- **Service cycle considerations**—providing guidance and in some cases notification of upcoming service to the employee. An example data marker is "time for furnace to be serviced."

Technically, there were many ways to implement data markers. However, as so often happens, when HiVolt/E-Hearth started discussing how data markers would be used, organizational issues —not technology—were the stumbling blocks.

Within HiVolt, like most organizations, the marketing team focused on the buy role—in this case, the new E-Hearth services. Customer service and operations people focused on the use role. The two groups were at odds, which created issues such as:

- **Segmentation rules**—Is a large family that pays late and frequently calls for service an "upper-income cross-sell opportunity" or a "high-cost customer?"
- **Operational feasibility**—Do call-center staff have the time and motivation to engage in meaningful conversations with callers?
- **Cost**—What are the direct and opportunity costs associated with gathering the needed information?

Often CRM strategies are marketing-dominated with too little consideration of the operational viability and the costs of implementation. Within large organizations, it is often technically challenging to incorporate the softer "marketing" processes with operational customer-service processes. The result can be "surprise" delays and significant additional costs.

At HiVolt, both sides realized that in the long term these two approaches would have to come together so that customer service and operations could take increased responsibility for customer recognition—engaging customers in the right conversations, and thereby extending those relationships. The ultimate goal was instant recognition of customers.

What Information is Needed

Being able to identify, recognize, and anticipate the needs of customers depends on reliable data and information. Without it, decisions concerning customers and the design of a business around those customers are really only shots in the dark. Discovery has a direct impact on discipline. HiVolt's initial market research of potential E-Hearth services provided a starting point. But information systems at HiVolt needed to be adjusted to keep the right customer information flowing into the organization.

As is typical for large organizations, HiVolt had many separate databases—each supporting different regions of the country. These separate information systems were built with a patchwork of legacy technologies. This created a lot of discussion about modernization and integration. Before the IT debate advanced too far, however, the heads of marketing and operations asked for a review of the actual data contained in these disparate customer information systems. The answer they got was:

- name and address
- monthly electricity consumption
- equipment purchased from HiVolt (usually space heaters and furnaces)
- billing and payment history
- credit rating (external service)
- dates of service calls and bills (infrequent).

This simple list forced management to face the reality that HiVolt's customer information system (CIS) was not exactly the gold mine it was assumed to be. Whatever the state of CIS technology, it was clear that it did not have the information required to produce customer and client profiles. Rather, it had electricity consumption and payment records for patrons—not the customer group that would eventually purchase and use E-Hearth home-management services.

To measure the magnitude of the challenge, the HiVolt and E-Heath project teams decided to "map" the information in the existing CISs against the definitions of key customer groups derived from the market research initiative. The results were:

- **Patrons:** The current information was adequate should HiVolt wish to continue with this type of relationship.

Screen formatting, organization for quick reference, and speed of access were the only issues.

- **Customers:** Precise information was lacking about attitudes towards the HiVolt brand, electricity as an energy source, or any price sensitivity. HiVolt call centers could not readily see the difference between patrons and customers. Some call-center agents knew the difference by instinct, but they could not link their instincts to shared customer definitions.

- **Clients:** Current information on service history for clients was adequate because clients often called with special requests. However, as with the customer group, HiVolt was missing clients' attitudes towards the HiVolt brand and electricity as an energy source, as well as any price sensitivity. HiVolt also lacked the demographic data needed to understand if there would be a demand from this group for home-management services. While call-center agents were able to distinguish between the client and customer groups, they did not record this information in the CISs. As a result, E-Hearth could not use the CIS to identify clients.

- **Partners:** E-Hearth did have what it considered to be a small group of partners. These were partners for its traditional product and services, but there were no partners for its new services. After deregulation, HiVolt expected to lose a large number of customers in this group. While they were partners of HiVolt, it was less likely that they would become partners of E-Hearth.

HiVolt's CIS is massive, but hardly a gold mine. The size was actually a problem for E-Hearth, since modifying these systems as requirements changed would be a difficult task. Establishing a basic CIS is likely to require a major investment, affecting business processes, organization roles and responsibilities, organizational culture, business and technology infrastructures, and legacy information systems. Wisely, HiVolt deferred. Instead, HiVolt decided that the growing E-Hearth organization would build its own interactive customer database using the Intranet and a Web site. All customer profiles in the E-Hearth database would have simple links to HiVolt customer information.

Customer profiles would be for both business-to-consumer and business-to-business relationships. The business-to-consumer profiles needed information on such variables as interaction data, lifestyle, attitudes, behavior, values, needs, and relationships. Business-to-business profiles needed to contain even more information, including whether each business was local or national or multinational; private or public; a major division; the business's size, financial status, major products and services; the market or industry sector it served; its strengths in the marketplace; its major customers and competitors; and critical success factors in the industry. As the E-Hearth organization matures, eventually supplanting HiVolt and transforming the basic nature of the company's business, E-Hearth's CIS will expand in step. The system will likely be designed and redesigned many times, including the processes for dealing with it, using it, and validating it, in many units across the organization. Its evolution will likely include:

- Development of a customer information strategy, to enable the supply of key customer information to the people in the organization who deal directly or indirectly with the customer through conversation. The strategy will address the collection of relevant information and ensure that co-existing operational and marketing objectives are satisfied.
- Validation of potential strategic solutions, using proofs of concept operating on a representative section of the customer base. These proofs of concept will include necessary modifications to business processes and the deployment of associated new technologies and systems. The information gathered from such exercises will be analyzed and extrapolated to shape the full-scale implementation of an appropriately modified and viable strategy.

- Development of a blended investment program that addresses all necessary process, culture, and technology changes. It will be supported by all impacted functions and secured with business sponsorship at the highest level. Inevitably, this program will involve the deployment of IT to support the processes of marketing and customer service. While it is possible to design a system capable of satisfying both needs concurrently, the cost and performance factors will make separate but linked systems the most likely scenario. This will promote the deployment of an operational CIS interacting with a data warehouse.
- Establishment of a holistic approach to knowledge management, one that will recognize that maintaining good customer information requires a blend of technology, people, and organizational capabilities.

The development journey will be long, with many twists and turns. But the objective is simple: when the customer calls, HiVolt /E-Hearth will look and feel like the mom-and-pop store on the corner—with instant recognition and accurate memory of every customer. The new company will know exactly who its customers are and, more importantly, it will have the processes it needs to change as its customers grow and evolve.

In designing customized solutions and personalized channels (conversation), HiVolt/E-Hearth will enable customers to contribute far more than money in exchange for service. They will contribute time, effort, and knowledge about their needs. They will become partners of the company. They will develop a stake in the solution and in continuing their conversations with the company. And HiVolt/E-Hearth will, in turn, develop a stake in delivering better solutions based on more intimate and current knowledge of their customer—the tools for continuing the conversations and strengthening the relationships.

Who's On First?

Abbott and Costello's famous comedy routine, "Who's on First," sums up the problem faced by the Relationship-Based Enterprise in identifying its customers. To start with, it has to define what the term "customer" means—in Abbott and Costello's terms, "who is" on first versus "is who?" on first—or it will just keep going around in circles. Without defining the participants, it is impossible to develop relationships. One way to do this is to classify customers by the style of relationship: as patrons, clients, customers, or partners. Each will be looking for a particular kind of conversation and value exchange, and it is the enterprise's task to focus on its ideal customer and structure conversations accordingly.

To maintain conversations and to create broader, deeper relationships, the Relationship-Based Enterprise also needs a way of anticipating what customers will need next. A customer characteristics profile, listing current characteristics and future relationship potential, is one way of doing this. In addition, everyone in the enterprise needs the ability to recognize customers on contact. A call-center agent, for example, must know right away that a caller is a patron, a client, a customer, or a partner. This kind of instant recognition is achieved by embedding data markers in the design of conversations. Each conversation can then become a response to some "condition" or opportunity linked to a specific type of customer, revealing who he or she is. Finally, the enterprise also needs to remember each customer so that whenever and however the customer contacts the enterprise, the customer is known and has a history. This is likely to be a gradual process, as information systems are reworked to support instant recognition and total recall of every customer.

All of the above is iterative, driven by dialogue, enabled by discovery, and realized through discipline. The result is a constantly current profile of customers, which informs and guides the Relationship-Based Enterprise in evolving its business.

Window on the Real World:

Avaya Inc./
Lucent Technologies, Inc.

Avaya, formerly the Enterprise Networks Group of Lucent Technologies, has a mission to provide the world's best communication solutions that allow businesses to excel. Avaya has 34,000 employees, with offices or distributors in more than 90 countries and territories.

In a large enterprise, the question "Who are our customers" is likely to have many answers. "Each function and department defines the customer from its own perspective," says J. Zachary Taylor, Director of CRM Solutions at Avaya. "One of the greatest hurdles is to get commitment from all functions from all product lines—with their own systems, objectives, and P&L centers—to join hands in building an enterprise-wide CRM strategy."

Many of the traditional fiefdoms in sales and marketing have been built around owning specific channels. For example, the marketing department might believe relationship-marketing strategies executed via direct mail are the best way to communicate personally and improve the customer relationship. The source of the problem? The typical enterprise has functionally aligned departments with disparate information systems supporting their core operations. Therefore, interaction and fulfillment of customer service are managed separately.

With enterprise-wide CRM, the picture changes. People need to recognize that the customer really deals with the enterprise as a whole—and also that the enterprise deals with the customer as a whole.

Further Thoughts

For the Manager

- Do I have an agreed definition of "customer" in my organization?
- Is there more than one definition of "customer" in use within my organization?
- Does everyone in the organization have the same understanding of "customer"?
- Do I have relevant information and data on my existing customers?
- Do I have information about my potential customers?
- Do I have information about customers who have defected to a competitor?
- Is my customer information up-to-date and accurate?
- Is my customer information accessible to everyone who needs it?
- Is my organization making the best use of the customer information we have?
- Do we have the processes in place to continually learn about our customers? From this position, it is fairly easy to move to the next step.

For the Manager's Organization

- What do we mean when we say customer? Define customers.
- Who are our ideal customers? Identify customers.
- What are their likely characteristics? Anticipate customers.
- How do we recognize them? Recognize customers.
- What information do we need? Remember customers.

7

CHAPTER

What Do Our Customers Want and Expect?

Elements of an Answer

- **The Offering**—What customers need from suppliers
- **Time**—When customers want help
- **Space**—Where and how customers want to have conversations
- **Roles**—How customer wants and expectations vary
- **Value**—Why customers choose suppliers

Long-term customer relationships depend on "getting inside the customer's head." Accomplished sales professionals, account managers, and consultants know this intuitively. Those who have formalized their intuition through rigorous professional discipline are often spectacularly successful—leaving the rest of us to wonder how their success can be duplicated.

In the early 20th century, with the rise of the sales culture in American business, trying to answer this question led to the very first books on how to succeed in business. Even today, authors continue to churn out books claiming this or that magic formula for creating successful long-term customer relationships. But in most of these books, the sections on what customers want and expect tend to be very generic and quite short. Advice such as "Work with the customer as a team," "Be responsive," "Keep your promises," "No surprises," and even the venerable "The customer is always right" are all of limited use when each customer, and each situation, is different.

Traditional organizations, unable to define customer relationships down to a one-customer-one-situation level, have done their best with market segmentation. The idea is to target the segment, based on the attributes, and measure quality expectations. Of course, the Relationship-Based Enterprise takes a different approach.

To answer the question, "What do our customers want and expect?" the Relationship-Based Enterprise depends on its preoccupation with discovery and turns the results of discovery into a constantly current profile of customers (Figure 7-1). This profile has three elements: a *characteristics* profile (Chapter 6), a *preference* profile (as presented in this chapter), and a *value* profile (Chapter 8).

Figure 7-1: *The Customer Profile—Preferences*

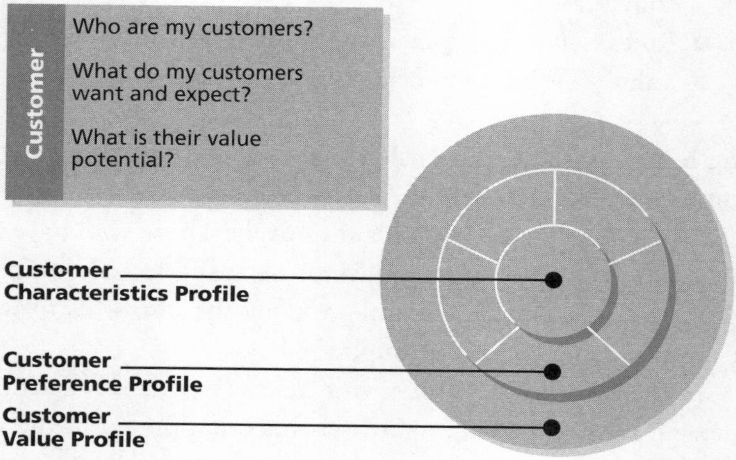

Customer: Who are my customers? What do my customers want and expect? What is their value potential?

Customer Characteristics Profile

Customer Preference Profile

Customer Value Profile

The continual interplay of discovery and dialogue, then of dialogue and discovery, allows the enterprise to work with customers, not segments, and to create solutions that generate value. In the process, the Relationship-Based Enterprise becomes a target for the customer, and not vice versa. The hunters have become the hunted.

All of this would not be possible if the enterprise were not preoccupied with continually discovering the customer through a true dialogue. For the traditional sales professional, this comes as no surprise. The investment firm of Morgan Stanley Dean Witter says it best: "We measure success one investor at a time." When conversation is with a single individual customer, the sales professional should be able to discover the precise needs of the customer. But what happens when the conversation occurs over the Internet with millions of customers? How does the business—not the individual sales professional—discover what each customer wants? How should this kind of dialogue be structured? The answer, as HiVolt Energy and E-Hearth found, lies in structuring conversations that reveal the evolving customer needs and enable action. Developing a customer preference profile is an important part of the process, but evolving that profile as the customer evolves is even more important.

Old Customers Become New Customers for E-Hearth

For 20 years, HiVolt Energy segmented consumers by amount of energy consumed, equipment purchased, and payments recorded. Unfortunately, this information did little to help E-Hearth understand its customers in terms of its new home services offerings. Home management has many more product and service components than electricity. E-Hearth wanted to provide its customers with customized solutions to a number of home management problems—from energy efficiency to childcare. This would require a much deeper knowledge of the customer than was required to track electricity consumption and payments.

The new operational challenge was to determine the best way to keep an accurate record of the products, services, and solutions purchased by key customer groups and by individual households. Customer Relationship Management (CRM) software was to play a core role in meeting this challenge. But the broader challenge was to make sense of the mountain of information and, in particular, to understand what drives customer preferences and the evolution of those preferences.

Where is the starting point? What are the current set of products and services? Where are these customers heading? How can they be influenced? To answer these questions, E-Hearth needed to relate "the facts" about product and service preferences to other elements of the customer profile. As a result, HiVolt/E-Hearth decided to build a profile of what individuals, households, and customer groups want and expect. These preference profiles would become information resources used by E-Hearth managers and electronic systems. Here's how it came about.

After a presentation by the CEO, the HiVolt board formally accepted the proposed plan to launch three pilot projects. These projects explored the market for E-Hearth services in a cross-section of suburban markets. During the discussion, one member asked the CEO for more details on how the diversification strategy would be put into operation. "Exactly how will you target the customers that have been identified in the research?"

The CEO replied: "We will not be trying to hit targets, we will try to make ourselves into a big, inviting target for our ideal customers." To do this, he said, E-Hearth will actually need better, more focused information about customers than was provided by its current market segmentation methods, which were designed mainly to support occasional direct-mail campaigns and periodic service quality-improvement drives. The better information would match the more complex set of services being offered to customers, and the more complex set of exchanges required to sell and to deliver those services.

The HiVolt marketing director and the Chief Customer Officer (CCO) attached to the E-Hearth project took to the boardroom floor to describe the essential elements of a preference profile. The purpose of the preference profile, explained the E-Hearth CCO, is to share knowledge quickly and effectively about the "customer side" of exchanges. These preference profiles would be different from traditional market segments. They would contain more information than traditional labels (such as Generation X-er, baby boomer, or upscale empty-nester), ratings (seven out of ten), and purely factual individual sketches. The profiles would describe customer preferences for products, services, and channels. But they will also probe for less tangible, more judgmental factors—customer attitudes to "value," their "experience" of the relationship, and the degree to which they wanted to cooperate with the company in creating value.

Several board members commented that the profiles appeared to be non-traditional and, most likely, very expensive to develop. The Director of Marketing responded by pointing out that the entire process of creating a customer profile reflects the innovative, mold-breaking character of the E-Hearth program. "We are making new assumptions about customer knowledge and trying to achieve higher standards in this area."

The success of the E-Hearth strategy continues to rest on building much richer relationships with customers. Richer customer profiles are critical to the success of exchanges and dialogues. The profiling process is more ambitious than traditional market segmentation, and much more closely linked to the actual process of "live exchanges" with customers. The process should result in a constantly current profile of what customers want from E-Hearth.

What Customers Need from Suppliers

The problem faced by E-Hearth as a nascent relationship-based organization is that customers are a fluid, ever-changing element of the business equation. The only way to discover what they want and need is to engage in a continual process of discovery and dialogue. As E-Hearth will find out in many ways, the customer relationship is even more like a marriage than a marriage—where long-term success requires more than occasionally saying to your spouse, "You're right *again*, dear."

Nothing about spouses—or customers—can be taken for granted. This does not imply that suppliers must respond to the customers' every whim, even though it may seem that way with certain dotcom companies, especially those that offer an incredible array of products and services. But it does imply new levels of responsiveness based on a new definition of relationships.

The relationship space, introduced in Chapter 5, lays the foundation for the new levels of responsiveness that are required. It does this by precisely identifying customer groups and the relationship style they prefer to have with the enterprise:

- **Patrons**—price-centered competitive relationships identified by everyday low prices for standard products and efficient shopping experiences
- **Customers**—product-centered cooperative relationships identified by customized products often co-configured with the customer
- **Clients**—need-centered cooperative relationships, identified by personalized exchanges and intensive dialogue
- **Partners**—value-centered collaborative relationships identified by jointly developed solutions, services, and products based on intensive dialogue, resource sharing, and rich discovery.

The needs and wants of these different customer groups can be categorized by relationship style. Each group can be engaged in a conversation appropriate to their needs and wants. Specific needs and wants will be different for each type of business. The following illustrates what customers need and want using the HiVolt/ E-Hearth example.

Patrons/Price-Centered Relationships

HiVolt/E-Hearth patrons need convenience and low prices for standard packages of energy and related services on a single bill. They want the simplest, most convenient buying experience with minimum interaction. Electricity and gas should just "be there," preferably without having to think about it.

Customer/Product-Centered Relationships

HiVolt/E-Hearth customers need packaged solutions that can be configured to meet specific needs. They want help buying and using E-Hearth products.

Client/Need-Centered Relationships.

HiVolt/E-Hearth clients need personalized "help desks" and contact centers. Their needs change frequently, they tend to have more issues, and they want information, advice, and consulting support.

Partners/Value-Centered Relationships

HiVolt/E-Hearth partners want solutions not products or services and they are prepared to participate in developing those specialized solutions by sharing knowledge and resources.

When Customers Want Help

Patrons, customers, clients, and partners all want help available 24 x 7 x 365—on their terms. This means responding not only to time-of-day issues, but also to their channel preferences; for example, a patron might prefer e-mail during the week and Web-site interaction on weekends. Clients and partners, on the other hand, might prefer telephone or fax support during normal business hours and Web-site interaction after 5:00 p.m. By profiling the time preferences of each group, managers can gain better control over when different customers are engaged in certain types of conversations.

Understanding when customers want help, however, goes beyond managing 24 x 7 responsiveness. Time also includes macro cycles for defining moments, such as buying a home or the birth of a child, and micro cycles of the routine, such as household chores. And from the supreme moments in life to the most mundane, timing is everything—as accomplished sales professionals know very well.

For example, selling home insurance works much better in the two months leading up to policy expiry than when, say, nine months are left. The same principle holds for mortgage financing and car leasing. At HiVolt/E-Hearth, each service in the E-Hearth portfolio has its own natural cycle. A household has one cycle for buying groceries, another for leasing cars, and quite another for choosing a home-heating company. But the expression "life cycle" conveys a false impression of uniformity. It is more accurate to think that a customer may have many cycles of search, acquire, use, maintain, and dispose. These cycles embody the natural pace at which people like to do business.

Knowledge of cycles is a valuable element of the preference profile. It contributes directly to the process of conversation design and to sustaining relationships. In particular, it helps E-Hearth anticipate when and how frequently customer groups may interact with the company. It helps them map customer cycles precisely, better matching company sales and service cycles with customer cycles; and it helps them better understand the dynamics of customer loyalty.

Where and How Customers Want to Have Conversations

Over the last decade there has been rapid expansion in the number of channels and, even more, in the variety of choices that customers have for the way that they do business with a company. This expansion was a result of changes in technology and the increased expectations of customers. Customers now expect to be able to interact with their suppliers in whatever way they choose. For example:

- person-to-person contact in a store or branch
- home visits
- telephone or fax calls
- correspondence through the mail
- near real-time interaction via e-mail
- get product information through interactive or mass media
- get information from friends or affinity-group partners via chat and virtual networks
- tap into informational databases—self-serve facilities
- use links to a company Web site.

This creates two challenges: managing new channels and profiling customers accurately when they communicate and exchange through these channels. Over the last few years, the number and variety of channels have grown faster than the enterprise's ability to manage them and, most important, to keep track of how customers use them.

A key component of the channel management challenge has to do with customer profiling. Large-scale organizations like E-Hearth need to keep track of customers as they make purchases, complain, ask for advice, or look for information through a variety of channels. Beyond tracking, these organizations also need to understand customer preferences for new, more complex patterns of interaction. This understanding can contribute to customer profiling and segmentation, and play a critical role in shaping the overall value proposition. This is the challenge of *remembering* and *instant recognition*. Organizations use CRM and channel integration initiatives to deal with this problem. For example, many businesses have created customer-contact centers that handle both Web and telephone traffic.

Most organizations view customers through the lens of a single delivery or marketing channel—branches, direct mail, call centers, and so on. To structure appropriate conversations with customers, it is vital to "morph" all these channels into conversations each customer can shape, depending on his or her comfort levels and personal preferences. It is part of the move from one-way delivery to two-way dialogue.

At HiVolt/E-Hearth, E-Hearth's new relationship managers offered the couples they interviewed free access to the Ehearth.com Web site. News, tips, e-mail, chat rooms, and emergency help were available to these couples. One of the differences to emerge among customer groups was the degree of Web literacy and general comfort levels of entering cyber-relationships with strangers.

In one pilot project, a number of households initially believed to be patrons and customers were encouraged to follow up on the interview through any combination of Web-based exchanges, call-center support, or more personal visits. There were vastly different responses (greater differences than the differences among the responses to the service packages proposed). Some proved to be cocoon dwellers, most at ease in the quiet customer zone of the patron space. Quite a few others became clients, using both the Web and call centers regularly and building strong bonds with E-Hearth.

These channel preferences were seen as an essential aspect of the relationship—often more important than the products and services selected. The channel preference was based on more than Web literacy or PC ownership. It involved the choice of a style of communicating—what might be called the conversation *experience*.

One of the surprises of the E-Hearth program was the number of people who became comfortable using the Web and, especially, the combination of Web, e-mail, and call centers. The key was to demonstrate that these flexible communications channels could help them solve problems—and get value. Some relationship managers started chat groups, sent e-mails, and posted information that might be of interest to households. Through a series of face-to-face and virtual conversations with these people, the managers started to develop information-sharing among small virtual communities interested in major themes, such as:

- energy conservation
- insurance and financial services
- clean urban transportation

- childcare
- sports
- home maintenance.

Some couples evolved into "e-community leaders", with help from E-Hearth, when they showed real interest in developing home-management solutions. Their knowledge and insight were fed back via the Intranet to marketing and product development experts who began to design services and "conversations" to meet the needs of these communities.

The result of all this activity was not just an increase in chat with no increase in revenues. The first result was the recruitment of a large number of households classified as clients. They came from the ranks of both patrons and customers. Over time, these clients showed a marked preference for a larger basket of E-Hearth services. Their preferences were mapped to individuals or customer groups to form the foundation of conversation styles. One of the biggest group definers was not so much choice of service, but choice of conversation experience.

How Customer Wants and Expectations Vary

It would be nice and easy if customers' wants and expectations stayed the same. Life, of course, is not that simple. As discussed in Chapter 4, real-life conversations become complex quickly. All groups of customers can play various roles in the exchange space —any combination of buy, use, produce, and service.

For example, customers for E-Hearth are made up of households with many members and each can play a different role. Each member of the household can play the buy role (shopping, selecting, and purchasing) or the use role (home management), depending on a number of factors. It was not possible to profile a typical household as a discrete unit, as it was for HiVolt (which just counted energy consumption at each address). When E-Hearth looks at households, it sees stay-at-home dads, mothers who are working professionals, kids who spend the weekend with one parent

and the weekdays with another, and so on. In an E-Hearth household, a mother could be an engineer partnering with E-Hearth as
well as a buyer using E-Hearth services.

For E-Hearth, knowledge of role dynamics is key to effective
conversations and channel management. The concept of the
exchange space allows E-Hearth to conceptualize the different
roles and develop conversations—from the simple to the complex
—that accommodate these shifting roles. Customers choose
which conversations they engage in based on the role they need to
play at the time. Greatly simplified, these role-linked conversations could include:

- shop and buy
- get information
- ask for service
- ask for advice
- ask for shipping and delivery.

What customers want and expect depends on which role
they choose to play and which conversation they decide to have.
And the Relationship-Based Enterprise is preoccupied with continually assessing and reassessing what customers want and need
based on the roles they play and the conversations they desire.

Why Customers Choose Suppliers

The answer, in a word, is value. Every conversation with a supplier
must deliver value, or there will be no further conversations and
no relationship. It is up to the supplier to develop value propositions, embed them in conversations, and deliver the promised
value (see Figure 7-2). A customer preference profile containing a
clear articulation of the value proposition links the customer profile to customer definitions, which can be modified based on
evolving knowledge of the customer's context.

Once a value proposition is defined, it forms the core of the
customer preference profile. By explaining essentially what customers

Figure 7-2: *Value Propositions*

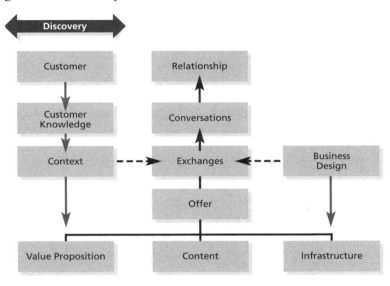

value—in their own language—the value proposition provides a cost-effective and accurate shortcut to understanding the product, service, and channel preferences of a customer group (or individual customer).

Figure 7-2 contains a short list of factors that often help shape value propositions.

Goals

Sometimes customers directly express goals, such as "hassle-free business trips." Those four words state one of the major goals of airline executive-class travel programs, which employ everything from e-mail alerts to customer profiling software and advanced seat design to deliver on that commitment. Similarly, the complex lean production supply chains in Japan have been designed around the very simple goal of "just-in-time delivery," not only of an individual part, but of the automobile. In the case of E-Hearth, some partners and customers will state a very clear goal: "Take these household tasks off my hands and deal with them."

Needs

Customers may also express goals indirectly, as needs. For example, a tired but loyal executive might complain bitterly to a travel agent about ticketing problems that cost him hours of scarce time. Or a potential client might let E-Hearth know that performing household duties after work prevents her from spending time with her young children. Often, needs are uncovered by closely observing customers rather than talking with them directly. A good example is the design of business travel hotels around the idea of a comfortable bed, luxury bar, and fast, hassle-free checkout—and not much else.

Results

Customers also express more general results or outcomes that they seek in their businesses or lives, rather than goals specific to a product or service. Companies focused on results give their customers structured opportunities—and conversations—to learn how their products and services are used to get measurable business results. This can help the company understand how it can become a partner with the customer in meeting specific performance objectives.

The results focus is most appropriate for business-to-business (B2B) relationships, as exemplified by a manufacturing supply chain or virtual network of retailers and their suppliers. But it can also be applied to relationships with entrepreneurs and households who conceive of themselves as meeting specific performance objectives—and therefore of delivering results.

Experience

Sometimes customers conceive of their exchanges with the company in terms of an end-to-end experience rather than of an identified result or goal. Going to the opera, for example, is a lot more than ordering the ticket or sitting in the theatre; it is the entire experience, including that created by the music, orchestra, and atmosphere. Experience-centered marketing can be used to sell suites of products, services, and solutions in many sectors, such as personal financial management, investing, health care, and luxury cars.

In the emerging e-economy, having a certain type of experience is an integral part of becoming informed, shopping, and buying. Virtual bookstores such as Amazon and e-tailers such as ZDNet are well-known examples.

Experience has a role in virtually any customer relationship or conversation in which the branding is important. To convey a consistent brand experience across many delivery channels or product lines, companies need to know how customers actually experience their interactions with the company, and often how they experience the products and services in daily life.

Community

At times, what customers value the most about products and services is the fact that they are delivered to a community to which they belong. This could be a neighborhood or a more dispersed affinity group, such as lovers of extreme winter sports or graduates of the same university. E-Hearth is an example of how virtual communities can create a friendly environment for marketing some home-management solutions.

There are no magic formulas for defining value propositions. However, it is clear that there are quite different value propositions for patrons, customers, clients, and partners. This reality has some practical implications for developing customer preference profiles.

One important implication is that organizations must develop very creative solutions for developing profiles of true patrons, those who only want to buy a product or service, ask few questions, make few special requests, and leave few clues about why they are buying or what they feel about the company.

Businesses very often deal with them as buyers only. It is difficult to know how often they will deal with a company in future and whether a more solid relationship might emerge.

In contrast, the return on investment from the time and money expended to learn about customers, clients, and partners is more obvious. Their value propositions are more easily discovered, and this knowledge can be used to develop a profitable relationship.

At HiVolt/E-Hearth, the following thumbnail sketches of value propositions were mapped to the key customer groups with whom HiVolt and E-Hearth were trying to build various types of relationships.

- **Patrons** want to minimize their dollar/energy ratio, which they see in terms of low prices, while taking account of reliability of supply, accurate billing, business integrity, and other less tangible factors. They are far more interested in the priced product than in any unpriced services or convenient channels. Their core value proposition is, therefore, cheap, reliable energy.
- **Customers** want, above all, a sense of security and control over their energy costs, which they see in terms of "all in costs," including repairs, worry time, and other intangibles. They prefer electricity to other energy sources. They are willing to invest upfront in things like home insulation, modern windows, and electric furnaces in order to stop thinking about these things and harvest some peace of mind—the core value proposition. This value proposition makes them naturally interested in various services surrounding home heating, such as plumbing and home insurance. They are possible E-Hearth customers.
- **Clients** may look like customers based only on knowledge of their energy purchase and usage patterns. But they take a very different approach to life. They are intuitive problem-solvers rather than seekers of long-term peace of mind. Their busy professional lifestyles mean

they have a lot of problems to solve: heating costs, plumbing, babysitting, shopping, car leasing, and environmental cleanliness. They can be quite open to the E-Hearth service offering, provided they can pick and choose—and do not have to spend time choosing a complex package upfront. Unlike patrons, clients feel that convenient channels and access to service can be more important to the problem-solving value proposition than the product or service itself.

- **Partners** are new arrivals on the scene, since relationships with them are just now being built. Like clients, they are willing to interact often with the company. Like customers, they are willing to invest time upfront in order to find long-term solutions to their problems. Because they are extremely busy professionally, they are willing to accept help from a company to find professional home-management solutions that extend beyond heating and plumbing. Yet, they want to design that solution to suit their families. Their core value proposition is integrated solutions.

With these value propositions fully understood, E-Hearth is able to embed them in conversations as basic themes. In particular, these themes appear as separate pages of the Ehearth.com Web site, which functions as a powerful way to recruit customers in the client group, who join and help shape Web communities.

Who Loves Ya', Baby?

In the hit 1970s TV show *Kojak*, actor Telly Sevalis played a New York detective known for his tough talk, lollipops, and bald head. His trademark line was "Who loves ya', baby?" Developing a customer preference profile pretty much answers the same question.

Discovering what customers want and expect tests the validity of that strategy with the people whose opinions ultimately count—real live customers. A good preference profile characterizes how customers expect to do business and provides an overall view of the value the customer seeks from the relationship. The best preference profile is one that everyone believes is never really complete. It reinforces the need for continual discovery—a continual repetition of a signature line not unlike "Who loves ya', baby."

Window on the Real World:

HomeSide Lending, Inc.

HomeSide is one of the largest full-service residential mortgage banking companies in the United States. Headquartered in Jacksonville, Florida, HomeSide services over $173 billion in home loans representing 192,000 loans. As a wholly owned subsidiary of National Australia Bank, HomeSide is on the verge of becoming the world's first truly international mortgage company.

What do customers want and expect when they apply for a home loan? HomeSide Lending of Jacksonville, Florida has the answer—and it's not just "more money."

One reason HomeSide is so successful is that it has been able to make getting a mortgage so easy. With its loans-by-phone service, customers can handle the entire mortgage process from the comfort of their home or office. One phone call puts customers in touch with a HomeSide loan officer who helps select the best home financing option. The loan officer takes applications over the phone and quickly responds with a final loan decision.

William Glasgow, Jr., executive vice president of HomeSide, finds it is difficult to build and justify a business case for implementing customer relationship management (CRM). Home loan customers are very price-sensitive—and will switch at any price movement. Price is the first buying criterion, followed by product breadth. A CRM strategy can only do so much in terms of customer retention in a "commodity" business. The question then becomes: how much should a company really invest in CRM, and will it translate to repeat business?

Nevertheless, Glasgow is committed to CRM. Why? "As customers begin to use the Web and e-mail in addition to the telephone, HomeSide will have to make sure that it continues to be easy to deal with—no matter how the customer contact is made. The critical issue," says Glasgow, "is that most companies are failing to create a holistic CRM strategy and instead are purchasing disparate EC/CRM products, services, and solutions that do not 'play' well together."

Further Thoughts

- What customers want is a moving target.
- What customers want must be continually re-discovered.
- Customers don't necessarily know what they want.
- Customers want everything and anything that increases their ability to realize the potential value of the core product or service.
- What customers want are products and services designed for the way they are actually experienced.
- What one customer wants is different from what another customer wants.
- What customers want is to be satisfied with all aspects of the conversation—value is beyond the good or service.
- Information on what customers want is needed by all parts of the organization.
- What customers want may not necessarily be determined by what the competitors are doing.

8

CHAPTER

What is the Value Potential of Our Customers?

Elements of an Answer

- **Sources of Value**—How conversations with customers generate value
- **Customer Value Profiles**—The value potential of specific customer groups
- **Most Valued Customers**—Prioritizing investments
- **Dynamics of Value**—How customer-value potential changes over time
- **Increasing Value Potential**—How to influence factors that can increase the value potential of customers

The value potential of customers directly affects the success of any enterprise—and is a central concern of management. To assess the value potential of customers, it is not enough to simply count the dollars of revenue, costs, and profit that may be generated by repeat conversations. Value potential is also contingent upon the willingness of customers to participate in the creation of products and services, on the degree to which they are prepared to share information and other resources, and on the degree to which they want to share control over the design and production of products and services. The question is, how can managers assess, track, and even influence the value potential of their customers?

The answer chosen by a Relationship-Based Enterprise is to create a value profile of customers. A value profile, when combined with an characteristics profile and a preference profile, as illustrated in Figure 8-1, gives the Relationship-Based Enterprise a sound and practical basis for evaluating its investments in customer relationships. It helps forecast how long the enterprise can retain the customers' business and how customer relationships will evolve. And it answers questions such as, "Can this relationship be sustained? Will it grow, and how? Or, should it be allowed to fade?"

These were exactly the types of questions faced by HiVolt Energy, the company introduced in Chapter 6, in its quest to transform itself into a Relationship-Based Enterprise—E-Hearth Home Services. HiVolt's business model before deregulation was based on providing one product to a customer base that was reasonably captive. The new business model for E-Hearth was to be

Figure 8-1: *Completing the Discovery of Customers*

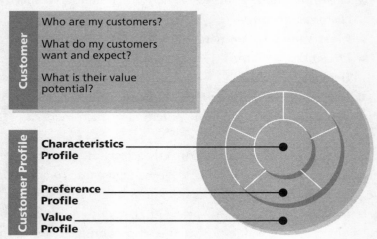

based on selling many services, in varying combinations, to different customer groups for which there were alternative sources of supply. With this new model, HiVolt/E-Hearth's customers would no longer look like one another. As a result, the matter of determining the value potential of customers became an issue that needed to be addressed because it affected investment decisions. As a consequence it became a matter for the board. Here's what happened.

The board of directors had already given approval in principle for the creation of characteristics profiles and preference profiles for each of the four key customer groups. But when they met to review the budget that would be needed to create these profiles, many questions were raised. Several board members made the observation that these profiles appeared to be very expensive, and some wondered why. One of the board members, who was an executive of an airline, had contacted the CEO to warn of the costs—emphasizing that while customer profiling was expensive, it was, indeed necessary. This led the CEO to ask, "What are we doing to ensure that we focus the profiling effort on only those customers who will bring significant value to HiVolt and E-Hearth?"

Two other board members expressed quite different concerns. They saw the mandate and brand identity of HiVolt as still linked with the provision of energy to the community at large. In fact, one director openly questioned the CEO about how they would handle customers who did not wish to acquire the new services of E-Hearth. It was a shock to everyone in the room when this board member said, "Are we going to ask these customers to find a new supplier?" The CEO responded decisively, "We will not dump any customer in the patrons group. They are vital to our success, especially during the transition." He said that they would continue to invest in this group of customers, and that the only remaining question was how much.

In tossing around this hot potato, the board members decided that the question of potential value needed to be addressed directly.

The characteristics and preference profiles would be complemented with a value profile.

The HiVolt and E-Hearth marketing directors were asked to create customer-value profiles that defined and measured the benefits and costs of relationships with specific customers or customer groups. Each customer-value profile was to cover not only financial benefits but less tangible ones; for example, savings in time, or even a suggestion made by a customer that turned into a brilliant new product. These profiles were to provide managers with a thumbnail sketch—a "Customer ROI."

The first step was to determine the sources of value, which meant understanding how new relationships with customers would generate value.

How Conversations with Customers Generate Value

In the new economy, relationships produce a much greater variety of benefits than was possible before. HiVolt Energy recognized that an effective CRM strategy for its E-Hearth initiative must include an understanding of not only "what was the value potential of their customers" but also "how customers generate value" because its new customer set can generate value in many different ways. There are the obvious: product sales, service fees, monthly installment payments, interest payments, increased production efficiencies, shorter cycle times, and reduced time to market. And there are the not-so-obvious: information sharing with production partners, opportunities to test and improve new product ideas, and faster transfer of knowledge.

The traditional, market-centric view is that customers generate value in response to advertising and sales programs. The job of the advertising agent is to connect with customers from a distance, with the aim of getting their attention, mind share, and wallet share, creating a simple relationship characterized by brand awareness and the completion of a sale. The job of the sales executive or account manager is to approach customers directly and leverage the company's marketing efforts to create more personal relationships—in essence, one-on-one loyalty programs—that result in repeat sales. The value generated by these marketing and sales relationships is measured in terms of higher prices, higher revenues, and higher profits. In this environment, value potential is easy to understand using conventional financial models—"Did sales make their numbers this quarter?"

In contrast, the Relationship-Based Enterprise takes the view that value is generated through the process, operational, and information economies created by competition, coordination, collaboration, and cooperation. This value-generation does not fit easily into a financial mold. For example, by working with customers, a supplier of industrial equipment may reduce its "total cost of after-sales service" by providing customers with better education on maintenance procedures. The savings are real, but hard to quantify. To take a more complex example, a financial magazine decides to "give away" its Web edition for two years. It is hoping to recruit Web-savvy readers (and writers) into chat rooms and into an Intranet where several virtual editions are to be created, and then sold in professional markets. The benefits of the relationships that are established with these Web-savvy customers include: getting the new edition to the market in a shorter period of time, better quality in the published editions, and more focused marketing through the networks established by the participants. If the plan works, the benefits are real—but, again, hard to quantify financially. And so a different approach is required.

Instead of focusing exclusively on financials, the Relationship-Based Enterprise identifies the many ways that customers can generate value, and then structures its conversations (and its CRM strategies) accordingly. The frequency with which conversations are repeated becomes an indicator of value potential.

The first step is to list the ways that customer relationships generate value. At HiVolt/E-Hearth, the marketing organization conducted a systematic survey to determine the how customers generate value. They then organized the list into four basic categories:

1. Financial
2. Operational and Process
3. Knowledge and Learning
4. Strategic.

These are categories where well-managed customer relationships can create value, by increasing benefits or reducing costs, or by a combination of the two.

Figure 8-2 maps the four value-generation categories to the relationship space. This mapping reveals that patron relationships, in which the customer is engaged in simple conversations with the enterprise and the enterprise knows the least about the customer, generate *financial* value. At the other end of the scale, partner relationships, in which customers have very rich conversations with the enterprises and enterprises know a great deal about the customer, generate *strategic* value.

At HiVolt, there were already basic CRM programs focused on financial and operational benefits. But these programs were not appropriate for moving patrons towards the customer or client zones of the relationship space. What HiVolt needed for its E-Hearth

Figure 8-2: *The Relationship Space and Value Categories*

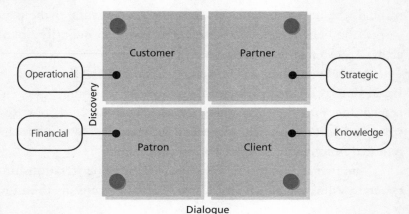

initiative was a CRM program that was broad enough to balance the potential value of relationships across all four quadrants. To do this effectively, it was important to know the value potential of specific customers.

The Value Potential of Specific Customers

Each customer and customer relationship brings its own value package ("net benefits package") to the enterprise. This value package can vary significantly, even within a single group of customers. Consider, for example, the relationship between a parts supplier (the enterprise) and an automobile manufacturer (the customer).

The traditional approach places emphasis on open-market negotiations with suppliers bidding for short-term contracts. To the supplier, the automobile manufacturer acts like a patron—trying to drive down the price while trying to maintain a reliable source of supply. The supplier pushes for the maximum price that can be negotiated, knowing that the customer may well switch suppliers in the next round of bidding. There is little opportunity for operational and learning benefits from this relationship—the value potential of the customer is based solely on financial criteria. As a result, the supplier maintains relationships with several car manufacturers or customers.

In contrast, the integrated Supply Chain Management approach, pioneered by Japanese lean producers, places emphasis on joint management of operations, free information flows, and frequent sharing of strategic product development plans. The shared goal of supplier and car manufacturer—indeed of the entire integrated supply chain—is to deliver maximum satisfaction to car buyers—"the customer's customer." In this case, the supplier gets a much more varied "net benefits package" from the customer. Negotiations may not always be easy, but they will cover a much broader range of issues than price and delivery schedules. The same principle applies to any assessment of value potential.

Finally, consider the supplier that not only provides parts to its customer, a major car manufacturer, but also convinces its customer to carry a link to its parts on its Web site for the benefit of its customer's customer. This simple act can increase the value potential of its customer by orders of magnitude. Now the supplier not only has the car manufacturer as its customer, but potentially all of the customers of its customer.

In this simple example we have seen three different approaches, and in each case, the value potential of the customer is dramatically different. These differences in value potential become visible when value profiles (Figure 8-3) are prepared for customers and customer groups. The value profile takes specific net benefits from a particular customer relationship and the associated costs, and lists them by the four categories—financial, operational and process, knowledge and learning, and strategic. (Figure 8-3 shows the generic benefits that must be adapted.) Evaluating the time and effort required to achieve each specific net benefit provides a sound and practical basis for evaluating investments in customer relationships in each of these four areas.

Figure 8-3: *Customer Value Profile*

Value Category	Benefits	Costs
Strategic	- Products - Value - Customer Satisfaction - Market Position	- Operations - Production
Knowledge, Learning, Information	- Customer Info - Product Development - Technology - Network Effects	- Operations - Learning - Production
Process and Operational	Marketing Effectiveness Predictable Demand - Referrals - Related Sales - Price Premium - Long-term contracts - Time to market - Product development	Operational Effectiveness Supply Chain & Logistics - Production - Logistics, Transport - Distribution - Cycle times - Other time savings
Financial	Revenue & Profit - Gross Profit - Net Profit - Unit Price - Volume	Costs - Variable costs - Fixed cost (allocated) - Unit cost

In Figure 8-3, it should be noted that "benefit" does not imply an advantage nor does "cost" imply a disadvantage. For example, an airline may "lose revenue" on the benefit side by giving its loyal customers price discounts. However, it might win a net benefit through a combination of increased marketing effectiveness (improved process) and improved load factors (reduced logistics costs). The value potential of a customer depends on the "net benefit" which the relationship generates for the enterprise.

The calculus of repeat purchases worked for the simple customer relationships of HiVolt Energy. For its E-Hearth CRM programs, however, HiVolt will need to prospect for value by assessing a much wider range of options to fully understand the value potential of customers. Because the value potential will vary across customer relationships, this prospecting must be done by customer group or by individual customer.

Prioritizing Investments

Competition, not just among offerings but among entire business designs and technologies, means that customers have more choice, and thus naturally divide themselves into smaller and smaller segments. Just think of what has happened to something as simple as buying coffee. There used to be just two ways to buy coffee—in the grocery store and at the coffee shop—and now there are at least five, with each "channel" being a separate business design. And these are not just different labels on the same package. Coffee-lovers can go shopping in a supermarket, take out a cup from the corner store, go to a Web café, buy a cappuccino from a machine, and order an exotic blend from a specialty Web site. A byproduct of this kind of competition is that exactly the same person can be seen as several completely different customers.

Different business designs for different customer groups are destroying the old paradigm of large-scale production and service factories. Getting as many customers to buy from the same store to lower average costs has given way to earning profit from many niches. This situation further reinforces the idea that to be of practical use to managers, customer value profiles must be developed for specific customer groups. With such profiles, organizations can prioritize their investments based on the return they expect these relationships to produce over a period of time. But to be successful they must be able to dynamically revise those value estimates as required, based on their continual conversations with customers.

Another concern is the variation in profitability of the different customer groups—and the gaps in knowledge about those variations. Preparing customer-value profiles can fill these knowledge gaps.

For each of the four customer groups—patron, customer, client, and partner—the HiVolt/E-Hearth marketing team put together value profiles that were linked to key business objectives and an investment plan. Here is a summary of their work.

Patrons

Patrons were the largest group (ten million) and they accounted for the bulk of HiVolt's revenue. While they were initially quite valuable in the days of regulated energy pricing, they would become less valuable in the future, as competitive pricing eroded profit margins and a significant number of patrons switched to competing energy suppliers. One of HiVolt's business goals was to stabilize the revenue base. To achieve this, HiVolt would have to retain 80 percent of its existing patrons during the first five years of free competition. HiVolt would invest in a simple loyalty program that awarded price discounts and points to patrons, based in part on the number of years their households had been HiVolt customers. Investments would also be made in improving service at call centers and in advertising brand-awareness. Patrons were regarded as having value potential not only because of the revenue generated by their numbers, but also because they could become a major source of future clients and customers.

Customers

Customers were valuable because of their brand loyalty. They were expected to become more valuable in the future, since HiVolt expected them to buy a range of specialty packages that would generate higher margins than did "plain old energy services." HiVolt's business objective was to retain 90 percent of the three million members of the customer group and recruit 500,000 more in the first five years of free competition. Its investments would focus principally on the development and marketing of new packages, mainly in the areas of home maintenance and energy efficiency. They expected that many customers would also be attracted by the loyalty program developed for patrons.

Clients

Clients were viewed initially as less valuable because they accounted for "more than their share" of call-center traffic. In the future, they would have the highest value potential because they were seen as prime candidates for "work and family" services, to be developed and marketed through intensive dialogue with parents. Their value potential was based not only on revenue forecasts but on their membership in affinity groups, Web-based communities, community groups, and referral networks. HiVolt anticipated clients would participate in the pilot programs, working with E-Hearth relationship managers to develop the new services. The business objective was to retain 80 percent of the existing one million clients and recruit one million more in the first five years of free competition. HiVolt's investments would focus principally on the development and marketing of the new "work and family" services. HiVolt expected that clients would take advantage of the loyalty program developed for patrons, but did not expect the programs to play a major role in retaining them.

Partners

Partners as a group were valuable, but many were expected to switch to competing suppliers. E-Hearth partners were expected to be a small group of professional households that would play a particularly active role in testing and co-designing new services, particularly in the "work and family" area. Partners were expected to emerge from the client group as new services were developed, though it was hard to predict the size of this group. HiVolt's primary investments would focus on development of the new services and the provision of relationship managers. While the partners group was considered a "loss leader," its participation was seen as strategically valuable in the creation of a new category of home-management services. Partners were also valued for their ability to increase the value potential of other customers through their influence in the community.

Clearly, the types of value that can be produced by each of these customer groups vary significantly. HiVolt's investments in relationship programs would have to be adjusted to each type of customer. To build a Relationship-Based Enterprise, HiVolt needed to carefully balance its investments across the four groups of customers. And HiVolt needed to understand both the current and potential value of its relationships with these customers.

The marketing team concluded that in a regulated environment both patrons and customers should be considered as having a high value-potential. The team felt that in the future the customer group might have the highest value potential because of the higher margins provided by its members and because of their apparent loyalty. However, they also suggested that clients could become even more valuable if they chose to play a role in developing the "work and family" services. What E-Hearth partners would or would not do was hard to assess—since none existed.

In a changing business, there are not only changes in the number of customers in each group but also differences between the current value of a customer group and estimates of future value, a fact that highlights the need to track the value potential of customers over time.

How Customer Value-Potential Changes Over Time

Unlike the quick exchange of cash on the counter, or the instant transfer of digital cash from customer to enterprise, customer relationships take time to create and to realize benefits. The length of time it takes has a major effect on the value of that relationship—hence the reason that organizations focus on loyalty and retention. More important is what happens to the relationship. Does it stay the same, does it continue to grow and expand, or does it contract? How will the value potential of customer relationships change over time?

The goal of a CRM program is to retain customers for as long as possible and to make the relationship grow. This increases the "lifetime value" of a customer. Valuing customers from this perspective helps organizations assess the expected profit streams that can be generated through different relationship scenarios. At the same time, these scenarios generate a net present value for a customer, providing the organization with an indicator of the amount of money that can be invested without impacting the profitability of the relationship. Such knowledge is key to the success of an entire CRM program.

Discounting future cash flows from customer purchases to obtain a net present value produces precise figures. But it is a forecast that depends on the assumptions that are made about the future of the relationship, and about the purchase pattern associated with that assumed future relationship. These factors are as changeable as those used to calculate the net present value of long-term bonds—the value fluctuates daily as it does for bond prices.

One of the keys to the successful identification of value potential is to have all assumptions about customer relationships clearly articulated. For this purpose, three different views of value potential can serve as a starting point:

1. **Historical Value:** This view provides a summary of the purchasing pattern and the revenues and profits produced by the customer to date. This summary provides essential background information.

2. **Current Value:** This view provides a summary of the customer's value today. This value can be projected with the assumption that the relationship is maintained and repeat purchases are continued.

3. **Potential Value:** As with current value, this view provides a summary of the customer's value today, but it assumes that the relationship grows through cross-selling, related sales, price premiums, and other factors, all contributing to an increase in future revenues and profits.

Each organization must also make assumptions about how long the relationship will last and the appropriate rates of return at which future cash flows are to be discounted, as well as the benefits that are to be included in any calculation. Calculating the lifetime value of the customer provides a way of answering this question with some realistic scenarios of what might happen to the relationship. As usual, the questions and assumptions prove to be as important as the answers. Customer valuation using the lifetime-value method tells managers in precise terms what profit the customer can be expected to generate if the relationship lasts and grows. While focusing management attention on the importance of retention and growth potential, it does not answer the question of how an organization is to deliver the customer relationships required to produce that value. In a sense, the only complete answer is "through dialogue"—which is the focus of the next part of this book.

How to Influence Factors that Can Increase the Value Potential of Customers

The value potential of customers and the resulting benefits stream can be expected to change frequently, along with the inevitable changes in the relationship itself. A Relationship-Based Enterprise does not simply track these changes; it works with its customers to increase their value potential.

The Relationship-Based Enterprise actively manage three sources of change in relationship value:

1 Relationship evolution
2. Market challenges
3. Demographic and lifestyle changes.

Changes in these areas represent both opportunity and risk. Here's how HiVolt/E-Hearth identified opportunities to increase the value potential of its relationships, and how it viewed the risk associated with those relationships:

Relationship Evolution

HiVolt had to face the prospect of fighting a price war to retain as many patrons as possible. Obviously, it could not expect to retain them all, since it was the target for the competitive actions of the newcomers. The prospect of a smaller customer base earning less per household would drive down the total estimated value of its base of patrons. The E-Hearth strategy opens a new opportunity: significant numbers of patrons could migrate into the customer and client quadrants of their relationship space, when offered new services. This opportunity increases the value potential of the entire base of patrons. Management would need to act on this opportunity and monitor the results.

Market Challenge

HiVolt also faced the threat that other companies through innovation would change the ground rules of its markets. If it chose to remain a conventional energy producer, it ran the risk of being caught in a corner—a market dominated by pure price competition. This prospect reduces the value potential of its customer base—fewer brand-loyal customers, fewer patrons, and so on. The E-Hearth services strategy was risky. It could have failed. However, it provided them with the opportunity to change the rules of the marketplace, and to have higher margins, and stable relationships with clients and customers. Viewed in this light, the innovative strategy taken by E-Hearth increased the value potential of its base of customers while reducing risk.

Demographic and Lifestyle Changes

The value of any customer group is very often tied to the current product and service offering. One way to increase the value potential of customers is to look at changing the offering to leverage a major change in demographics and lifestyles. This is what E-Hearth did with its "work and family" strategy. While this strategy would affect everything from the services it offered to its brand positioning, it would also increase the value potential of its customer base by increasing the projected revenues per customer.

In many ways, the E-Hearth home-management services strategy might appear foolhardy to experienced managers. How could a public utility reinvent itself in this way? Yet, considering all the options in a rapidly changing industry, HiVolt/E-Hearth's relationship-based strategy was one of the surest ways to increase the value potential of customers.

Valuation: A Sound, Practical Basis for CRM

Clearly understanding the value potential of customers and customer relationships is fundamental to any CRM strategy. An enterprise that seeks to operate CRM without at least a basic understanding of the value potential of their customers, whether the customer is an individual or another enterprise, is unlikely to be successful in realizing its optimum profit potential. Worse still, any enterprise that attempts to operate CRM with an inaccurate or misconceived view of its customers' value potential is likely to go out of business.

To manage value potential, the Relationship-Based Enterprise maintains a model of the value potential of its customers, synchronized with the organization's business and target markets. The example used in this chapter, HiVolt/E-Hearth, focused on a business-to-consumer situation, but a similar model could just as easily be created for business-to-business situations. The model requires processes for assessing the revenue received from individual customers, the cost of servicing those customers, their likely lifetime as customers, and the degree to which the enterprise can help them achieve that potential.

Any such approach is only capable of generating a theoretical model of customer value, which must then be tested in real markets with real customers in order to evolve into a model capable of accurately forecasting the loyalty and defection behaviors of the organization's target customers. The process of refining potential needs to be continuous—and linked to the organization's aspirations for working with its customers.

Window on the Real World:

Cadillac Jack

"Cadillac Jack" Hendrix, of Little Rock, Arkansas works at the top-rated dealership in customer satisfaction out of over 1,500 Cadillac dealers in the United States.[1] He's been number one in sales for the dealership for eight of the past ten years. How does he do it?

Cadillac Jack is Mr. Relationship. He does not sell cars per se. Rather, he owns and solves his customers' problems, using a variety of products and services—some offered by his employer, some by related suppliers. He bills himself as "your personal transportation specialist," available by cellphone any time of day or night to deliver an amazing array of services, from taking you to the airport and having your car serviced while you are away, to bringing you gas if you run out.

1 **Source:** *Industry analyst J.D. Power customer satisfaction index*

Cadillac Jack excels in understanding his customers' needs, owning them, and bringing together various car-related services (towing, garage, car rental, mobile phone rental, etc.) as well as integrating the supply chain into a seamless customer service strategy. The perceptions of his customers are to be envied by any Fortune 500 corporation. So is his retention rate. About 80 percent of his business comes from 20 percent of his customers, which means that he sells cars to the same people year after year.

His underlying strategy is based on avoiding head-to-head competition with other dealerships, especially a pricing war. He understands that customers prefer having someone take care and ownership of their problems as opposed to simply selling them products. He is plugged into people's needs and problems, and knows how to keep emotion in play.

Cadillac Jack is a prime example of how value is in conversations with customers and not in the product or service. And of course, the name helps too!

Further Thoughts

For the Manager

- Can I identify all of the revenue emanating from my customers?
- Can I identify all of the costs of servicing my customers?
- Do I have a realistic view of how long my customers tend to remain with my organization?
- Do I know which non-monetary factors are important in assessing the value of my customers within my business?
- Can I measure the profitability of my customers on an individual basis?
- Do I have a model of customer-value potential, which is relevant to my business?

- Is the value potential of our customers consistent with the goals of our business?
- Should my organization consider assessing the profitability or value potential of consumer groupings?
- What steps are we taking to increase the value potential of our relationships with customers?
- Is the same kind of ROI calculated for my customers' value potential as that of any of our fixed assets?

For the Manager's Organization

- How do our relationships with customers generate value? (Source of value)
- What is the value potential of specific customer groups? (Customer value profiles)
- Who are our most valued customers? (Most valued customers)
- How will their value potential change over time? (Dynamics of value)
- What factors can we influence that will increase the value potential of our customers? (Increasing value potential)

PART

Dialogue — An Engaging Conversation

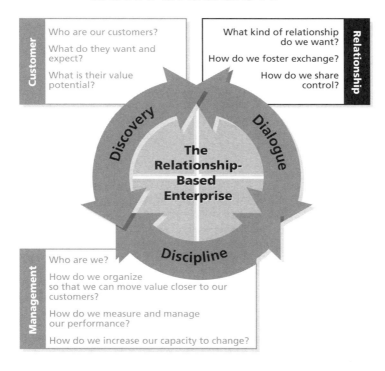

Customer
Who are our customers?

What do they want and expect?

What is their value potential?

Relationship
What kind of relationship do we want?

How do we foster exchange?

How do we share control?

Discovery

Dialogue

The Relationship-Based Enterprise

Discipline

Management
Who are we?

How do we organize so that we can move value closer to our customers?

How do we measure and manage our performance?

How do we increase our capacity to change?

"Work, in fact, is a continual dialogue with a vision of what is to be made, knowledge of how to make it, and the creative results of a combination of the two ..."
—Charles M. Savage, **5th Generation Management**, 1996

9

CHAPTER

What Kind of Relationship Do We Want?

Elements of an Answer

- **Relationship strategy**—Relationships as the path to growth. Match the relationship style to the customer.
- **Price-centered relationships**—Everyday low prices for standard products and efficient shopping experiences create value for patrons. The relationship is *competitive*.
- **Product-centered relationships**—Customized products create value for well-defined customer segments. Precise *coordination* is often required to co-design products.
- **Need-centered relationships**—Personalized services based on requirements create value for clients. Extensive *cooperation* is required to solve problems and co-design service channels.
- **Value-centered relationships**—Partnerships create value through jointly developed solutions, services, and products that benefit both the enterprise and its partner. Close *collaboration* is required to share knowledge and resources

When similar companies talk about building "stronger relationships" with their customers, they can mean different things. For example, a telecommunication company that sells long-distance minutes to a business customer might see relationships as based on discounts, often as part of a "loyalty" program. Even if the loyalty program has been customized for a particular customer, it still involves *classic value delivery:* a standard product delivered for a lower price (or cost). In contrast, a telecommunications company that sells custom-designed services (such as voice, data, and multimedia) to a business customer's sales force might see relationships in terms of a communications package—one that requires the customer and carrier to work together to create the service. They become involved in joint planning to determine which services the sales force needs and how those services will be used. The relationship is based on the *creation of value* and involves conversation that is richer than the conversation about long-distance minutes.

The business case for working together and building a stronger relationship is simple: both the customer and the enterprise will create more value by cooperating and pooling resources than by engaging in more traditional forms of competitive behavior—haggling over price, terms, and conditions.

The classic example of "lowest bidder wins" was developed in Detroit. It gave the customers, auto assemblers, value in the traditional economic sense: standard parts produced to specification for the lowest price. While this seemed like a good deal, it did not encourage a long-term commitment to efficiency. Japanese lean producers proved that treating suppliers as partners created an integrated supply chain, one that was more cost-effective and more innovative. This type of supply chain was able to win a larger share of the global vehicle market, and provided each of the partners with more value and greater opportunities for growth.

The principle underlying this integrated supply chain, in the words of game theorists Adam Brandenberger and Barry Nalebuff (*Co-opetition*, page 4), is "cooperation to create the pie and competition to divide it up." And the new economy is opening numerous opportunities for enterprises and their customers to create and grow such opportunities through cooperation.

Other examples of creating a bigger pie can be seen in the software industry and e-commerce. Sun Microsystems developed collaborative relationships with programmers, and these programmers helped develop the Java programming language. The programmers not only helped develop applications, they acted as technology opinion-leaders. As such, they helped expand the network of Java users more rapidly than Sun could have done through traditional marketing. In the e-commerce world, Cisco Systems and America Online have developed chat rooms and user groups where sophisticated customers play a leading role.

In all these cases, the relationships are more complex and they create value for both the enterprise and its customer. These kinds of relationship create new products, new industries, improved processes, and better service. And in some case they reinvent marketplaces. Don Tapscott, David Ticoll, and Alex Lowy in their article "The Rise of the Business Web," (*Business 2.0*, November 1999) say the key to "winning in the New Economy is not in creating an agile sales force or innovative marketing pitch"— traditional ways of competing for market share. Rather, the key lies in "reshaping how you do business" and "with whom." When it comes to customers, "reshaping how you do business" can mean only one thing—reshaping customer relationships.

To illustrate the implications of reshaping a business, consider the following story of Cosmos Communications.

Cosmos Communications, a communications industry conglomerate, was created in the merger wave of 1998–2000. This is when it diversified into cable TV, the Internet, a number of wireless services, and financial news. Its vision was to become the 21st century's leading supplier to "the wired home." But this vision was slow in materializing and, as a result, both investors and analysts were cautious about its shares. To reshape its business, Cosmos began to consider the growth opportunities that started to appear in the business market; in particular, small businesses, entrepreneurs, and mid-sized businesses in advanced technology sectors. Here, there were a number of high-growth opportunities. One of those opportunities was the "wireless office"—where mobile employees get laptops, cell phones, wireless information appliances, and a phone number, but no desk or land line. Another opportunity was the "networked sales force"—totally mobile, with no office at all. It seemed to Cosmos that it was these businesses, and not households, that had the money to buy broadband communications solutions.

To gain market share with small businesses, Cosmos began to leverage its extensive market research capabilities; its existing call centers and e-commerce Web sites; and its complete portfolio of services, which included plain old long-distance services plus cellular, Internet, wireless Internet, multimedia, e-commerce support, Web site management, and the outsourcing of 1-800 services and small-scale call centers. Early indications suggested that business owners were concerned with a few basic questions. How do we select among all the options available? What is the competition doing? How much will all this cost and can you give me a readable bill explaining what we are buying? To the head of marketing, these questions looked like relationship builders—or busters.

The challenge that Cosmos faced was building new relationships. As the head of marketing commented, "We have all the product and technology you want... broadband, wireless Internet, portable, mobile and wearable. But we do not have the relationships or the credibility to market those products to real-live customers. We have to find out what they want from the communications solutions that we offer."

Cosmos Communications is a company whose story illustrates the critical questions around *dialogue*—the second preoccupation of a Relationship-Based Enterprise. These critical questions include: What kind of relationship do we want to have with our customers? How do we foster exchange? and How do we share control? Answering the first of these questions is the subject of this chapter, and answering questions two and three the subject of Chapters 9 and 10.

Relationships as the Path to Growth

It is one thing to recognize the growth opportunities arising from stronger, better relationships. Many organizations can easily envision a number of growth-through-cooperation scenarios. It is quite another to figure out exactly how to build relationships that will produce growth. What is meant by a "more intimate relationship" or "closer cooperation" or "partnering with our customers"? How do these goals become operational? What benefits will they produce?

A relationship strategy is needed to answer these questions. To put together such a strategy, organizations can use the relationship space discussed in Chapter 5. The relationship space identifies four separate relationship styles and four different groups of customers. Each relationship style delivers or creates value in its own distinctive way. Each involves a distinctive pattern of conversation and a distinctive way for an enterprise and its customers to work together. Each is suited, therefore, to a different customer group. Patrons prefer a low price and limited conversation, while partners can only develop joint solutions after a series of involved conversations and intimate collaboration. Customers prefer conversations that focus tightly on the product, while clients readily sustain conversations that are broadly focused on a wide variety of service problems and processes. Following is an overview of the four relationship styles that are a part of the relationship space illustrated in Figure 9-1.

- **Price-centered relationships.** Everyday low prices for standard products and efficient shopping experiences create value for *patrons*. The relationship is *competitive* in tone and conversation is limited in scope (mainly about completing transactions and pricing issues).
- **Product-centered relationships.** Customized products create value for well-defined *customer* segments. Precise *coordination* is often required to co-design products and conversation is tightly focused on product design.
- **Needs-centered relationships.** Personalized services and channels create value for *clients*. Extensive *cooperation* is

required to solve complex, changing problems and to design personalized service channels. Conversation is personalized, far-reaching, and lively.

■ **Value-centered relationships.** Value is created through jointly developed solutions, services, and products that benefit both the enterprise and its *partner*. Close *collaboration* is required to share knowledge and resources. Conversation is rich and multi-faceted.

The relationship space illustrates that "closer cooperation" and "more intimate relationships" can mean quite different things, depending on the type of customer and the style of the relationship. This framework can help organizations focus on the style of relationships they want to build, and with what objective. It can also help cut through the rhetoric of loyalty programs by helping answer questions like these: "What kind of relationships are these customers looking for? Why and how do they want to work with us? And we with them? What kinds of relationships do we want

Figure 9-1: *Relationship Space: Four Styles*

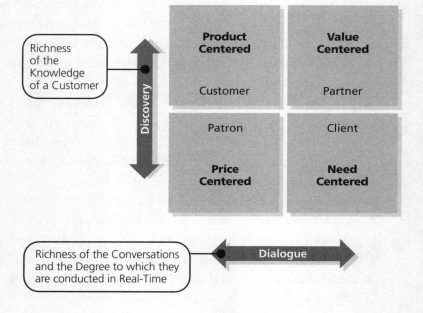

today and what kinds do we want in future?" Specific answers to these questions can help organizations meet the challenge, described at the beginning of this book, of building relationships with today's customers, who may not be bound by traditional loyalty, but instead are looking for value-creating conversations.

The Relationship-Based Enterprise defines distinct relationship styles and molds them to each unique customer group. It is adept at handling a variety of relationship styles simultaneously and, moreover, at focusing resource commitments on those customer relationships with the highest growth potential. It has a customer relationship strategy, one that links each relationship style to:

- a customer group (or individual customer)
- processes to create value for customers
- growth opportunities for the enterprise
- the types of competition, cooperation, coordination, and collaboration needed to support the relationship
- the types of conversation preferred by the customer.

The relationship strategy is not set in stone. In fact, it is continually adjusted to reflect the ongoing conversations with customers.

Cosmos: Relationship Styles Must Change

Cosmos has aggressive growth, technology, and product development plans. Now it needs a relationship strategy so that it can connect with customers and realize those plans. At the moment, there is a disconnect. The story of this disconnect can be told by looking at relationship styles.

The small businesses and entrepreneurs with whom Cosmos wants to build relationships are interested in getting everything on one bill. This need misleads Cosmos into thinking they are patrons, only interested in price-centered relationships, because Cosmos believed that wanting the simplicity of one phone bill was a patron characteristic. However, unlike patrons, the small businesses Cosmos want as customers are maintaining several lines: not just local and long-distance telephone, but DSL, cable, and wireless as well. What they need is not just one *phone* bill, but one *communications* bill. The complexity of their communications bills (not to mention the expense) is skyrocketing. They need simplicity to get a handle on it—but simplicity means answering questions such as, "Can the business eliminate local long-distance in favor of an all-wireless solution?" And dealing with all the competing offerings, not to mention to pages and pages of billing summaries, is hopelessly time-consuming and frustrating. Small businesses felt they were being taken advantage of, but didn't have the time and energy to devote to the problem. Some viewed Cosmos with distrust.

To discover all this, Cosmos needs to go out and converse with customers in a new way. They need to strike up conversations based on new product prototypes and service visions. In the process, they see the possibilities of new relationship styles and begin to develop a game plan.

Price-Centered, Competitive Relationships

Imagine a day trader using a software agent to scan the market for the best prices on his planned portfolio of securities. Or an experienced shopper scanning the aisles of Wal-Mart for the best deal on a basket of back-to-school items. These are members of the patron group, people who derive value from "everyday low prices" and efficient shopping experiences.

What do patrons look for? Nothing less than the best deal in the marketplace. And how does the enterprise that serves patrons make money? By learning to deliver standard products at competitive prices and by making shopping comparisons easy. The key is efficient production, marketing, and distribution—management of highly efficient exchanges.

Conversation is limited. It usually consists of only the exchanges required to complete the transaction—information, product, and money. Communications are mainly one-way from company to customer via traditional marketing and advertising channels. Monologue prevails over dialogue. Limited conversation reflects the traditional value-delivery model, in which patrons need accurate information on price and product features to promote accurate comparisons and efficient shopping.

Price-centered relationships (illustrated in Figure 9-2) can be characterized as "competitive." The customer is seen as an average statistic. The enterprise knows a great deal about such customer segments, but very little about individual customers. Products and services for those in the patron group are created with very little dialogue or feedback.

Patrons can be loyal to an enterprise that consistently offers them a good deal. But that loyalty is conditional—on getting the best price, perhaps not every time but most of the time. The enterprise that targets patrons must ensure that it focuses all of its energy around the idea that customers are aggressive, price-sensitive shoppers—and that these customers will insist on getting the best deal that the market can offer. Examples of such enterprises

Figure 9-2: *Price-Centered Relationships and Competition*

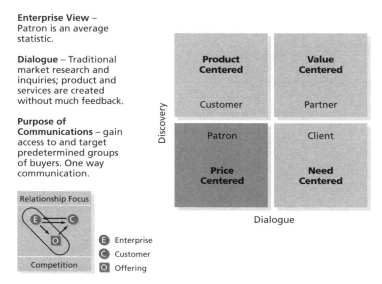

are Wal-Mart, eBay, priceline.com, and some of the e-discount brokers.

The relationship is price-centered because it is focused on efficient operations in a free market—where there is perfect information, perfect competition, and standard products. The goals shared by the enterprise and customer center on completion of short-term transactions. Typically, these exchanges are "final" when they occur and require little follow-up or service.

The added value provided by the enterprise in this kind of relationship is a result of its "operational leadership." It produces high-quality products and services at the lowest possible cost, and the focus of the enterprise is on "selling."

Price-Centered Relationships

- Delivery of the "best deal" in the marketplace
- Solid profit margins for those enterprises that are operationally efficient
- Competition based on the price of standard items
- Company and customer are marketplace adversaries —the classic economist's model
- Patrons are treated only as buyers.

Product-Centered Relationships and Coordination

Imagine a veteran business traveler who wants her trips organized precisely to reflect a long list of "do's and don'ts" covering everything from flight times to seating arrangements to meal preferences to wake-up calls. Or an extreme sports enthusiast who has an intricate list of equipment specifications for a trip into the Andes. Or a manufacturing production line that must be stopped if parts do not meet predetermined quality specifications. These people are members of the customer group, and they derive value from the customization of products and services to meet very specific needs and preferences.

What do members of the customer group look for in a relationship? In simple terms, the delivery of customized configurations of products, services, information, and solutions that precisely meets their needs. Customers may have problems with standard formats and configurations, for reasons that range from mundane to mission critical. Jeans do not fit. Today's jet engine designs do not match new jet prototype. "Plain old" cellphone and wire-line Internet services no longer meet the needs of a network of investment bankers, securities lawyers, and venture capitalists. In all these cases, customers see a "once and done" solution to their problem in the form of a self-contained product or package that can be configured to meet their needs.

How do companies make money and generate growth opportunities from the kind of product-centered relationship illustrated in Figure 9-3? Typically, they become adept at (1) market micro-segmentation, (2) directly observing customers and understanding their needs, (3) providing ways for their products and services to be reconfigured, and (4) customizing and mass customizing their offers.

Figure 9-3: *Product-Centered Relationships and Coordination*

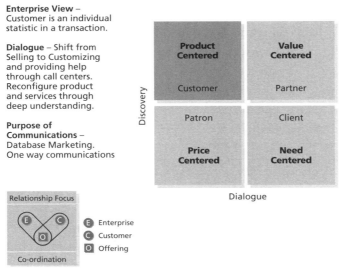

Intimate knowledge and information on customers is required to support customization of products, services, or solutions to precise customer specifications. Companies build such customer knowledge in three main ways. The first method is excellence in market segmentation using traditional market-research methods. This enables the company to learn about the segment in depth without engaging individual customers in direct conversation. The second method is to scrutinize a customer's buying and usage patterns, a form of indirect conversation that becomes part of sales and service routines. The third method is to engage customers directly in delivery of the product or service. These conversations are very efficient, since they are usually limited in time and tightly focused on the customization of products and solutions.

Product-centered relationships involve precise coordination, specifically when the enterprise creates processes that enable customers to co-configure products and services. The customer is seen as an "individual statistic" in a transaction. Long-term relationships with those in the customer group provide a framework for precise harmonization, synchronization, and coordination of processes, as well as specialization of roles.

Coordination requires yet more information and knowledge sharing, and the precise sharing of control over key business processes. It reflects long-term shared goals that are specific in focus, synchronization, and specialization. Examples include longer term agreements in supply chains to use JIT and other methods to coordinate production processes and operations; and a financial Web site that enables customers to design a portfolio and change its composition by trading.

◎

Cosmos: Customer-Focused Product Development

The product development teams at Cosmos found that technological change in the communications industry had created a huge potential for customization and the development of product-centered relationships. In market research and focus groups, more and more small-business owners expressed the desire for "simple solutions" and "integrated solutions" to their communications needs. Many of these included a variety of wireless and Internet-based applications in addition to "plain old" telephone service.

There were two basic drivers behind this demand for solutions. The first was that busy entrepreneurs were somewhat intimidated by the time it took them to learn about broadband, multimedia, third-generation, wireless internet, optical networks, and so on. The second driver is that they were not sure how to buy these new services, or how to use them.

Cosmos responded with a number of proposed solutions designed to meet specific, documented needs in many businesses. These solutions mobilized all the relevant technologies into packages that met a specific business need. Many focused on the needs of mobile workforces. For example:

- **The Wireless Office**, which enables traveling employees with laptops and cellular phones to "plug in" at any office location and use the company network
- **Networked Car Fleet**, which enables employees to use their cars for the full range of voice, data, and multimedia communications; also supports navigation and roadside assistance services
- **Connected Sales Force**, which employs many of the mobile applications to support the networking and communications needs of sales forces
- **Telepresence**, a high-quality broadband teleconferencing service that functions as a virtual meeting room
- **Lone Wolf Program**, which provides independent entrepreneurs who operate outside a traditional office with a customized package.

Some solutions, like the wireless office and networked car fleet, were prototyped with a few select companies and then rolled

out in a traditional way. Market demand was strong and customers came quickly. Other services, such as the connected sales
force, needed to be designed with customer involvement. In these
cases, Cosmos co-designers worked for months with a handful of
customers. These customers got free service for a year, in return for
their input to the design teams.

All this was several steps beyond traditional customization
for brand-loyal long-distance customers. Such innovations as the
"friends and family" program were simple in comparison to the
design and installation of a wireless office.

Product-Centered Relationships

- Focus on delivery of customized products, services,
  and solutions
- Achieve solid profit margins by segmenting customers
  precisely, observing their behavior, or involving them in
  the product-design process
- Coordinate activities to support precise harmonization,
  synchronization, and specialization
- Put the company and its customer on the same team
- Treat customers as buyers, users, and limited producers.

Need-Centered, Cooperative Relationships

Imagine a busy entrepreneur who can get access to credit, foreign
exchange service, and market data "anytime, anywhere,"from a
personalized combination of Web access, call centers, and his personal account manager. Or a microbiologist in a pharmaceutical
research laboratory who uses a B2B exchange to place her orders
for exotic combinations of chemicals from up to 30 suppliers, all
in a single order. Or an e-shopper using a portal site's search engine
to build a personalized Web-scanning interface. These people are
members of the client group. They derive value from the ability to

personalize service processes, channels, and interfaces to help them solve complex, changing problems.

What do members of the client group look for in the relationship? In simple terms, access to personalized service and advice through convenient channels that save them time and money. Their problems are not with standard products but with the fact that there may be too many products to choose from, many different ways a product can be used, or many complex after-sales service issues. They may also find it hard to use standard service and delivery channels.

To deal with these issues, clients need suppliers who can converse with them freely, intelligently, and on a wide range of issues. Clients want personalized service channels and processes that put them in the driver's seat when it comes to selecting the when, where, and how of service. They prefer suppliers who are willing to participate in a shared forum rather than traditional channels. Personalized conversation helps keep members of this group in control of the situation, deciding when and where various services are needed. The enterprise must respond quickly to changing requests. Examples include expert service from help desks, skilled account managers, and outsourcing firms.

How do companies make money and generate growth opportunities from the relationship? They need to be adept at (1) conversing freely with clients and understanding their problems, (2) working with clients as channel co-designers, and (3) personalizing channels, market spaces, and service processes.

Need-centered relationships (illustrated in Figure 9-4) provide stable frameworks for cooperation over long periods of time. The three typical drivers of cooperation are that (1) joint action is required to solve complex problems that often arise in unpredictable ways, (2) it takes time for members of the client group to select, buy, use, and dispose of the products and services in question (quality, warranties, after-sales service), and (3) it takes time for suppliers to learn what members of this group need.

Figure 9-4: *Need-Centered Relationships and Cooperation*

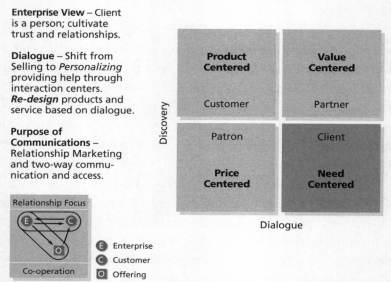

As cooperation grows, conversations become rich, free-flowing, and interactive. Conversations focus on a variety of buy and use challenges, issues, and problems.

Companies do not need to learn the intimate details of customers' lives and operations. They just need to listen closely and respond flexibly to an ever-changing stream of requests for advice, navigation aids, information, and problem-solving.

Traditionally, need-centered relationships involved high levels of personal service by people like account managers, boutique owners, and customer service departments. Today, modern communications technologies combined with CRM create a variety of options. For clients experiencing problems with shopping, selection, and ordering, B2C portals and B2B exchanges can provide personalized search and selection aids. For clients experiencing difficulty with after-sales service, advanced call and contact centers can provide what amounts to virtual help desk services. Personalization and cooperation via the new technologies of conversation are some of the major business opportunities for relationship-based growth.

Cosmos: Virtual Hand-holding and Cooperation

Cosmos marketing teams began to discover potential clients as they tested the solutions developed for customers on some mid-sized businesses, businesses with more complex needs. Typically, these organizations did not need a single customized solution. Often they asked for parts of several packaged solutions, say, a wireless office for some work groups combined with a small wired sales force, and so on. Some of these potential clients also wanted to outsource their call centers, contact centers, and Web-site hosting.

These companies' needs were complex and changing. A "once and done" packaged solution was not practical. Service was needed continuously. The challenge was to deliver it on an economic basis. Cosmos' marketing and account management teams responded by designing the Virtual Communications Help Desk Service. It enabled clients to personalize their "space" for dealing with Cosmos from the following options:

- account teams and consultants
- Web site support
- call-center support
- membership in an extranet-based Advanced user group
- outsourcing of client call and contact centers.

The client was in the driver's seat when it came to choosing which parts of the help desk to use for which purposes. Over time, the client and Cosmos co-designed a help desk that linked their processes, systems, and communications experts into a personalized service network.

Need-Centered Relationships

- Offer personalization of channels, interfaces, and service processes
- Offer solid profit margins for companies that can listen to clients, respond quickly, engage them in interactive conversation, and enable them to co-design "the store"
- Entail cooperation over long periods to solve complex problems and personalize
- Mean that company and client are in the same network
- Treat clients as buyers, users, and producers (including design activities).

Value-Centered, Collaborative Relationships

Imagine the traditional integrated supply chain in which suppliers partner with their upstream customers. Or the intimate relationship between a customer and an independent professional (lawyer, investment banker, venture capitalist). Or a small Web-enabled community in which graphic designers and their suppliers work on common projects. These people are members of the partner group, which creates value through jointly developed solutions and long-term collaboration.

What do both partners want? In simple terms, they want value that can only be created through the joint design of solutions that involve products, services, channels, and interfaces. To develop these solutions they need to achieve high levels of collaboration. The conversations are rich, free-flowing, and interactive. Exchange of knowledge, information, and other resources is extensive. The enterprise and its partner develop intimate knowledge of each other. All this forms the basis for sustained collaboration, supported by joint investments of resources, over time.

Value-centered relationships come in many forms: partnerships (formal and informal), joint ventures, strategic alliances, Web-enabled communities, integrated supply chains and supply networks, B2B exchanges that involve extensive customization and personalization, and product developers that team with suppliers and their customers.

Value-centered relationships depend on intensive and extensive collaboration. Collaboration among members of a value chain is not new, but the primary focus has always been collaboration with suppliers. Or collaboration among a group of independent organizations that produce something of value—products, services, information, knowledge—that could not possibly be produced by a single organization or single entity. But collaboration with customers in this way is a new idea.

A collaborative, value-centered relationship (illustrated in Figure 9-5) is a series of conversations between an enterprise and a customer that occurs over an extended period of time. The conversations are personalized and spawn customized products and services. In this type of relationship the added value from the enterprise is that it provides each of its customers with the right combination of supplier relationships. Collaboration embraces the

Figure 9-5: *Value-Centered Relationships and Collaboration*

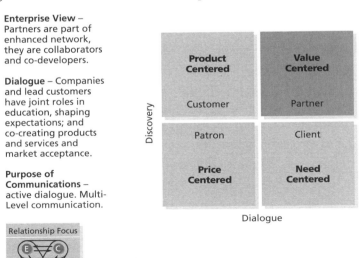

joint action needed to achieve complex shared objectives over extended periods of time. A collaborative relationship goes beyond the normal collaboration that occurs among suppliers, since here collaboration is with a customer. And that customer is a partner.

◎

Cosmos: Moving Towards Partnerships

Over time, Cosmos account teams developed relationships with several clients who began to look like potential partners. These clients wanted more than personalized service; they wanted sophisticated customized solutions as well. For example, some mid-sized companies that dealt with Cosmos are "primary nodes" in their supply chains and virtual supply webs (in advanced manufacturing, pharmaceuticals, etc.). Cosmos decided to recruit these customers as lead partners in designing, prototyping, and marketing service packages to the entire supply chain, involving anywhere from 10 to 30 business partners. The business case for this type of arrangement is that state-of-the-art networking is a critical success factor for all the partners, who see the advantages of adopting a broadly shared solution.

Cosmos wanted to develop network architectures and services for supply chains and supply webs. It also considered investing in B2B exchanges for small groups of enterprises in travel, news, and several other sectors. Collaboration is required to create this type of partnership. Both customization of products and extensive personalization of the "conversation space" (channels) is the goal. Dialogue becomes rich and complex. In essence, this is a joint venture to provide customized communications solutions to integrated supply chains. Account teams work with enterprises for which state-of-the-art networks are a critical success factor (CSF) —linking them to B2B exchanges, key customers, and integrated supply chain partners. The goal is to develop networks that cover supply chains and networks (usually regional in scope).

As the Cosmos example shows, in value-centered relationships strategic knowledge and control sharing are needed to support integration of communications operations and processes. All partners must invest resources not just in product development and solutions, but in a long-term relationship. And joint action is required to achieve complex shared objectives over long cycles (financial cycle of household, growth cycle of an enterprise, fitness cycle of an individual). Collaboration involves customization of products and personalization of shared workspaces.

Value-Centered Relationships

- Involve design of solutions that create value for all partners and community members
- Enjoy solid profit margins for companies that can customize products, personalize channels, and freely share resources with outside organizations
- Feature conversations that are rich and multi-faceted
- Extend collaboration over long periods
- Blur the boundary between enterprise and customer; partners can fill any role in the exchange space—buy, use, produce, and service.

It's All About Style

A relationship strategy clearly identifies the relationship styles preferred by key customer groups. It also answers the basic question: "What kinds of relationships do we want today and what kinds do we want in the future?"

As the relationship-based enterprise goes about answering these questions, by actually conversing with customers, a relationship strategy emerges. Marketing and product development teams start with a focus on "full-service" and "integrated" solutions. But they quickly realize that these expressions mean very different things to different customers. They could mean a simple phone-cellular-Internet package for the corner store. Or they could mean a sophisticated wireless office for a group of young lawyers.

The problem could easily be defined as one of market segmentation. But the Relationship-Based Enterprise realizes that it cannot segment the market that exists based on traditional market research. Both customer needs and technologies are constantly changing. Trial-and-error plays a role in testing new solutions, which focus on the need for dialogue and well-designed conversations with customers—a key to marketing success.

Back at Cosmos, the marketing director was able to create a Cosmos Relationship Strategy, which was revised and adjusted regularly. Cosmos realized that its business spans all four quadrants of the relationship space. Therefore, knowledge gained in one quadrant can be used to meet the needs of customers in other quadrants. For example, Cosmos might work closely with clients to develop customized solutions, but then realize that these solutions could be packaged as a set of options for customers. Or they might recognize that customers consistently configure products in a certain way, opening up a market opportunity to develop such configurations as standard products for patrons. The following status report, which documents activities to be undertaken in all four quadrants of the relationship space, sums up the Cosmos relationship strategy.

> *Price-Centered Relationships*—Cosmos will offer patrons two standard packages of land line, mobile voice, Internet, and Web-hosting services. Cosmos is slightly ahead of the competition in its reputation for network reliability and the ability to offer a single bill. Market share is steady to date.

> *Product-Centered Relationships*—A large base of customers who want Cosmos wireless office and wired car fleet products have been identified. New sales of these products and

customer retention are strong across most business sectors. Marketing is working with several customers to reconfigure the wired sales force solution, which needs to be refined. Account executives report reduced switching to specialized competitors.

Need-Centered Relationships—The sales force has met hundreds of rapidly expanding firms that expressed interest in more than three of our products and lacked in-house communications expertise. As planned, sales persons completed handoffs of these clients to Cosmos account teams, who convinced them to co-design personalized communications help desks. About 150 help desks and 20 outsourced contact centers are currently under development and have been generating revenue for an average of four months. So far, growth potential appears to be strong.

Value-Centered Relationships—Experience to date shows that Cosmos will be able to recruit partners for whom advanced networking is mission critical. As expected, these customers want high-bandwidth solutions linking them to their downstream business partners in supply chains, B2B exchanges, and Web-enabled business communities.

Window on the Real World:

Quebec Institute of Statistics

Like all governments today, the government of Quebec (Canada) has various programs in place to attract foreign investments and knowledge workers to its territory in order to develop the economy, support job development, and broaden its financial resource and tax base. Attracting foreign investment is just one of the Quebec government's many economic development strategies.

When the Quebec Institute of Statistics (QIS) wanted to increase foreign investment in Quebec, it identified the kind of relationships it wanted with foreign investors. In essence, QIS wanted to do a better job of building value-centered relationships with partners who would co-create value for the province of Quebec. To do this, it needed to engage each investor more personally and make it easier to obtain current, correct, and relevant information. This turned out to be a complex process.

Today, QIS relies on a network of 2,000 economic development agents stationed across the province and overseas, all charged with promoting Quebec among investors and building promotional documents and analyses that "sell" Quebec. These economic development agents come from agencies at various levels of government. Over the years, the government has created a multitude of organizations responsible for supporting this large network and supplying it with all sorts of information: statistics on employment, unemployment, salaries, financial resources, taxation, industrial zones, labor, transportation networks, demographics, and so on.

Agents consult a continuous stream of reports, studies, and brochures produced by various contributors and contact many government customer-service points to build promotional documents and analyses. And the process is the same for potential investors— they are forced to deal with multiple customer-service points, multiple reports, and multiple information sources. Getting personalized information was difficult.

To overcome these complexities and deliver personalized information, QIS decided to take customer service to the Internet. It created a Web-enabled solution that integrates the processes of the various agencies into a flexible electronic network linking points of service to the supply chain. According to Michel Gauthier, director of department statistical operations and technology, this was accomplished in three major steps:

1. QIS organized focus groups among the various contributors in the supply chain, including representatives of their primary target market, to better understand the information needs, key messages, and best ways for interacting with them.
2. QIS created a restricted-access extranet for economic development agents around the world, providing instant access to all analyses and promotional information, statistics, and selling points about Quebec and its regions.
3. QIS developed a public Internet portal for foreign investors, offering "views" of Quebec tailored to the target customer's interests.

As a result, the 2,000 agents can build their analyses and promotional documents faster with much higher quality information. "The left hand is now coordinated with the right, and both of them are firmly on the wheel," says Gauthier. More importantly, "Foreign investors can access a central portal on the Internet to access the information they need, instantly, with varying views—and initiate a dialog with a centralized source."

Further Thoughts

For the Manager

- Have you made the commitment to customer dialogue?
- Have you identified a champion for the vision?
- Have you institutionalized the vision?
- Have you demonstrated that you are interested in and understand the customers' needs and concerns?
- Have you maximized customer dialogue at all touch points?
- Have you enabled your employees with the proper tools?

- Have you empowered your employees?
- Have you created a seamless environment for success?
- Have you demonstrated to the customer you can add value?
- Have you gotten ahead of (or behind) your customer?

10
CHAPTER

How Do We
Foster Exchange?

Elements of an Answer

- **Listen**—Go beyond the delivery mindset
- **Engage**—Create value exchange by exchange
- **Enable**—Share channels, places of business, and meeting spaces
- **Learn**—Learn with customers through sharing information, knowledge, and product design interfaces

Three hundred years ago, at the start of the 18th century, a new way of fostering economic exchanges appeared: the coffee house. The new, black brew, fresh from the New World, stimulated the evolution of a different sort of meeting place with a new set of rules that closed the gaps between certain levels of society. Businessmen—commodities traders, financiers, and brokers of all sorts—went to the coffee house to hear the latest news and trade information. And as relationships and trust grew, they began to trade stocks and other pieces of commercial paper across the table. Gradually, those coffee houses grew into the London and New York stock exchanges.

The foundation of these exchanges was discrete conversations in which economic exchanges occurred one by one, offer by offer. Aggregated, these conversations evolved into lasting business relationships. And as those relationships became more and more economically valuable, they formed the base for organized marketplaces. The relationships that were created eventually became stock exchange memberships.

In simple terms, the financiers of London and New York discovered that coffee houses gave them a place of business, a meeting place or forum, where it was convenient, efficient, and congenial for them to conduct business. In the coffee houses, they created shared ground rules and understandings about how to do business—how to buy and sell, how to settle accounts, how to clear transactions, and which information to trust (or not). All this was needed to foster exchange.

In the formal language of this book, the London and New York financiers faced the challenge of conversation design. Their response was to develop a system of stock trading, financial accounting, information exchange, and "exchange membership" that proved successful in attracting more and more business. They were able to work intuitively over many decades to develop all these conversation designs and the supporting systems.

Today, conversation remains a powerful force in the creation of marketplaces. The basic questions are: How do organizations foster economic exchange? How do they turn those exchanges into conversations that will become relationships that create value?

To start answering these questions, consider that the Internet serves a similar function to the coffee house—except on an instantaneous, global scale. Conversations still occur, except in an electronic forum. However, because of the speed and scope of e-business, enterprises do not have the luxury of developing these conversations intuitively, over a long period of time. Instead, conversations must be *designed*.

There are two fundamental principals to conversation design:

1. Conversations must be designed exchange by exchange.
2. Each exchange must create value.

The essential context for conversation design is to define broadly the relationship styles preferred by various customer groups — patrons, customers, clients, and partners. As explained previously (Chapter 9), each of these styles—price-centered, product-centered, need-centered, and value-centered—involve a different type of conversation, and what might be called a different "working relationship"—competition, coordination, cooperation, and collaboration, respectively.

Using high-level insights into the relationship styles preferred by customers, the relationship-based enterprise can then design conversations that support the target relationships. This activity can usefully be viewed as translating a strategy into a tactical design. It is important to remember, however, that the process is interactive—the relationship styles and conversation designs will evolve together, both in response to "live conversations" between the enterprise and the customer.

At Cosmos Communications, the telecommunications company introduced in Chapter 9, conversation design is a pressing issue. Managers faced the task of translating their relationship strategy into actual conversations with customers. They have already determined what each type of customer—patron, client, customer, or partner—wants from Cosmos and what to expect from them.

Patrons want standard service packages of telephone, cellular, and Internet services—for a flat fee—and can be expected to switch for lower prices. Customers are expected to buy customized solutions, such as the wireless office and the networked sales force, that use advanced communications technologies to meet specific business needs; they want conversations focused on these so-called expert solutions. Clients want more than expert solutions; their needs are so varied and changing that they need virtual com-munications help desks to handle lively dialogue on a wide range of subjects. Partners want to do mission-critical business using advanced networks, B2B exchanges, and Web communities; the relationships they seek are more like joint ventures and business alliances.

Here's how Cosmos began to take their relationship strategy to the next level.

"The Big Picture of these target relationships needs to be turned into practical blueprints," says the marketing director. "Broadband solutions and all-optical networks will be like trees falling in the forest with nobody listening ... unless we connect with our customers."

In response, four Cosmos teams are formed to handle con-versation design, one for each customer group and relationship style. The four teams start by trying to imagine what types of "conversation" are involved in delivering the various packages.

The patron task group has no problem visualizing the con-versations supporting price-centered relationships. There are plenty of precedents—long-distance competition, the launch of cellular services, the launch of Internet services. If the truth were told, Cosmos still intends to use the techniques developed in the old long-distance wars to deliver basic communications service packages to small businesses. Classic market segmentation, tar-geted advertising, targeted Web casting, targeted print and TV advertising, e-mail, and direct mail campaigns, will all focus on one-way delivery of marketing messages and price-product infor-mation to buyers. The conversations will not be interactive (except for the award of points under traditional loyalty programs).

The task groups exploring customers and clients have a harder time designing the fine details of product-centered and client-centered relationships. After all, they are exploring unfamil-iar terrain. What is involved in selling and installing a wireless office solution or a connected car fleet? How does one determine whether a business really wants a virtual help desk, or how they would want one to work?

To answer these questions, the customer and client task groups sponsor some focus groups. The results are incomplete and inconclusive. Most participants are interested by the proposed Cosmos solutions, but the issues raised are too complex to be discussed in a few hours. Moreover, it is hard to get decision-makers to take an afternoon off for a Cosmos focus group—most business people do not believe Cosmos will listen to them!

A few conclusions emerge. First, Cosmos employees had better "get out from behind their desks" and begin actually conversing with customers. Second, they will not know what most businesses want until they get out with prototypes and ask for feedback.

The focus of the task groups shifts from the products and solutions they are trying to develop to the process of generating business conversation around those products and solutions. Entrepreneurs are not used to being approached by Cosmos to discuss product development issues. Cosmos does not have "listening posts" and forums for discussion. The sales force is respected, but there are not enough sales people to market and develop all the new products in the hopper.

Work begins on the problem of "making our channels more friendly and accessible." Representatives come together from all groups that "touch the customer"—the sales force, road service crews, technical support, call centers, Web sites, various help desks involved in serving business accounts and marketing research. The team takes on the job of finding the best mix of channels and "touch points" for conversing with clients and customers. It looks for the best combination of messaging channels to support a specific relationship style: face-to-face, telephone, wireless, e-mail, video-conferencing, chat rooms and user groups. The focus is on opening channels of conversation with customers—to open doors for the sales people.

One offshoot of this work is the Cosmos credibility problem—the fact that its relationships have been impersonal in the past, "so why should that change now?" One workshop explores the list of the "top three irritants" for small-business customers.

One of those items is "the monthly phone bill"—errors, inaccuracies, and, above all, the inability of call-center agents to give simple explanations of rates and charges. Some participants think back to focus groups where the big questions about new solutions like the wireless office is: "How much will it cost? Will your bills tell us what we are buying? How will you help us manage the costs?" Mundane billing problems, it turns out, could be one of the big barriers to marketing innovative Cosmos solutions.

Both teams start to focus on two key aspects of conversation design. One is interactive verbal communication—dialogue in the ordinary sense of the word—about the Cosmos offer. The other aspect is complex economic interaction—such as the automated, manual, and verbal interactions involved in billing for a complex offer like the wireless office.

The Cosmos teams begin to experience, at a gut level, the importance of "conversation" to their business success. They begin to understand that conversation design may be as critical to their success as product design or technology configuration.

All this is a good start. But to complete its conversation designs, Cosmos will need to focus more strongly on four primary management activities

1. **Listening**—Sharing perspectives and knowledge. Listening is a type of exchange that is critical to conversation. To foster exchange, organizations need to create listening posts and forums for customers to express their opinions and suggestions. Listening processes must be designed into conversations.

2. **Engaging**—Linking value-creation processes in order to engage customers in conversation. Every exchange needs to create value to sustain a conversation. Value is created exchange by exchange, with each exchange linking

the value-creation processes of the customer and the enterprise.

3. **Enabling**—Sharing channels, places of business, and meeting spaces to ensure that exchanges create value. Making conversations seem personal wherever, whenever, and however customers do business with you enables them to converse freely. Clients want to do business in shared meeting spaces and forums for dialogue rather than traditional one-way "delivery channels" owned by the company. They are ready to co-design those spaces.

4. **Learning**—Sharing information, knowledge, and product design interfaces to ensure that exchanges create value. Customizing products and the content of offers rests on learning about, and from, customers. Customers can teach the enterprise about their product preferences or go further to act as direct co-designers of products.

As discussed below, these four activities of conversation design focus managers' attention specifically on how to foster more interactive types of exchange with customers. The emphasis is on the processes of sharing—like the processes in the financiers' coffee houses.

Go Beyond the Delivery Mindset

To converse effectively with customers, relationship-based enterprises need to get beyond the traditional "delivery mindset." This change in management emphasis is symbolized by two types of transactional Web sites. One has excellent product information, an easy-to-navigate catalog, and buttons to select and purchase—it is excellent at traditional information and product delivery using a new channel. The other site has all these delivery features *and* one other button: "Click here to talk to us" or "Click here for the status of your order" or "Click here if you have a question."

In traditional terms, the second site is just trying to offer better customer service. In terms of conversation design, this site is taking the first step towards combining delivery with conversation in a new virtual forum.

Listening is obviously vital to the success of any conversation. And if a relationship is a series of conversations, as defined in this book, then listening is also vital to the success of a business relationship. But listening is not necessarily a prominent capability of every organization. And because of this, customers face an interesting dilemma, especially in a period that has been characterized as nothing less than a communications revolution. They have many more channels through which they can contact their suppliers, and yet it seems difficult to get through. The inability to make contact is often referred to as "bad service" when, in fact, it probably results from an organizational hearing defect. The organization is not listening.

Why is listening a problem? For the most part, listening problems are largely related to the way businesses have been designed. Most large-scale organizations, including service organizations, are designed to deliver. Their channels are there to "deliver" and "distribute" products and services to customers—they were not necessarily built to hear from customers. And delivery is primarily a one-way process. Products, information, and productized services are delivered to customers. The channels are not designed as meeting places and they are not forums for discussion. And so, the way that a business is designed makes listening to customers a low priority. Listening is most certainly done, but listening, in real time, has for the most part been a secondary concern, something that has to be done when there is an after-sale problem. But many try to eliminate even this kind of listening through programs that focus on the quality of products. The goal of these programs is to eliminate such problems before the product is delivered.

Having a delivery mindset is not necessarily a bad thing. But it makes it harder for organizations to listen. A revealing example is the way that many organizations approached the Internet. The first instinct was to build Web sites—and manage them in the same way as other channels—as a vehicle for delivering information, advertising messages and products to customers. Because of this delivery mindset, one of the problems that many organizations face is handling the e-mail that is generated through these Web sites. In many ways, this is no different from the problem that organizations have had over the last decade handling customer complaints that arrive by regular mail. It is a listening problem.

A good example of this is provided by Cosmos Communications. Cosmos hoped to make its corporate Web site a hub for customer discussion.

Cosmos and Chat Rooms: Channels or Listening Posts?

To probe small businesses about their communications needs, the marketing group from Cosmos Communications ran a series of focus groups to test customer response to ideas for integrated solutions. As often happens, the results were incomplete and inconclusive. There was not enough time to review the details of both the wireless office and connected car fleet programs and, adding to this, many key decision-makers were unable to attend. A telephone survey of the decision-makers who could not attend the focus groups proved even less informative. And although sales calls were producing good information, the sales organization could not generate enough hot leads.

In order to more quickly open customer doors, a "friendly channels" task force began to explore new way of starting conversations with customers, conversations about service issues, unmet needs, new communications technologies, and so on. One of the programs undertaken by this task force created a chat room for entrepreneurs and business users. It was located on the Cosmos corporate Web site. However very little traffic materialized, even though the site developers had advertised the room in a number of choice locations.

After a few months, one of the younger representatives from customer service (and a member of the friendly channels team) navigated her way into an answer to the chat room problem. While browsing the Internet she wandered into an independent "complaints and solutions room" that was maintained by business users of telecommunications and ISP services. The participation was lively and the volume heavy. To her surprise, many of the complaints were about the services of Cosmos. The focus was on problems with billing, routine service, software maintenance, and a range of private-network configuration problems. The discussions were technical one day, freewheeling the next.

After several return trips to this independent chat room, she realized that all the issues and problems that were being thrown out on the virtual table were a potential gold mine. The chat room could provide Cosmos with the inspiration needed for developing new products, billing systems, and service facilities that businesses were looking for—and not finding. Moreover, the context of a chat room favored frank exchange about problems and issues, more than was possible in staged focus groups or executive interviews. It was also obvious to her that the customers whom Cosmos was trying to attract to *its* chat room had another place to go; but more worrying was the thought that competitors would show up too. Some Cosmos employees, from marketing and product development, began to participate in these chat room discussions. They would follow up on complaints and issues, and then come back with proposed solutions. At appropriate times they would throw a new product ideas on the virtual table. Over time, the conversations around the Cosmos proposals became lively and the ideas were either quickly refined or discarded. Cosmos had entered into a dialogue with its customers.

The chat room escapade was not universally popular within Cosmos. Some were nervous about handling complaints "outside the normal channels." They would have been more comfortable "owning the site" where these conversations were taking place. "Why should we trust the people running this room?" commented one of the critics. But after several discussions of ownership, everyone began to realize that the chat room was not a "channel." It was a "listening post." The Cosmos participants were not delivering service in this forum. They were doing market research, testing product ideas, and handling customer-service issues all at the same time—through conversation. And the customers were coming back because they knew that they were being heard: someone was listening.

The lesson to be learned here is that, in the midst of a communications revolution, the ability to listen can be a major advantage. More importantly, learning to listen and listen well can give companies "early mover" competitive advantage.

Create Value, Exchange by Exchange

Good conversation designs foster interactive exchange. Interactive exchanges fuel dynamic conversation. And the whole process creates value. In fact, the key requirement for a successful conversation is that exchanges between the enterprise and a customer create value.

When designing conversations exchange by exchange, it is important to remember that each exchange must create value. Without value, a conversation cannot be sustained.

Here is an overview of the key types of exchange that can make up conversations:

- talk (selling, bargaining, negotiating, consulting, chat)
- messaging (structured information exchange)
- knowledge creation and transfer
- resource sharing and pooling
- working together
- buying and selling
- returning goods
- exercising warranties
- placing and confirming orders.

Some conversations involve money and some do not. Value can be created through the exchange of such valuable resources as time, knowledge, and information.

The principle becomes more interesting and helpful to organizations when applied to more complex conversations, especially those that rely on technology. For example, the IT departments of separate organizations may need to ensure that their order-processing systems can talk to one another. The exchanges of this conversation—order, confirm, pay—will be executed many times each day. Conversations can include many interactions; some of these involve the exchange of information, others product, and still others money. It is important to ensure that each exchange in the series of exchanges creates value, and that it does so, as shown in Figure 10-1, by connecting the right value-creation processes.

Conversations must be designed to create "the shortest route to value" for both the customer and the enterprise. This means ensuring the best connections possible between the two value-creation processes. There is no need to integrate or merge these value-creating processes. Instead, conversation connects the processes, ensuring that each conversation has an optimum combination of value-creating exchanges.

Figure 10-1: *Exchanges Linking Value-Creating Processes*

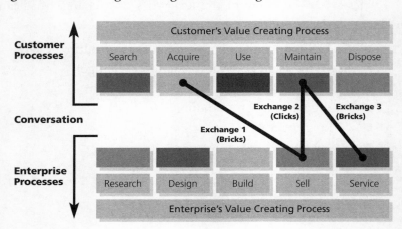

Billing and payment systems provide one example of the value of connecting processes more effectively. Billing and payment can be viewed as a complex conversation between the enterprise and customers—a conversation that often wastes valuable time and resources. For Cosmos' small-business and entrepreneurial customers, "the monthly phone bill" is a major irritant. Focus group tests and call-center traffic all confirm the mundane truth: business owners do not appreciate the errors or the inaccuracies, and they find especially annoying the inability of Cosmos' call-center agents to give simple explanations of rates and charges.

These problems were hurting the credibility of Cosmos as it tried to reshape its relationships, leading Cosmos to the conclusion that it needed to find a better way to design "the billing conversation."

Cosmos Designs a Billing Conversation

Information gathered through its new ability to listen told Cosmos that a single bill, itemized in detail, was viewed as providing significant value to businesses—like travel agencies and software development houses—where communications costs were high. These were the same businesses with which Cosmos wanted to build new relationships.

A Cosmos team went to work on the billing issue. The problem, they concluded, was that Cosmos' billing systems and customer payment systems were like islands—preventing the exchange of relevant information and data. The team responded with a plan to create software links between its billing systems and the accounts payable and finance systems of some companies. The idea, proposed to a handful of customers, was to "get our billing and payment systems to talk to each other."

When an interested client agreed, Cosmos and the client mapped the conversation exchange by exchange. This detailed view enabled the teams to ask the key conversation design questions; for example: Which processes need to be connected to save time and money? Which connections are needed to make customer cost-tracking and management easier? Which exchanges should be automated? Which require face-to-face contact and bargaining? Which can be electronic with human assistance when needed? And so on.

◉

There are many and varied value-creation processes in business. Many of them can be connected to create valuable conversations between a Relationship-Based Enterprise and its customers. Billing and payment processes are central to many relationships, especially business-to-business relationships. Other key processes, reviewed in the next two sections, revolve around the design of channels and the design of products. Linking these processes creates value through personalization through cooperation (client-centered relationship) and customization through coordination (product-centered relationship).

Share Channels, Places of Business, and Meeting Spaces

If value needs to be created exchange by exchange, then personalization of service processes and delivery channels with clients represents a major opportunity to foster exchange and link value-creation processes.

New communications technologies and CRM personalize the places, spaces, and times in which clients and enterprises deal with each other. "Channels" and "marketplaces" and "portals" are becoming infrastructures that clients are co-designing and sharing with enterprises. Meeting places and forums for dialogue are replacing traditional one-way "delivery channels" owned by the company. The potential to wrap exchange spaces around clients opens the door to even tighter linkages—and to customer involvement in the design of service processes and channels.

What does this new capability mean to clients? What difference does it make? The answer depends significantly on the value clients attach to the service experience. Personalization can be a simple matter of convenience. Take the example of "my bank"—that special combination of ATM, Web site, call center, and branch access that meets the need of a loyal mortgage customer. The convenience is nice to have—but not essential.

At the other extreme, personalization can be mission critical. The client may need personalized service—or none at all. Personalization of the channel or interface is closely linked to personalization of services, information, and advice. Day trading investors, for example, want more than fast, convenient access to stock market trades using e-trading services. They need to control the pricing information, formatting and menus, the precise timing of stock trade execution, and so on. Without personalization of the screen interface and several key services, the trading service has little value.

In designing conversations, it is important to ask: How important is personalization to the client? When is it essential to foster exchange? How involved does the client want to be in designing channels and conversation spaces?

A common sense answer to these questions is the *driver's seat principle.* Personalization is key to value creation and fostering exchange when the client really wants to be in the driver's seat when it comes to deciding the where, when, and how of service. For these clients, service processes are critical to their success. Personalization enables high levels of cooperation. Conversation is lively and interactive, creating the fabric of a need-centered relationship.

Mission-critical personalization is illustrated with a fictional example, Export-Import. This is a business that survives—and profits—based on its agility; in particular, its ability to close deals and make critical commitments faster than multinational clothing industry giants.

Chan Export-Import: The Deal Maker's Conversation Space

The Challenge: CEO Betty Chan wants speed, fast access, and control over financial decisions from access points around the world.

She thinks, decides, and manages on her feet, along with her three adult children living in different cities.

This family of entrepreneurs faces a variety of split-second decisions that must be made virtually every working day: whether to buy a lot of clothes from Malaysia; whether to pay in U.S. dollars or local currency; on which terms to negotiate a long-term supply contract with a retail chain. There are financial issues and risks associated with many of these decisions. Fluctuating credit needs, currency values, and the availability of short-term trade financing all affect the family's choices.

The Solution: Betty needs specialized support from her bank for international trade transactions, both real and virtual. She says she wants reliable service, flexibility, and to keep banking issues in the background of our business. "We need to stay focused on the business, not our lines of credit and foreign exchange rates," says Betty.

So, what does she really mean by "reliable service" and "flexibility"? The family's core requirement is timely access to credit and information, which can make or break export/import deals. It is a game of seconds and inches. In more specific terms, they need a combination of standard products and personalized access:

- credit-line draw downs, accessible within minutes via phone or click on extranet-supported banking facility
- credit line authorizations, that is, access to decision-makers who can revise authorizations with a phone call to account manager or local bank
- foreign exchange and forward contracts, instantly accessible via extranet or phone
- specialized information services (trade, shipping, and foreign exchange reports), via Web site or voice-response system
- personalized "alerts," by phone or e-mail if traveling to international meetings with bankers, family members, and occasional clients who want to know who is backing the company
- access via advanced video-conference facilities
- traditional advice from the bank account manager

- opportunities to negotiate discounts on fees and interest rates from time to time; meetings with account manager.

All these exchanges combine into a series of conversations between the Chan family and the bank—with each conversation tending to focus on banking support for a trade deal. In order to conduct these conversations, Betty Chan needs her bank to, in effect, travel with her around the world. "Her" bank is actually a personalized banking conversation space that is accessible—via Web, phone, or teleconference—to family members in Bangkok, San Francisco, and Antwerp. (It is the family's shared banking space.)

Driver's Seat: Betty has another requirement. She needs to call the shots and take fast decisions—with the confidence that she will have fast access to service and that her bank will back her. She does not need exotic, customized financing support but she does need a flexible set of "authorizations" to conduct standard credit, trade, and foreign exchange operations—and a flexible set of access channels to activate those authorizations.

The Chan family "banking space" is a mission-critical element of the information, money, and service that makes up "our bank." Foreign exchange quotes and credit are useless in closing deals unless access is immediate. Betty does not see her challenge as involving channel management. "That's my banker's problem," she laughs. What she wants is the required banking service—anytime, anywhere, anyhow. For the bank, however, this level of service represents major investments in Internet, call-center, paging, and wireless e-mail technologies that allow Betty, her banker, and her family to share the same meeting space several times a week, or even in a day, year-round.

The bank need not become involved in the business—it sticks to banking. But excellent execution is critical. Betty will pay a premium and remain loyal in order to have a stable but flexible service arrangement. She knows "loyalty" does not always mean "low everyday prices."

Cooperation and the Driver's Seat: The banking arrangement involves more than convenient access to service. The personalized banking space is a key element of a framework of cooperation. It enables personalization of conversation spaces that helps members of the client group stay in control of the situation—enabling them to decide when and where various services are needed.

For each transaction, fast response and instant access are critical to success. Over time, cooperation is required to meet the banking challenges of Betty's company. A stable relationship that lasts years is required. Shared goals are necessarily broad and vaguely defined. Betty wants an open-ended banking arrangement and the bank must be ready to respond in a flexible, open-ended way. Cooperation is needed to create the service framework for problem-solving, service delivery, and information exchange over long time periods. A long-lasting relationship makes good economic sense.

To sum up, Chan Export-Import is being served via many channels. In classic CRM terminology, this involves channel integration—giving the customer the same service and a consistent, branded experience when being served in any or all channels. This type of service can be presented in a different, more powerful way using the new language of relationships. What the Chan family has come to expect is a "team conversation" with the bank—its account managers, Web sites, extranets, and call centers. All these members of the bank team, whether human or electronic, are equipped to "converse" with the Chan family and respond to service requests.

Traditionally, conversation meant personal service—either face-to-face, or point-to-point contact on the telephone. But person-to-person conversation is no longer the only option for interactive business exchange between an enterprise and customers. As the Chan family shows, there are a number of "personalized conversation" alternatives that can provide value to customers.

A simple example is the team of call-center agents who can "converse" with an individual customer over a period of days. When they share access to a good customer profile that is updated regularly, team members can listen and respond intelligently to the customer from one call to the next ... and hopefully solve the problem.

When conversations are personalized (as distinct from personal), clients do not always deal with the same person in the organization. Yet they can still have the impression of dealing with an integrated team of people and customer-facing systems. "Conversations" (in every sense of the term) can be personalized using CRM technologies and customer profiles. The team members can keep track of the customer, recognize, remember, and exchange information with him or her on a personal basis.

Of course, personalized conversations need to be designed. They can only happen consistently when supported by human and technological systems. Here is a short list of conversation design ideas:

- "Team conversations" between a client and a virtual team. These teams can include many units of a large organization—call-center agent, Web-site agent, sales person, account manager, delivery driver, sales clerk, order processing agent, supplier representatives.
- "Many-to-many conversations" between clients and call-center agents. The agents are supported by efficient switchboards and shared customer profiles that enable them to recognize clients and respond quickly.
- Interaction in a conversational mode between a client and a Web site, an "intelligent" software agent, and an efficient e-mail response system.
- Messaging in a conversational mode between two "intelligent" software agents, one representing the customer and another the enterprise.

Personalized conversation represents a big change in the costs and organization of "personal service." Traditional personal service required a sales force or corps of account managers to provide personal attention; this was considered the highest cost service-delivery channel, and reserved for large corporations and wealthy individuals.

Personalized conversation can offer interactive exchange to many more customers, creating a competitive opportunity by enabling patrons to become clients. Creating conversations in this way is one of the main purposes of CRM and relationship-based strategies.

Learn with Customers

By sharing information, knowledge, and product-design with customers, customers can contribute value as product co-designers. Customization of products and solutions (the content of offers) creates major opportunities to foster exchange and link value-creation processes.

Like personalization, customization can be a simple matter of convenience. It is nice to have jeans that fit better, a hotel room outfitted to your specifications, and a blend of coffee that tastes just right. Nice to have, but not essential.

At the same time, customization can be a matter of life and death. People need pacemakers that are precisely adjusted to the rhythms of their bodies. Medical equipment manufacturers need parts that fit precisely with their designs, just as plane manufacturers need jet engines designed especially for a specific model.

Obviously, it is mission-critical customization that most fosters interactive exchange and value-creating conversation. In designing conversations with customers, it is important to ask: What factors make customization more or less important to a customer?

Three key factors stand out. One is *value*. Is customization critical to the value of the product or solution? The answer varies a lot. A pair of jeans can be worn (by most) without fitting perfectly. It can be important to customize the features of a mortgage—interest rate, maturity, life insurance—but you can still buy a house with a plain-vanilla mortgage loan. In contrast, a household financial plan must be customized to generate any value at all; if it is prepared using a standard formula, it is not really a financial plan but just a set of useful guidelines that many households can use.

Another factor influencing the importance of customization is the *nature of the exchanges* required to customize a product or solution. Some products and services can be customized with little or no exchange. For example, hotel chains discreetly observe regular customers' behavior from visit to visit, and then customize room features and services to match their exact preferences; but the verbal exchange required to do this is quite limited. Other products can be customized to the needs of very small customer groups through a combination of traditional market segmentation and conversations with only a few "lead customers" who represent the segment accurately. Examples include affinity-group credit cards and the suite of Harley Davidson products. Yet other products have enough adjustable features built into them that customers can do the customization themselves through a process of experimentation; examples include computer-controlled lighting systems and features-rich personal computing interfaces.

In all these cases, the company needs to develop intimate knowledge of individual customers or customer groups, and especially of their product requirements. But none of these types of customization involve a significant amount of interactive exchange.

In contrast, there are varieties of customization that require customers to play an active role in teaching enterprises about their product requirements—whether for a certain type of jet engine, a customized news service, a certain type of insurance policy, or the configuration of a corporate communications network. Even more intense exchange is required when customers become active product co-designers. This approach has been used for the design of products ranging from eyeglasses to home windows, daily news scanning services, and auto parts.

When customers play the roles of teacher or product co-designer, time must be spent in highly focused conversation and experimentation. The company must often invest in the development of computer-assisted product-design processes and design interfaces, which create the environments in which conversations occur. The roles of the customer and the enterprise must be precisely defined and coordinated to make the design process work.

A third factor influencing the importance of customization is the *scope* of customization. What is being customized? The product itself (an automobile) or certain cosmetic features (doors, air conditioning, color) or just the packaging and presentation?

In designing conversations, it is important to ask: How important is customization? How does it affect the value of the offer? What is the nature of the exchange required to customize? How deep is the customization?

As with personalization, a common sense answer to these questions can be found by applying the *driver's seat principle*. Customization is key to value creation and fostering exchange when the customer wants to be in the driver's seat when it comes to deciding the "what" of the offer. For these customers, product design and performance are critical to their success. Advanced customization requires high levels of coordination. Conversation is tightly focused on the product, solution, and content of the offer.

Mission-critical customization is exemplified by the development of household financial planning software for use by independent, computer-literate professionals. These customers— accountants, business lawyers, day traders, investment bankers, and stockbrokers—do not want to pay a financial planner. They do not want their hands held. But they do need help and guidance in preparing a complex financial plan. Direct involvement in designing their financial plans provides a solution for this hands-on customer group.

Sit Down and Have a Cup of Coffee

But don't relax. In the global version of the 18th-century coffee house—the Internet—conversations have to be designed to create relationships that deliver value to the enterprise, to patrons, to customers, to clients, and to partners. Relationships and trust across the Internet are slow to grow and fast to go. And instead of centuries-old institutions, like the London and New York stock exchanges, relationships fostered via the Internet empower the Silicon Valley Fast-50 index of companies. Which of these will be around 100 years from now? The answer may well be the ones who are best at fostering exchange through good conversation design.

Further Thoughts

Questions for the Business Manager

- Context: who is the customer?
- Infrastructure: where and when does exchange takes place (in space and time)?
- Content: what is being exchanged and for what price (or cost)?
- Value proposition: What is the value provided by the exchange?
- Business design: how is the exchange conducted?

Questions for Those Designing Conversations

- Who? The customer or customer group involved in the exchange.
- Why? The value created by the exchange (value proposition to customer).
- What? The content of the offer (product, service, solution, information, etc). Customization.
- Where? The combination of physical places and virtual spaces that is preferred by the customer. Also the matching combination of "interfaces" that provide access to those places/spaces (offices, telephones, wireless and handheld appliances, kiosks, personal computers). Personalization.

- When? The appropriate combination of business hours for personal service and 24 x 7 access (extended hours) via the Web, call centers, and stores. Personalization.
- How? The mix of traditional one-way exchange (delivery) and interactive exchange. Type and tone of conversation. Personalization.

11

How Do We Share Control?

Elements of an Answer

- **Planning**—Develop a control-sharing game plan
- **Decisions**—Share decision-making
- **Information**—Share information, knowledge, and expertise

William C. Durant created General Motors by acquiring and merging automobile manufacturers and their suppliers into a single organization that dominated its market space for a very long time. Contributing to General Motors' success was its ability to control a significant portion of the automobile-manufacturing value chain.

For most businesses, acquiring control to this extent is no longer possible. But many business executives, government officials, not-for-profit administrators, and entrepreneurs still recognize that their success is often contingent on what happens outside of their immediate control. So they take a different approach to achieving similar results. For example, Sears Roebuck did not buy their suppliers; they invested in them and secured relationships with contracts. Marks and Spencer adopted an approach that was based on contracts alone. The production chief of Toyota, Taiichi Ohno, created a new supply chain, replacing ownership and contracts with cooperation. And cooperation among upstream suppliers in the supply chain became the new model for success.

Just as important as control of the supply side is control of downstream activities. Every enterprise exists between its upstream suppliers and its downstream customers, as is illustrated in Figure 11-1. It is not isolated. This is true in both business-to-consumer (B2C) and business-to-business (B2B) domains. The enterprise buys products, services, information, and other resources from its suppliers and uses these to produce products and services for its customers. Control must be exercised over both upstream and downstream activities. Control of upstream relationships, that is, relationships with suppliers, has been a focus of attention for quite some time; more so than for relationships on the downstream side, relationships with customers. CRM is about the downstream

Figure 11-1: *The Value Chain—Upstream Suppliers and Downstream Customers*

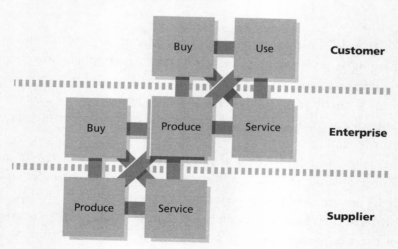

side. This brings us to the last of the critical questions concerning the Relationship-Based Enterprise's preoccupation with dialogue: "How can an organization share control with its customers?"

The value of control is obvious to everyone—improving quality and profit, reducing cycle-time, and cost. In their book *Co-opetition*, Adam M. Brandenburger and Barry J. Nalebuff make the following distinction: "Business is cooperation when it comes to creating a pie and competition when it comes to dividing it up." It can be added that sharing control with customers is a fundamental part of cooperation, and at the same time it positively influences everyone's perception about the fairness of the competition that divides the pie.

But actually sharing control is not easy in practice, even among the divisions and work groups of a single organization. Most are willing in principle. However, when push comes to shove, many executives, managers, administrators, and officials will move in the opposite direction, toward centralized control. Their reasons are known to all—avoiding uncertainty, reducing risk, and eliminating surprises. Economists describe these situations as Prisoner's Dilemma, Battle of the Sexes, and Chicken: all nerve-wracking games of self-interest versus group benefit. This delicate balance between centralized control and shared control is not only difficult within an organization, but also beyond the bounds of the organization, and especially with customers.

Businesses face a strategic choice. They can adopt the mind-set of fighting this trend, giving up control to customers inch by inch. Or, they can leverage the customer's desire for greater control as a way of building relationships. Giving customers the brush-off or the "functional shuffle" in today's marketplace is a high-risk option. So many enterprises have moved toward shared control, with little or no downside, perhaps spurred on by competition, the demands of customers, or because they simply recognize the ultimate benefit and value of sharing control. The bottom line in the new economy increasingly depends on the ability of enterprises to share control with customers.

The immense possibilities opened by the Internet enable businesses to build new, innovative types of business networks and supply webs. As a result, there are many opportunities for sharing control. For instance, specialized electronic news agencies syndicate their news packages to hundreds of different Web sites, and these sites then combine these packages with other information to create customized information services for yet other audiences. There are endless combinations of these kinds of partnerships, alliances, and networks that bring together both dependent and independent organizations, all recognizing the very practical need for sharing control of the value chain, and as well, for sharing the spoils—sales revenue, subscription fees, and advertising revenues. Make no mistake, the agreement to share control of the value chain is as crucial to the success of these business networks as is the use of Internet technologies.

From the point of view of an enterprise, sharing control can mean relinquishing control over product design, channel management, and sensitive business processes such as pricing, selling, financing, and billing. AT&T shares control by allowing consumers to decide the resolution of disputed charges through self-crediting. BMW allows customers to control the selection of certain features. Dell Computer went farther; it allows its customers to control the actual configuration of its products. Sun Microsystems went to the next step, by sharing control of the creation of products. GM allows its customers to select among alternative processes—the Saturn no-haggle process or the dealership negotiating process. Progressive Insurance gives its customers the ultimate in control by providing them with empowering information—quotes from its competitors. There are many possibilities, and many options for sharing control with customers.

The case for sharing control can be particularly hard to make in traditional product and service factories that are trying to implement large-scale CRM programs. A good example comes from the telecommunications company introduced in Chapter 9, Cosmos Communications. At Cosmos, executives were concerned that too much personalization and partnering would turn their clients into telecommunications experts and lead to a "loss of control over networks and intellectual property."

Cosmos has spent several years learning how to customize communications solutions such as the wireless office and the virtual communications help desk to meet the needs of customers. The more progress Cosmos teams made in these areas, the more they changed the operational reality of telecommunications services. This led to some heated internal discussions and debates.

But most customers expect to connect with more than one network. If they have a preferred communications supplier, they do not care whether or not that supplier owns the entire network through which it provides service. In fact, customer perceptions are gradually being turned upside down. Customers view the best solution not in terms of a connection to a specific supplier's network, but in terms of "their network"—a unique communications solution. The solution is assembled for their purposes from many network options.

Cosmos has leveraged this customer perception in marketing its integrated solutions, particularly the wireless office and its help desk—a personalized communications control center. In some situations, the Cosmos team has even helped its clients connect to competitors' networks. Cosmos also routinely leases bandwidth from other suppliers and purchases "spot" bandwidth on B2B exchanges in order to plug gaps in its own networks. Cosmos' strategy is to build relationships with customers, not by acting as a gatekeeper to a single proprietary network, but by acting as the gatekeeper to a wide universe of network services. Many within Cosmos think of this as their network portal strategy.

Senior executives have noticed the change, and it continues to stimulate intense discussion. Following are some of the comments overheard at a recent management committee meeting. "Whose network is it anyway?" asks the head of operations for the traditional wire network. "We almost have to answer that question one customer at a time," responds the head of marketing.

"Customers no longer want access to our networks," comments a senior account manager. "They just want to control the access points and services that they see and use. It is their network."

Develop a Control-Sharing Game Plan

In Chapter 9, "What Kind of Relationship Do We Want?" the types of relationships that an organization may choose to develop with its customers was fully described. It should be no surprise that the degree to which an organization shares control with its customers and the areas where it chooses to share control will depend on the nature of those relationships. Defining relationships is the first step towards a viable control-sharing game plan.

Sharing control is often thought of as a matter of willpower, or good intentions. This is a very limited view. Sharing control has now become an important part of every business relationship, and it is an important part of conversation design. Shared control is also an important aspect of the value that both the enterprise and the customer obtain from their relationship. As such, the way that control is shared needs to be considered in every exchange and

Figure 11-2: *Sharing Control: An Operational Reality*

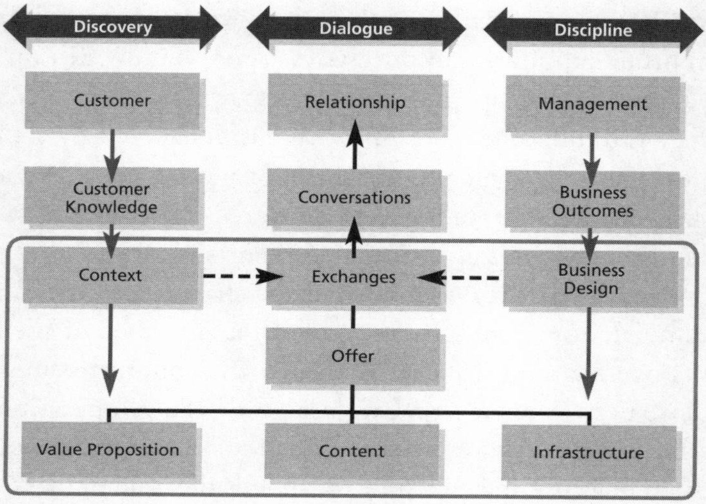

every conversation. In fact, to be successful it must be a part of the value proposition of the offers that are a part of those exchanges and conversations, as illustrated in Figure 11-2.

Sharing control must become an operational part of each exchange for it to be useful to an organization. Broad statements of intent, style, and design do not provide an organization with very much benefit. Sharing control needs to be an operational reality. To converse effectively with customers, the enterprise needs to be "open" or "agile" or "networked," today's most common buzzwords. From an operational point of view, this means designing conversations and exchanges that provide customers with control in one or more of the following five areas.

- **Decisions**—Key issues and decision processes where control can be shared
- **Information and knowledge**—Control over sensitive business information, customer information, and knowledge
- **Infrastructure and business design**—Channels, infrastructure, conversation spaces, and the business designs supporting them
- **Resources**—Critical and scarce resources including people, money, physical plant, equipment, and technology
- **Rewards (benefits)**—The full range of rewards, results, and benefits that both customers and enterprises derive from economic exchanges and conversations.

The Relationship-Based Enterprise is expert at answering the three basic questions regarding each sphere of control: Where does the enterprise have control? Where does the customer have control? Where is control shared? By answering these questions systematically, as exchanges occur, the enterprise develops a control-sharing game plan.

Such a game plan might seen like common sense in simple cases, such as mass customization using new computer-controlled design and production systems. Even here, however, giving customers new decision options can have far-reaching effects on the company's control of resource allocation and infrastructure. Control-sharing game plans are critical to the success of complex business-to-business relationships.

A successful example of sharing control is provided by the franchise business model. It shows how thousands of organizations can share the control of a value chain. Under this business model, the franchisers of McDonald's Restaurants, 7-Eleven Stores, and Midas Muffler Shops control the strategic decision-making, ideas, and information that make those businesses unique. These ideas and information for the most part determine the success of the entire network of franchisees. At the same time, the franchisees finance and manage the elements of the infrastructure required to turn those ideas into viable business operations. Franchisers and franchisees each control the resources they need to do their respective jobs—and reward-sharing arrangements reflect the resource investments of each partner in the value chain. All this is possible because the line between what the franchiser controls and what the franchisee controls is well defined. This is a key to the success of this business model, which incidentally is one that accounts for close to 50 percent of all retail sales.

In general, managers need to define the degree and type of shared control that is to exist with each individual customer or with each group of customers. This game plan is one of the distinguishing features of crisp, effective conversation designs and solid relationship-based strategies.

Focusing on the five possible areas for shared control—and reviewing, revising, and adjusting these control-sharing arrangements—enables the organization to develop some of the core competencies of the Relationship-Based Enterprise. These competencies include:

- measuring the value of shared control and making clear linkages between specific arrangements for sharing control (where something is "given up" by managers) and value creation (where something is "gained" by both the customer and the enterprise)

- balancing the requirements of internal integration (supported by enterprise control) with those of external connection (supported by shared control)
- matching the form of shared control with the needs, wants, and expectations of customers
- building trust and commitment.

It has already been pointed out that customer trust and relationships are won conversation by conversation, exchange by exchange. Trust and commitment are dynamically created, over time, as customers and suppliers work together with the question "Who controls what?" in each of the five areas of control. Gradually, a shared view emerges and a relationship is born. That relationship, in turn, provides a framework for confidence and shared expectations. This can become what some call a "virtuous circle" or a "self-reinforcing system of positive feedbacks." Whatever it is called, it makes for continuing conversations and long-term relationships.

Cosmos Asks, "Can We Trust Our Customers?"

One of the promises that Cosmos made in marketing its wireless office was that customer satisfaction would be "guaranteed." Operationally, this meant that one of the value propositions associated with every conversation was: "Our wireless network quality will be as good as the quality of your current land line." The guarantee didn't add much to the value proposition until Cosmos put some teeth in it—by offering to refund minutes of substandard network time. The refund would take the form of a rebate on the following month's bill. After some acrimonious billing disputes, during which Cosmos lost several customers, most account managers realized that, in the end, only the end users could judge network quality. And that attempts to cross-check those judgments would prove to be insulting to the customer and costly to Cosmos.

Finally the account managers approached the vice-president of marketing with the following advice: "Either drop the guarantee or let business customers take control of these decisions." It was agreed that this issue was not about the quality of the network technology. It was about people and giving them control—"Can we trust customers to self-credit responsibly?" The interim decision was that account managers would have to answer the question customer by customer, or conversation by conversation.

Share Decision-Making

Today's customers want to make decisions. They want to make decisons about more than when to shop and what to buy from predetermined menus of choice. Priceline.com created value for many customers by allowing them to control the one decision they could not control before—price. For a century, it was companies, not customers, that "named the price." Priceline.com does more than give customers the power to bargain and negotiate—it gives them total control of the price.

The eBay auction space has been successful by enabling buyers and sellers to share control over prices in a new way—by negotiating, the way people did in the old village markets, and by going to auctions, but with the advantage of a much wider "market" of buyers.

Enabling people to control buying decisions in new and interesting ways can actually draw them into a long series of conversations within the exchange space. The key is letting go of traditional administered pricing as a business model and giving customers either exclusive control or shared control of prices, discounts, rebates, and so on.

These few examples are relatively simple. Much more elaborate conversations and relationships are built when customers become involved in the decision-making processes of the enterprise regarding production, design, and service. For example, when the engineers of jet-engine makers set up joint design teams with the engineering teams of airplane manufacturers ... or when auto-parts companies become involved in new model design with

their customers, both the auto assemblers and selected end customers, the car buyers and users.

The operational details are different in each case, and they
need to be "sweated" by the people who will need to share control
or give it up outright. But the guiding principle is unchanging:
new kinds of conversations can be designed to create value *with*
customers by opening up decision-making processes—and sharing
control over decisions. To abide by this principle requires a change
of management focus.

Enterprises have traditionally thought of decision-making
processes as being internal and largely invisible to customers. In
fact, this can only be true of traditional patrons who control only
that single decision: "To buy or not to buy."

That was fine, as pointed out earlier, in the relatively simple
world of value delivery. Today, the other types of value creation
must involve the customer more deeply in management decision-
making processes. A glance at the relationship space shown in
Figure 11-3 illustrates only a few of the decisions where customers
may want greater control. Each enterprise will need to work with
its own customers to determine what areas require shared control.

Figure 11-3: *The Relationship Space—Sharing Control*

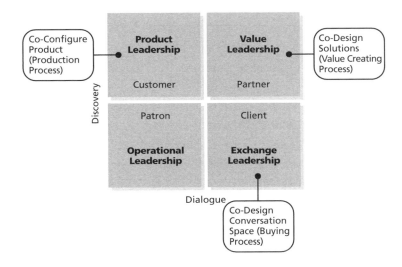

Customers may want to control aspects of product design. The company may have to create a design process and an interface that enable the customer to participate in things like product configuration (not just choice of features). Clients want to share control over the conversation space, including access points, interfaces (Web, phone, store) and time (24 x 7, store hours, home visiting hours). Their control may grow from the interface to include core business processes for purchasing (B2B), shopping (B2C), and selling. In such cases, an enterprise may need to redesign those processes to enable customer involvement. Partners, of course, want to share control over many facets of the relationship, including shared value-creation processes.

When resources are invested in complex CRM solutions, it is important to check the hidden assumptions about the customer's role in decisions. Does the solution provide for more customer control, or does it depend on the assumption that the enterprise will give up no control? At Cosmos, the decision was finally made to share control of network management.

Cosmos Shares Control of Network Management

A core competency of traditional telecommunications carriers was "network management," the control of traffic flows and loads through complex communications networks. This complex operational task used to be under the exclusive control of Cosmos. Now, the tables are turning. Clients no longer feel they are gaining access to the Cosmos network. Rather, they feel Cosmos is being paid to help them configure and manage "*our* network." In reality, control-sharing is the order of the day, given the superior technical expertise of Cosmos.

A case in point is Cosmos' specialized network management service, sold under the label "tailored bandwidth solutions." It helps companies solve problems such as "We have high-capacity fiber-optic networks at headquarters but we cannot share big files with our sales offices and plants because they are linked to us through regular phone lines."

Cosmos knows the real problem is a lack of local fiber-optic connections—the so-called "last mile" problem that prevents high-speed multimedia services from being delivered to many homes. To solve such problems, Cosmos has acquired a start-up company. Its expertise is to locate segments of under-utilized fiber-optic cable (so-called "dark fiber") that can be leased from the owners and connected to other networks to increase their bandwidth (transmission capacity) with gigabit Ethernet.

One client's problem was to link its head office network with expert consulting teams who moved frequently from city to city, and needed access to multimedia services provided by head office. The new Cosmos group had leased fiber in 20 major North American cities. It made the bandwidth available to clients, granting access to a personalized dashboard via a secure extranet facility. That enabled the client to provision its own bandwidth, on demand, cutting costs both to the client *and* Cosmos—while personalizing network-management service at the same time.

This solution worked not just because of the technology but also because Cosmos gave the client a large sphere of control over network-management decisions. It was a case of shared control over day-to-day network management, with the client in the driver's seat.

Share Information, Knowledge, and Expertise

Today's customers want more information and knowledge. One of the big reasons is that they need to support the new decisions they are making—by themselves and jointly with enterprises. Information is part of the much-discussed shift of power towards customers. Better access to information on product quality, price, and other customers' experiences is a big part of the role reversal, described earlier, in which customers become the hunters rather than the hunted.

How can businesses leverage this expansion in customer control? The simple answer is to make "information hunting" easy, focused, and fun. This is the approach taken by the successful Web sites. Sharing information is essential to the new types of conversations that are struck up with Web browsers. At Amazon.com and other book sites, for example, the client can harvest far more information in one visit to a site than in one visit to a mega-book store—book reviews, reader reviews, what others have bought, and more. The client's costs in time and money for accessing information are driven towards zero. In effect, this remote virtual conversation with software agents is superior to a face-to-face conversation with a harried customer-service representative, who cannot possibly read, review, and catalog all that is published today.

Everyone talks about the information that is available from certain e-stores and portal sites. Not noticed are the changes that were made to the business and its technology to support this information-sharing. Companies invest a lot of money to develop the information systems, including CRM solutions, which actually make this information available. They then share the information—or give it away outright—without insisting that the customer make a purchase in return.

Not too many years ago, most organizations would have tucked away price and quality comparisons in a confidential file somewhere in the marketing department. Today this kind of information is readily available, enabling easy comparisons of prices and features across many sectors. Should any individual supplier try to control this information, by hiding it, the portals that make the information available would become even more valuable to consumers. In fact, the portal may become more valuable then the supplier's own Web site. Of course, providing information of this kind follows a change in mindset in which "free information" is viewed as the start of a conversation.

More elaborate control sharing is required to benefit a high-growth opportunity, as in the use of the Internet to create information value-chains and networks where information itself is bought and sold like a product. The specialized electronic news agencies identified at the start of this chapter provide a good example. For their information-sharing arrangement to work, the news agencies must be willing to let the downstream Web sites control the information product, its distribution, and the relationship with the end customer. At the same time, the downstream Web sites must let the upstream news producers control the information content of the packages.

Such syndication arrangements are the e-commerce equivalents of the franchising networks described earlier. There are endless combinations of partnerships, alliances, and networks that bring together both dependent and independent organizations. And make no mistake, the agreement to share control of the information value-chain is as crucial to the success of these business networks as is the use of Internet technologies—as are, of course, the arrangements to share control of the spoils, including sales revenue, subscription fees, and advertising revenues.

Whatever the specific control-sharing arrangement, it looks a lot different from the value chain of a traditional newspaper. It insisted on "end-to-end control" of information—from its shaping in news rooms to its packaging in lay-out rooms to its production and delivery to newsstands and doorsteps.

Sharing control of information requires a major change of management focus, a change that is vital to the success of many CRM initiatives. What is this change all about?

Enterprises have traditionally thought of "their information" as being proprietary. That applied to customer, product, cost, financials, design, and many other kinds of information. "Information is power" was a slogan that was widely believed to be true in business. And most managers thought it meant hiding information rather than sharing it, strictly controlling information rather than "giving it away."

What was true of information was even more true of knowledge—knowledge of production processes, formulas, work methods, customer preferences. This was viewed as the intellectual property of the enterprise.

These ideas were part of the value-delivery model, in which knowledge and information were embedded in a product or standard service that was then sold to patrons who needed only to know the price and certain key features. Naturally, commercial advantage seemed to flow from exclusive control of the designs and knowledge that were used to develop the product—including information and data concerning customers and their preferences.

To converse effectively with customers and clients, however, there must be much freer knowledge and information-sharing. Some customers will want to have information about the design and configurations of products customized to meet their needs and specifications. Clients expect to have access—on demand —to extensive information about products, services, and the enterprise. An essential quality of good sales people, and a user-friendly Web site, is that they know how to share information freely, quickly, and at low cost (or free of charge). They know what information to share, how, when, and why; and they know the value that sharing creates.

Knowledge-sharing reaches a new level when customers become partners of the enterprise. In this case, it is more accurate to talk about joint knowledge creation by the partners. A simple example is the community of practice that develops when pharmaceutical companies outsource research and development work in genomics to a small network of university and private laboratories. The partners jointly create scientific databases and knowledge in order to create value (in the form of improved R&D guidelines or perhaps new experimental drugs). From the standpoint of intellectual property, the partners act like employees of the same company. The development community is "where" the knowledge resides.

Nothing to Fear but Fear ...

Paradoxically, in the connected economy, the more companies try to maintain control, the more control slips away. The Internet outmodes monopolies—as Microsoft foresaw with regard to its operating system, and, as a consequence, made investments in Internet technologies. Another case in point is Napster, which passed the control over copying of music to its community of users, challenging the music industry's monopoly over music sales and distribution. It was a wake-up call to the industry, which is now seeking new business models—and, eventually, better ways to share control.

As Howard Sherman and Ron Schultz wrote in their book *Open Boundaries: Creating Business Innovation Through Complexity:* "... a conventional company ... has to recognize that in order to continue to grow and develop, it must find a way of relinquishing the centralized control that it holds on to out of anxiety and fear."

The new type of business, the Relationship-Based Enterprise, only thrives on true relationships with its customers and suppliers, relationships characterized by intensive dialogue, partnering, and shared control. It too believes that "information is power," and more powerful when shared.

Further Thoughts

Control-Sharing Activities for Managers

- Define exchanges with customers.
- Outline choices that customers have in each exchange.
- Define limits and cost implications of choices.
- Outline company's strategic position on customer control.
- Create a customer-in-control atmosphere in the company.
- Define measurements to track the implementation of the strategies' revenue, expenses, and customer satisfaction.
- Popularize success stories around customer control.

PART

Discipline — About the Choices of Management

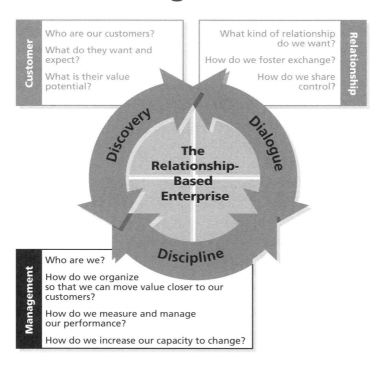

Customer Who are our customers? What do they want and expect? What is their value potential?	**Relationship** What kind of relationship do we want? How do we foster exchange? How do we share control?

Discovery   Dialogue

The Relationship-Based Enterprise

Management
Who are we?
How do we organize so that we can move value closer to our customers?
How do we measure and manage our performance?
How do we increase our capacity to change?

Discipline

"Until a business team is somewhat stabilized by disciplined interaction, people are consumed by crises."
—Susanne Kelly and Mary Ann Allison,
The Complexity Advantage, 1999

12

Who Are We?

Elements of an Answer

- Business mission and customer relationships
- Management and branding
- From channel integration to conversations

For the Relationship-Based Enterprise, answering the question "Who are we?" means branding conversations. The challenge is to design conversations for different relationship styles without diffusing brand identity, either internally (for employees) or externally (for patrons, customers, clients, and partners). As in the old story of the blind men and the elephant, each touch-point should have a different "feel." But the elephant still knows it is an elephant.

Business Mission and Customer Relationships

Traditional organizations often tailor the message about who they are to suit the various markets that they serve. A Relationship-Based Enterprise takes this standard practice a step further. It will position itself in one or more of the quadrants of the relationship space and engage in different conversations with patrons, customers, clients, and partners. Each group may be presented with a different view of the enterprise, based on the type of conversation the enterprise has structured for that relationship. The answer to the question "Who are we?" can be different for each of the different relationship styles.

To the patron group, the relationship-based enterprise may present itself as the provider of standard, low-cost products and services. To customers it may present itself as the owner of industrial-strength products and services that can be customized to meet the needs of every customer. To clients it may present itself as the supplier who understands their need intimately and is prepared to help them find unique solutions to their business problems and opportunities. And of course to partners it would present itself as a supplier willing to share knowledge, information, and resources, an equal partner in the development of business solutions. The implication of this is that there may be no simple answer to the question "Who are we?"—especially if the enterprise chooses to serve more than one customer group. For example, certain customers may be looking for a bank that is conservative and stable, while others may be looking for a bank that is dynamic, changing, and flexible. Such diametrically opposed messages would look odd sitting next to each other in a brochure rack, but there is no reason why either of the two groups of customers should ever have to see both brand strategies.

Another important factor in creating brand strategies is that information, support, products, services, or whatever that is needed, can be obtained in real time or near real time. Customers want to do business on their time and on their turf. Under such conditions the organization must deliver the message about "Who we are" instantaneously and consistently across all possible channels. This is one of the challenges of Customer Relationship Management. Some executives have reported this as their biggest concern in the emerging world of electronic commerce. It is a goal that can be achieved, albeit with significant effort. But it does no good—unless the message about "Who we are" is clear, understandable, and *synchronized to appropriate relationship style*. The members of each customer group—patrons, customers, clients, and partners—will not "hear," or will misconstrue, messages intended for other types of customers seeking different relationships with the enterprise.

Window on the Real World:

Clearnet

Clearnet, a highly successful Canadian-owned communications carrier, was born out of deregulation. Clearnet provides wireless communications services in Canada. Initially entering the market-place with analog dispatch services, it launched its digital services (Mike) in the mid 1990s. Clearnet is a good example of a leading service industry company that uses information technology to provide better customer service and simultaneously handle more customers in less time.

According to Kevin Salvadori, vice president of client opera-tions, one of the key elements that Clearnet considered at the beginning of its CRM program was the question, "Who are we?" The answer—to become a "Future Friendly" company—settled many of their CRM-related issues, including how to convey the branding experience to customers through the various CRM touch-points.

Adopting a "Future Friendly" philosophy meant that every-thing Clearnet did had to be as clear and as simple to understand as possible to its customers. That philosophy affected all its product lines—from the way employees and call-center agents interact with customers, to education material for customers, to how the market-ing material is written, to the messages conveyed in advertising campaigns. "Future Friendly" became the branding experience Clearnet wanted to convey through its CRM touch-points.

Clearnet's touch-point strategy included five call centers in three locations: retail outlets, dealers (for the business segment), and a Web site—all built around two product lines. Call centers are used for servicing, collecting, and marketing. The interactive Web site is used for product support, learning, and purchasing.

Clearnet's future plans include a new Internet strategy to increase and divert customer traffic to their Web site in order to serve retail customers. They see their leading-edge Web site as performing some of the key functions currently performed by the call centers, especially as its target markets become increasingly Web-savvy.

Management and Branding

Organizations that have been successful at branding have done a few things, very well. These few things include creating a new category, being first in that category, promoting the category, leveraging publicity, and promoting the company as the leader of that category. There are many examples of organizations creating new categories of businesses on the Internet, for example, on-line booksellers, on-line e-tailers, and on-line reservations, just to name a few. The organization that creates the new category positions its organization as the first in that category. Because it is the first in the category, it is able to leverage any of the publicity that may be associated with that new category. The publicity will clearly encourage others to enter this market, and in doing so, will help propel the first in the category to a stronger position. Successful organizations continue to promote the category and they position themselves as the leader in that category.

While all of this sounds relatively simple, there are some traps to avoid. One of these traps is the loss of focus and dilution of brand. An organization such as Amazon.com, which has established itself as the first in the category of on-line bookselling, must carefully manage how it extends its brand. Offering to sell barbecues, for example, can reduce the effectiveness of the brand and result in a loss of mind share. In Amazon's case, while the scope of the products offered is expanding, the experience of personalized conversations on the Web—Amazon's first-in-category value proposition—continues to offer the value customers seek.

Any organization that expects to establish long-term relationships must ensure that focus and scope are obvious to all. To achieve this goal, most organizations will want to conduct recurring reviews of their business design and their products and services. Without this ongoing attention, CRM has little chance of delivering long-term relationships and mind share, one of its primary benefits.

In reviewing the strategic options there are a wide variety of approaches to choose from, marked by two extremes. An organization may choose a conventional approach, in which conditions are given and an overall strategy is modeled along competitive lines; this framework centers on beating competitors. With such an approach the organization leverages its existing assets and capabilities, making every effort to maximize the value of its products and services for its customers. Growth is achieved, believe proponents of this approach, through retaining and expanding upon the existing customer base with segmentation and customization of products and services.

At the other extreme is an innovative approach, documented by Chan Kim and Renee Mauborgne in "Value Innovation: The Strategic Logic of High Growth" (*HBR*, January 1997). Kim and Mauborgne suggest that the competition is not the benchmark, and that an organization must independently seek a quantum leap in value for its customers. This approach targets a mass of buyers and is willing to drop some potential customers. Its focus is on finding the common things that customers value through considering all the factors or features currently being offered, and is based on an understanding of what is important to customers.

The idea underlying the innovative approach is "What would we do if we were starting all over again?" The result is new products and services that go beyond the traditional boundaries of the industry, as the enterprise seeks new business solutions for its customers. With an innovative approach, an enterprise spends less time and effort on those features of its solution that may not be important to its customer and more on those that provide the customer with the critical components. There are many examples of organizations that have employed this strategy. It is their way of retaining focus and managing the scope of their business.

Expanding on one of these strategic options is a pragmatic view of how to convert business designs from strategy into a tactical reality. As illustrated in the following figures, the exchange space (introduced in Chapter 4) reveals that there are two distinct approaches: offerings provided by the produce role of the enterprise (Figure 12-1) and offerings provided by its service role (Figure 12-2). A third approach involves a combination of these two. These approaches are further described in the following.

In an initial relationship with a customer, an organization can adopt a strategy centering on how the producer would relate to the customer's buyer role. If the industry is mature, then this strategy may become refocused around servicing that product. An example of this strategy is occurring in the finance industry. Banks are repackaging their services into products to increase customer loyalty. The industry has found that if a customer acquires products from a number of different product lines (such as checking,

Figure 12-1: *Produce-Based Growth Strategy*

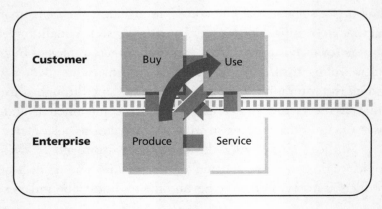

savings, tax-deferred retirement, mutual funds, and insurance) then the likelihood of changing banks is lowered. The bank can then change the services that are associated with these products to improve the customer's experience.

In other cases, the enterprise may see little interest on the part of the customer to purchase more products. This may have been caused by saturation of the market or some similar condition. But it seems clear that the relationship is not functional or may not be growing through the sale of products. This could have occurred because the market is in a later part of its life cycle, where the relationship is very mature or needs to be considered to be mature. The main effect on the business strategy would be a need to increase the type of services provided to the user.

A good example of an enterprise with a service-based strategy is Carrier Corp. They now offer a service level agreement on heating and air conditioning needs. They will manage all the components of the system, from electrical to mechanical, and provide a stable environment for a monthly fee. This change affects the nature of their product lines and refocuses their energy on satisfying the needs and experience of the customer.

The combined strategy, providing both products and services, is generally the most common. It attempts to leverage the exchanges among all four roles: produce, serve, buy, and use. The

Figure 12-2: *Service-Based Growth Strategy*

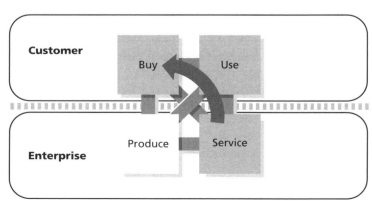

conversations that would occur between the enterprise and the customer are characteristic of a growth stage of the relationship. This stage is exciting and fun for both parties; both parties are learning, and each is challenging the other about how the products and services might be improved to everyone's advantage.

From Channel Integration to Conversations

The key difference between the old business places and the new exchange space is choice. The software-created parts of the exchange space are flexible and can thus be "wrapped around" the customer. Customers gain the ability to choose where, when, and how they do business with an enterprise—in effect, to co-design the forums where they meet to do business. These forums resemble meeting places, and old marketplaces, rather than today's enterprise-controlled channels. Conversations in the exchange space combine elements of channels, marketplaces, meeting rooms, and even stock exchanges. The space is flexible and can take on different forms—depending on the customer and the conversation.

The personalization of these spaces presents major growth opportunities. But it also challenges traditional mindsets in many organizations. These organizations think in terms of "managing channels," which they own and control, not of sharing an "exchange space" with customers and of designing that space jointly with those customers.

Most organizations are challenged by the Internet and all the changes it brings to the where, when, and how of building relationships with customers. They are used to delivering products and services to patrons, not to organizing two-way conversations with clients and partners. Customer involvement in value-creation processes, fueled by new forms of conversation (dialogue), presents a major challenge to organizations. They must open up processes that were traditionally controlled by marketing, customer service, and operations management. Conversation design requires a change of management mindset. It is not enough to build new Web sites, upgrade them, and then do "channel integration." Organizations must learn how to present who they are through conversation, which employs these channels.

Business on the Holodeck?

In the famous Star Trek series, created by Gene Roddenberry, characters enjoy highly realistic, computer-generated vacations in an area known as the "holodeck." They hold real conversations and have real experiences with characters and situations tailored from their imaginations. The Internet is the business world's holodeck—"wrapping spaces" around customers, substituting clicks for bricks, providing a satisfying exchange in a virtual zone, without diminishing the customers' real-life experience.

Of course, the holodeck itself is pure science fiction. But it is interesting to note that the clicks that wrap spaces around customers are already starting to be patented. For example, Amazon applied to patent its 1-Click technology, which allows returning customers to buy a product without repeatedly filling out personal information—and the patent was approved. Amazon views this 1-Click technology as their intellectual property.

More traditional places of business—bank branches, casinos, stock exchange buildings, meeting rooms, and commodity trading pits—cannot be changed quickly. Each has become associated with a particular type of business transaction, and relationship, over long periods of time. But communications and CRM technologies do make it possible to design and redesign conversation spaces to reflect the choices of individual customers and customer groups.

In architectural terms, communications technology gives both customers and enterprises the ability to create a variety of "places of business." They can change location, street address, and access point. They can also design flexible buildings, with adjustable walls, ceilings, and interior decors depending on the occasion. They can be designed and redesigned to help the enterprise and the customer create value together. And these places of business include conversations tailored to deliver consistent messages and a consistent image that answers the question "Who are we?"

Further Thoughts

Questions for Executives

- Who are our customers and what is our market?
- What are the products and services that we provide?
- What is our geographic domain?
- What key technologies do we employ?
- How will we conduct ourselves to ensure our survival?
- What is it that we believe?
- How do we see ourselves?
- How do our customers see us?
- How do we want our customers to see us?
- What is our responsibility to the larger community?
- Do we project our brand consistently across all of our existing channels?
- Do we project our brand consistently within each conversation with customers?

13

How Do We Organize to Move Value Closer to Our Customers?

Elements of an Answer

- **Relationship strategies**—Organizational designs for customers *and* stakeholders
- **Balance**—Local *and* global
- **Use of standards**—Flexible *and* stable

Moving value closer to customers through organization is all about the power of AND. Traditional organizations have structured themselves to support the demands of integration. But the Relationship-Based Enterprise structures itself to focus on both integration *and* connection. This structure is, of necessity, organic, multi-dimensional and self-reorganizing. It's how the Relationship-Based Enterprise resolves a unique organizational dilemma.

This dilemma arises from the Relationship-Based Enterprise's assumption that a perfect organizational structure, like perfect products and services, will never exist. The answer is to create an organization that reflects AND thinking by being adaptive, flexible, and inclusive. Creating such an organization is a delicate balancing act among many contradictions. The structure must take into account the interests of all stakeholders while constantly shifting and morphing as priorities and objectives change. It must balance the needs of the customer with the needs of the enterprise.

To walk this tightrope, the Relationship-Based Enterprise accepts the need to be multi-dimensional. Like the Internet itself, the Relationship-Based Enterprise allows structures that are simultaneously simple and complex; that enable the kind of connections required; and that are self-organizing and never finished. The growth of these structures is guided by three main imperatives:

1. Visible customer orientation
2. Moving closer to the customer
3. Delivering personalized services.

Visible customer orientation means that anybody viewing the organizational structure from outside gets the sense that customers are important. This message, communicated internally and externally, can significantly alter the corporation's culture and operation. In the past, many organizational structures were focused on the internal influences over product-design and/or supply-chain management flows. In contrast, the Relationship-Based Enterprise aims to select a design that demonstrates its commitment to the customer. But at the same time, it also knows that it must be structured to respond to other stakeholders.

Moving closer to the customer suggests that a balance exists in the organizational design between centralization and decentralization. The enterprise is structured to leverage the demands from one customer into an offering for another customer. One example might be an architectural firm that organizes its designs into reusable objects. Its design offering would then offer its clients inexpensive plug-and-play options or more costly custom drawings. This approach also increases the total amount of business value available, creating a bigger "pie," allowing the architectural firm to appropriate some of the value generated through its actions.

Delivering personalized services enables the corporation to reap the benefits of its relationships. Personalized services transfer control over the service to the individual by providing a series of choices that make the service unique to one person. For example, a personalized Web site is one that the individual can change to display only what he or she wants to see. Personalization is distinct from "customization" in that customization, though offering choices such as different colors for a car, does not transfer control to the individual, nor does it allow a unique set of choices. A personalized car-buying service would let each person design his or her own dream car from the ground up: choosing how many wheels and what size, the style of the fenders, an electric or gas engine, and so on.

Personalized services demonstrate that the enterprise can deliver the conversation wanted by its customer. The Relationship-Based Enterprise leverages its personalized services to increase its value proposition in the relationship. But it also understands the cost and risk associated with personalized services.

To achieve success with these three imperatives, the Relationship-Based Enterprise focuses on balancing its organizational design, local and global authority, and use of standards—topics to which we will now turn our attention.

Organizational Designs for Customers *and* Stakeholders

We start by asking, "What are the critical factors in organizational design? How do we transform organizations to be more customer-focused without making it more difficult for internal organizations and suppliers to perform their functions efficiently?" To answer these critical questions, we turn once again to our definition of the relationship space, in which the X-axis, *discovery*, represents richness of knowledge about the customer, and the Y axis, *dialogue*, represents richness of the conversation. As shown in Figure 13-1, four types of organizational styles can be plotted on these axes in the relationship space:

1. Operational leaders
2. Product leaders
3. Exchange leaders
4. Value leaders.

These four types of organizational styles overlay the four main types of customers—patrons, customers, clients, and partners—as well as the four types of customer relationships—price-centered, product-centered, need-centered, and value-centered. In essence, each quadrant of the relationship space is a domain with three objects: enterprise organizational style, type of customer, and customer-enterprise relationship.

Operational Leaders

Operational leaders are organized to facilitate price-centered relationships with patrons. The organizational style reflects the need

Figure 13-1: *The Relationship Space: Organizational Leadership Styles*

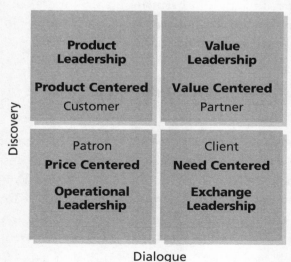

for very limited conversations with no significant dialogue. There is no need to facilitate value-based relationships because there is no need to know much about the individual buyer to be successful.

Product Leaders

Product leaders are organized to engage in conversations with customers, usually centered on customization of products. For example, a product leader might have a dedicated customer relationship group whose charter is to facilitate the configuration of a new product with participation from consumers and suppliers. Product leaders also have market-research groups whose job is to employ sophisticated methods of tracking customer buying patterns and loyalty.

Exchange Leaders

Exchange leaders are organized to engage in far-reaching, complex conversations with clients to co-create value. A good example is a professional services consulting organization where senior account managers are organized into territories and maintain ownership of long-term customer relationships in their territory.

Value Leaders

Value leaders are organized to undertake very dynamic conversations with partners, in which the organization and the partners determine the repertoires that are necessary for them to interact. It is a joint venture or community mode of operation and involves blending and balancing different organizational styles. Value leaders choose, on a very dynamic basis, to work with their customers to create the repertoires that are necessary to co-create value. This is critical because the enterprise may have customer segments in all of the other quadrants, and choosing the right model of interaction is necessary to achieve not only customer satisfaction but also profitability. For this reason, a marketing function may occupy the central coordination role between product development and customers, and between customers and fulfillment. Value leadership is more of a stewardship role because the business rules, which govern product generation and customer interactions, must be accessible to all in a very transparent and manageable way.

The value-leadership organization maintains a model of its markets, customers, and operations. It manipulates these to predict what effects new products and customer segmentations (including segments of one) may have on the operational and financial well-being of the enterprise.

Because value-leader organizations place marketing in a central role, the development of brand tends to be very sophisticated. Branding is based on the articulated needs of the customers and influenced by their unarticulated needs. The enterprise is in the business of developing relationship collateral with the customer, and the head of marketing may even be thought of as the Chief Customer Officer, a title and position that reflect the company's outward-looking focus. Previously, positions such as the COO and CFO have had a decidedly inward focus to them. The CEO has an outward focus but one more frequently directed at external agents such as capital markets, regulators, and, more recently, the business media, rather than customers and markets. Where is the customer represented at the most senior levels of the company? Customer relations vice-presidents are rarely part of the senior executive team.

In sum, in the value-leader organization, marketing functions as the steward of the brand, building relationship equity and organizational empathy with its customer and wider partner communities. Organizationally, it is positioned to provide total value focus.

Local *and* Global

Another critical element when considering organizational design is the need to develop a balance between local and global concerns. How does an organization start to leverage the knowledge of the local market and still adhere to a global branding strategy? In the past, there has been a natural tendency to adopt a structure that chooses one or the other. Localization has been seen as equivalent to decentralization, and globalization as equivalent to centralization. The new economy challenges companies to seek out structures where there is a balance between these two opposing forces.

At one extreme, an organization with a complete focus on the customer may continually attempt to provide its customers with unique offerings. These offerings are designed to meet every requirement identified in its exchanges with customers. But the costs associated with this kind of value proposition make the exchanges expensive. As a result, organizations come under incredible market pressure to convert the learning associated with the unique offering into a commodity so that they can harvest the benefits of their investment.

At the other extreme, the enterprise may establish policies to never supply a unique product—citing real-life concerns about the management of quality, potential liabilities, and the position of its brand. Common sense suggests that those companies that do not deliver a consistent product may appear to be unfocused, undisciplined, costly, and perhaps wishy-washy. Because such an image could quickly destroy a company and its added value, this extreme is generally avoided.

The goal then is to develop the organizational mechanisms that balance these two extremes, providing the organization with the capability to respond to the demand for unique offerings in each of the exchanges it has with its customers, while retaining a focused product strategy. The critical question becomes, "How does an organization produce a consistent product and at the same time be truly responsive to the needs of its customers?" Globalization drives products, services, and messages towards standardization while localization drives them towards customization.

However, before proceeding with a discussion of how globalization and localization can help an organization produce a consistent product, and at the same time, respond to the unique needs of its customers, it is important to understand a second delicate balance—back-office functions versus front-office functions. The back office will attempt to optimize the resources of the organization and its infrastructure to help the front office deliver value to customers. When an organization has a global presence, driven by the need to effectively manage critical resources, the back office will be segmented and distributed. For example, the human resource function will be segmented into functions handled at the corporate level and at the regional level. Because of the scope of operations, there may be a need for the human resources function to also exist in a number of different geographic locations. Segmentation and distribution apply as well to the other functions of the enterprise: finance, technology, and so on. Certain functions, like marketing, may be highly centralized, but even here final assembly of marketing campaigns will occur at the local level.

Figure 13-2 illustrates an organizational structure with responsibilities that are both global and local. At the core of the illustration are those elements that need standardization throughout the enterprise: financial records, HR policies, marketing strategies, and so on. The connections to the outside world come mainly through the customer.

The most important design aspect of this diagram is the strategic function. The strategic function has the primary goal of

Figure 13-2: *Enterprise Organizational Structure: Local **and** Global*

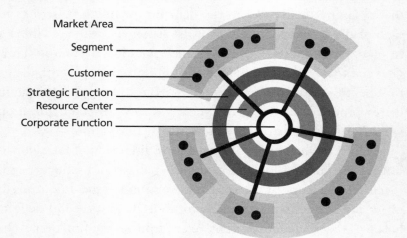

communicating between two competing forces: globalization and localization. The strategic function must also operate divisionally so that the person can localize the context of the responsibility. In the context of the value chain, the strategic function will operate between the front-office and back-office functions. This function will need to bridge these two essential parts of the value chain. It is a function that is rarely discussed—the "middle office," as opposed to the front office or the back office.

The circle surrounding the strategic function in Figure 13-2 depicts the resource center. Its primary function is to manage its value-added assets for the enterprise. These assets include work-in-process (WIP) and inventory, and are processed for external sale. Therefore, the mission of these resource centers is to optimize the accumulation and the execution of the operational elements related to these resources.

A cross-sectional view of the organizational structure (illustrated in Figure 13-2) reveals that the strategic functions or middle office consists of a series of layers. These layers provide the one-to-many communication connectors necessary for the enterprise to balance operations between the global and local requirements. These strategic functions are assigned the task of capturing the learning from the local market demands *and* ensuring that the globalization policies are being accomplished. It is this function that enables a local *and* global approach.

There will be a constant demand by the localization forces to bring the resource centers closer to the customers to increase sales. Corporate functions concerned about globalization will attempt to centralize the resource centers to control the messages and product proposal to the market. A simple way to illustrate this concept is to consider where the following functions would likely reside in this model:

- **Legal/Finance/Shared Service/IS** reside in the corporate functions—with distributed links throughout the organization (market segments, resource centers, and corporate) to gather and disseminate information. Control over legal

and accounting policies should be centralized. Shared
services/IS would establish local and global service-level
agreement for necessary infrastructure services.

- **Production** resides in the resource centers. These
  resource centers would then have primary responsibility
  for functions like purchasing, material, and inbound
  logistics. However, policies or guidelines should exist at
  the corporate level for these sub-functions, allowing the
  company to benefit from certain economies of scale or
  for quality-control purposes. Again, the resource centers
  may be geographically mapped independent of the mapping of the market segments. Sub-contracting/supplier
  services would normally be managed on a daily basis by
  the resource centers. Note: another classical name for
  resource center is strategic business unit.

- **Alliance/Partners** must be managed at three different
  levels: market segments (due to local demands), strategic
  functions (to manage the strategic messages around the
  product offering), and corporate (to provide direction for
  enterprise strategic decisions).

- **Product Offering/Configuration** will normally be identified at the corporate level, but should be functionally
  developed and managed at the strategic functions level.
  Investments in new product offering should be balanced
  between global and local demands.

- **Human Resources** primarily resides in the resource
  centers but complies with policies established at the
  corporate level. Regional considerations for skills, compensation, and issue management require this statement
  of work distribution. Common infrastructure tools
  should be centralized at the corporate level.

Product value will be a reflection of the tension between the
delivery of value from the resource centers and the strategic alignment. The strategic functions must strive to find the balance
between the local desires and global concerns.

Without the strategic functions to help arbitrate between the global and local concerns, product costs can escalate. The resource centers will naturally gravitate towards satisfying the demands of the customer. Solutions will be unique, and so the company will gain a reputation for not doing anything very well—though they will be capable of doing most things in an acceptable manner. The brand value of the company will not be able to be leveraged or supply any rational value-add.

With the increase in the complexity of organizations, which span both disparate and integrated value chains, there is a need to loosen the operational constraints while keeping a common brand image. This appears to be the case with a reorganization announced by AT&T, which enables four different customer-centric organizations to operate under a single brand at the same time. The structure allows each of the operations to establish delivery structures that are integrated at various points and yet operate independently.

Negative reaction in the press regarding the announcement was caused by the newness of the concept, rather than the logic behind the concept. But the logic and approach associated with this new model are quite creative. It presents a new alternative when considering implementing new customer-centric organizations. The model allows for a set of cascading organizational designs that leverage an AND design and not a static OR design. This new design does not eliminate the complexity and conflicting priorities but does attempt to establish a responsive framework that promotes a focus on the customer. The new structure allows for a organizational design that is responsive to new *and* existing customers.

Tension between various customer priorities and concerns is a natural result where areas overlap between the various businesses. However, these tensions existed before the new organizational structure was laid out. In the old organizational model, the internal bureaucracy may have caused sub-optimization of the value chain. Now with the new design, each business will be required to resolve the differences in priority based upon market-driven (external) *and* partnership agreements (internal) needs.

Flexible *and* Stable Organizational Standards

The final critical element of an organizational design involves a discussion of standards. Often standards are characterized as being bureaucratic and costly. However, there is a strong correlation between product/service quality and value delivery. The process of an organization to adopt the various standards can be dynamic; there just needs to be an objective and compelling business case surrounding the selection and adoption of the organizational standards. If the organization cannot state these objective and compelling business cases for the degree of standards then it might need to take a fresh look at its adopted standards.

For the Relationship-Based Enterprise, organizations that assume the role of value leadership will need to adopt and promote the concept and use of standards. Value leadership combines and balances standards from all the other quadrants to achieve:

- product quality and platform flexibility
- accounting systems that promote and reward collaboration
- processes that are adaptable to the customer segment
- communications standards that promote a consistent set of brand messages to the marketplace
- people skills tuned to transforming the unarticulated needs of the customers into viable product or solution hypotheses.

Value-leader organizations extract standards out of applications, manuals, and internalized learning of values and behaviors, and codify them in a set of business rules that drive processes, workflow, product configuration, and customer communications. When these rules change, the enterprise has effectively listened, learned, and leveraged its capabilities. This is the essence of double-loop learning. The frame of reference has changed from enterprise-centric to customer-centric, from being static and amenable to revision only through large and painful projects such as

Business Process Re-engineering, to being flexible, dynamic, and evolutionary.

At any point in the organization's evolution, focusing on particular standards reveals what kinds of behaviors are valued and what management is concerned about. At the enterprise level, standards are completely visible to the customer through the company's brand, which is its credible promise of value to the customer. This is because the brand encompasses so many of the attributes of the company's values, which define for the company—and its customers—"who we are." Mintzberg (1993) describes three basic types of standards that an organization can rely on for management controls:

- output or product standards
- process or workflow standards
- skill standards.

A balanced emphasis on all three types of standards—extracted out of applications, manuals, internalized learning of values and behaviors, and codified in a set of business rules that drive processes, workflow, product configuration, and customer communications—is what identifies the value-leadership organization. The resulting standards are both flexible (open to change) *and* stable (enforced and meaningful while in place).

Output or Product Standards

Companies that emphasize only output standards, exemplified by strict quality controls on products leaving the assembly line, are typically mass producers. If your organization pays great attention to its products but expends little effort in systematizing its interactions or creating new opportunities to converse with customers, then it is likely to be in the first quadrant, *operational leadership.*

Note that workflow standards, a type of process standard, are also in place, but they are internal and directed at product quality rather than at being able to replicate quality or have consistent interactions with the customer over different channels. For *product leadership* organizations, there has to be another class of output standards focused on communications. These take the form of marketing communications standards, to present a consistent image to the marketplace, and technology standards to seamlessly share and distribute messages whenever and to whomever they are needed, or in whichever media the recipient chooses.

Additionally, skill standards (also discussed below) will be found in the operational leadership or product leadership organizations, but focused on individual craftsmanship and product quality. Operational leaders or product leaders may produce expensive one-off products, such as fine furniture, but they are not built specifically for one customer with whom there has been any dialogue. The products would be built to a specific style, such as Chippendale. As a result, skill level and price can be measured, quantified, and justified by industry experts and standards. The organization prides itself on the skills of its employees to create quality products.

Skill Standards

Skill standards focused on product craftsmanship occur in operational leadership (see above). But a second type of skill standard, people or relationship skills, characterizes *exchange leadership* organizations. These organizations specialize in complex solutions, possibly unique to the client. Typically there are a few clients from whom the great majority of revenue is realized. The knowledge to recognize an opportunity, propose a solution, and then sell and produce the solution, is garnered through very skilled resources who typically interact in a face-to-face setting. Professional services and consulting organizations are examples of this type of company. Another example is the electronics company that has gravitated away from producing commodity electronics components towards producing unique configurations in response to detailed requirements. Both rely heavily on client executives to build long-term rapport. These executives intimately understand the culture of the client and their industry, for example, the defense or telecommunications industries.

Process Standards

Process standards may be internally focused and directed solely towards workflows and product quality. But they may also be directed at consistency of interaction with the customer, which is the type of process standard that characterizes value leadership and, to a lesser degree, product leadership. Process standards drive value leaders and product leaders to invest substantial amounts of money in call centers, which are directed at handling not only customer-service issues but also cross-selling and up-selling opportunities within the company's catalogue of products.

Put Everyone on the Same Team

Successful sports teams exhibit a high degree of teamwork—but what does this "teamwork" really mean? It means that a player takes on a role in play, knowing with a very high degree of certainty what the other players will do. The outfielder knows that the short stop is prepared to take the relay throw from left field, or the center knows the wings are racing to the corners. There is no guessing about it—it is fundamental. When necessary they anticipate the need to fill the role of another player—and the decisions are made in a split second, without waiting for an approval from head office. The team constantly self-reorganizes in response to events and the situation.

Similarly, the Relationship-Based Enterprise changes and morphs as both the situation and priorities change. The mature Relationship-Based Enterprise uses its ability to sense and measure to anticipate what its customers need and proactively organizes itself to help them achieve their goals and aspirations. It becomes a value leader that puts both the enterprise and the customer on the same team. This is the essence of collaboration and community-building, which is the next organizational plateau for companies who operate in the connected economy.

Window on the Real World:

Nortel Networks

Nortel, with revenues over US$20 billion and 75,000 employees, delivers value to customers around the world through Unified Networks solutions, spanning mission-critical telephony and IP-optimized networks. Customers include public and private enterprises and institutions; Internet service providers; local, long-distance, cellular, and PCS communications companies; cable television carriers; and utilities. Nortel Networks offers a fully integrated suite of software solutions in three areas: call-center business, customer relationship management, and e-servicing.

Susan King, vice-president and general manager of customer care at Nortel Networks, summarizes what's practical for CRM in the immediate future:

"The promise of CRM is the ability to satisfy customer needs (i.e., provide customer value) to such an extent that they remain customers for life (i.e., retention). However, the practical application of CRM to the problem of building a sustainable competitive advantage remains tied to the underlying enterprise applications that support such a strategy.

"For organizations that strive to fully embrace a CRM business strategy, both front-office (sales, marketing, and customer support) and back-office (finance, HR, materials management, manufacturing, data warehousing/marts, business intelligence, and data mining) applications are required, and unified at all customer-facing touch-points. Indeed, back-office application vendors are increasingly extending their offering to front-office applications in order to support seamless integration. And vice versa for front-office vendors. However, the true benefits to customers lie in the integration of all front-office applications. This is where customers will see immediate benefits."

14

How Do We Measure and Manage Performance?

Elements of an Answer

- **Why measure?** Understanding and adjusting plans
- **Assessment:** Measuring the amount of value current conversations generate
- **Projection:** Organization potential and the ability to do things differently
- **Focus:** How to do things better
- **Tools and Techniques:** What's available
- **Measurements:** Selecting measures

In spite of everything that has been written about measurement and performance, it is not uncommon to encounter a business manager who expresses the performance of his business based on a gut feeling about how the enterprise is doing. This feeling may be the result of an assessment of literally hundreds of different signals, or perhaps some combination of the office politics, economic performance, and the present inventory levels sitting on the shop floor. Or the feeling may be based on a single indicator—the response from customers to an invitation to attend a demonstration of a new product. In many cases, the instincts of seasoned business managers are a good indicator of performance. They are able to map out situations that are both complex and dynamic, seeing their business as a whole and making the necessary decisions where it may not have been possible to have all the facts. These instinctive assessments can be useful to those who understand the full context of the business, but may not contain all of the data needed by others. In addition, only taking into consideration one manager's instinct can lead to misunderstanding the trends, patterns, and events unfolding in a dynamic marketplace. The manager's gut feeling may be based on observations and the repetition of business cycles or the pattern of the business over an extended period of time, rather than what is happening at the moment.

In the new world of the Relationship-Based Enterprise, relationship opportunities are leveraged from conversations and exchanges that take place in real time. As the customer's requirements change, so must the supplier's understanding and responsiveness to those requirements. This is the starting point for a relationship, the ongoing conversation occurring in the white space between the enterprise and its customer. It is here that performance must be measured. However, this is a place where it may be difficult for the enterprise to obtain accurate measures. To complicate matters, traditional financial measures may not be adequate, and in some cases even misleading, because, like all other information, measures have a best-before-date and are perishable. All measures do not have exactly the same best-before-date, and most financial measures are out of phase with events occurring in real time.

The following light-hearted story about Call-Us-Painters illustrates the difference between two businesses: one that intuitively manages its performance as a Relationship-Based Enterprise (Ladders-R-Us), and one that does not (We-Do-Ladders).

On Monday, Fred Jones, from Call-Us-Painters, signs a new contract with City Hall. Mr. Jones knows that the job requires special ladders and so, in an effort to ensure his success, he orders two ladders—one from Ladders-R-Us and one from We-Do-Ladders.

Ladders-R-Us and We-Do-Ladders have been in business for years and both produce high-quality ladders. Each order has a note attached, indicating that the ladders are needed for a special job. Both companies assume that everyone thinks his job is special, and so they deliver their standard product to Mr. Jones. The next day, both companies receive a call—and it is clear that Mr. Jones is red with anger—both ladders failed.

Amy Smith, from Ladders-R-Us, is surprised and somewhat alarmed by the call. Being the president of a quickly growing business, she arranges to meet Mr. Jones at the site—to check why her company's ladder had failed.

The ladders were needed to help paint the city's drab metropolitan bridge, the one that carries some 20,000 commuters back and forth to work each day. Fred Jones's firm, Call-Us-Painters, was hired by City Hall to spruce things up for all those taxpayers. Attractive signs at both ends of the bridge announce the new contract with Call-Us-Painters. Mr. Jones tells Amy that when he ordered the special ladders, his intent was to hang them over the edge of the bridge and use them to suspend both paint and painters. Fortunately, he says, no one was hurt when the two ladders failed.

Ms. Smith knows that this special case was not considered during the design of the products that her firm provides. She informs Mr. Jones that he really does need a special ladder for this kind of job, and that the cost might be fairly high. Mr. Jones is not happy and suggests that they discuss the situation "some other time."

John Black, from We-Do-Ladders, is also surprised when he hears about the situation. He arranges to meet Mr. Jones over lunch rather than at the jobsite. He believes that it is important to keep a client happy—and therefore a good lunch would be in order. At lunch, Mr. Jones tells Mr. Black the story. Mr. Black is amazed that his company's ladder was even considered for this kind of job. Mr. Black promises to provide a "replacement ladder" on the following day, and deems the lunch a success.

When Mr. Black returns to the office, he arranges for exactly the same ladder to be sent over to Mr. Jones's company. He also gives instructions to his staff to attach a special orange label to both sides. The label reads, "Warning: Do Not Use to Paint Bridges." Mr. Black is pleased with his company's decision to replace the ladder for Mr. Jones at no extra charge.

Across town, Ms. Smith returns to the office to meet with her staff. Operations confirms that there would be a substantial increase in costs to manufacture a ladder to handle the special needs of Mr. Jones. Marketing suggests that few, if any, other customers would purchase these special ladders, and the Legal Department is distraught and immediately releases a new policy for reviewing all special orders. Ms. Smith pushes her team for alternate suggestions, and for ideas about how they may bring the costs down. She wonders if there are any opportunities to leverage the advertising signs that Mr. Jones has hanging on each end of the bridge.

The next day, Mr. Jones and Ms. Smith again meet at the job site. By this time, Mr. Jones had received the replacement ladder from Mr. Black. He was not happy. Ms. Smith, on the other hand, made a proposal that would seem to benefit both parties. She would have a special ladder delivered within 24 hours, one that was specifically designed to meet the needs of this job. She explains that the price for any future ladders of this type would be much higher than the cost of a standard ladder. However, her firm would be prepared to waive those additional costs on this first ladder, provided Mr. Jones agreed to a more creative relationship on this project. Ms. Smith would like her company's name added to the signs at either end of the bridge.

The arrangement is agreeable to both parties and the signs at both ends of the bridge are modified to carry both company names. The future picture for Call-Us-Painter and Ladders-R-Us seems bright. Profits continue to climb. However, over at We-Do-Ladders, sales have flattened, and Mr. Black does not have a good reason why.

Understanding and Adjusting Plans

The only purpose for measurement is to create understanding and therefore enable an organization to adjust its plans based on that understanding. While the above story is completely fictitious, it is one that can be told about the white space between any enterprise and its customers. The questions to be answered are, "How does an organization measure the value added of its products and services?" "How does an organization measure its performance?" In essence, the issue is how to measure the exchanges that occur in the white space between the organization and its customer.

The Exchange Space illustrated in Figure 14-1 identifies the focus of measurement in a relationship between an enterprise and its customers. That focus involves the four types of exchange that occur between the enterprise and its customers.

1. Producer (Enterprise) to Buyer (Customer) Exchange
2. Producer (Enterprise) to the User (Customer) Exchange
3. Service (Enterprise) to the Buyer (Customer) Exchange
4. Service (Enterprise) to the User (Customer) Exchange.

In some cases, these exchanges can be standardized and structured, such as those that occur when one interacts with an ATM. But

Figure 14-1: *Exchange Space and Measurement*

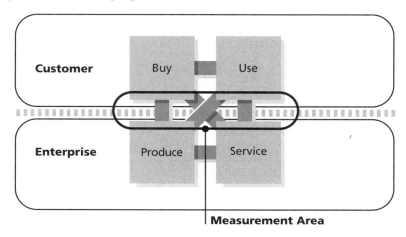

in many cases, they are fluid, dynamic, and a part of a constantly changing conversation. So how can their effectiveness be measured so that the organization gains the understanding necessary to adjust its plans? The following basic steps offer a practical approach:

- Assessment—"How am I (are we) doing?"
- Projection—"What is my (our) potential?"
- Focus—"What can I (we) do better?"
- Tools and Techniques—"What tools and measurement methods are available?"
- Measurements—"What measures should we use?"

To correctly measure the exchanges of this space, indicators are needed on both sides. However, it can be difficult to obtain such indicators because measuring anything that is not completely under one's control can be, to say the least, awkward. For example, how does an enterprise measure the value that it adds to the products and services provided to its customer? The responsiveness of an enterprise to the overt indicators provided by its customer will increase the level of understanding, but this is not a complete or accurate measure of the value added or of its performance.

This chapter will address each of these basic steps from the point of view of an enterprise engaged in conversations with a customer, focusing on the white space that exists between them.

Measuring How Much Value Current Conversations Generate

Assessment deals with understanding how much value each exchange and each conversation is currently generating. Customer satisfaction ratings can help provide a reference point for this assessment, though the limits of such ratings have been well documented. Some have even suggested that ratings of this type measure *dis*satisfaction rather than satisfaction. Ratings only provide insight about the current situation or the current business model. When an organization is constantly changing in response to the needs of a customer, the ratings will always lag behind the current value being generated.

As with measuring anything relating to value, there should be a stake in the ground from which to move forward. Value is an indicator that is relative to something or to some point in time. The most important task is to establish this reference point. Establishing a reference point may not be simple—it can take a lot of time and energy to develop an appropriate assessment indicator. In some cases organizations will have assessment methods in place but these methods are not being used for that purpose.

An illustration of this can be taken from the Call-Us-Painters story above. The way that special orders were originally handled by both organizations was by exception rather than as part of their overall business process. However, there was an indication that the situation (market) had changed and that there was a need for quick reaction. This indication was not easy for the organizations to perceive. Establishing a process and a culture for listening for exceptions can help a company identify whether conversations are generating value, and can lead to a productive dialogue between the customer and supplier.

In fact, the changing requirements of a customer's customer can be the cause of many of these exceptions. Gaining an understanding of the conversations that occur in this space can only help improve the relationship. The following are questions that can help start the journey:

- How do customers perceive the organization's responsiveness?
- Does the organization meet the expectations set by published information?
- What is the current value proposition of the organization's offerings?
- What are the customer retention levels?
- Does the organization consider the total value chain for products and services?

- Does the organization understand what its customers' customers are trying to achieve?
- What are the profit patterns of the organization's products and services telling me?
- Where are enterprise profits being generated versus individual organizations?
- What new business models are customers trying?
- Does the organization fully understand the profiles of its customers?

Sometimes questions are more powerful than answers. Asking these kinds of questions can help an enterprise understand how each exchange and conversation are currently generating value.

Projecting Organization Potential and the Ability to Do Things Differently

Projection addresses the next level of questions: "What is the organization's potential?" and "What can the organization do differently?" These can be thorny questions for any organization to address because simply asking such questions can appear to some as a challenge to what the enterprise has already accomplished.

Figure 14-2: *Value Chain*

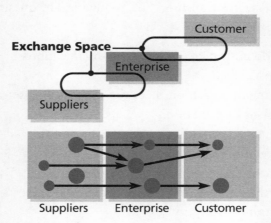

This is not the case. Such questions must be seen, by all, as an opportunity to respond to the needs of a customer. The exchange space that exists between the enterprise and its customers demands this kind of responsiveness. Leveraging and leading in this area are opportunities to demonstrate a responsive behavior. Economic benefits will provide solid feedback.

To fully address the questions that are a part of projection, it is important to understand the nature of a value chain, as discussed in Chapter 4. As illustrated in Figure 14-2, a value chain is a rather simple structure at a high level. However, as one examines the details, the exchange spaces that are a part of a value chain become complex. The enterprise must have a clear understanding of how its products and services fit into the value chain and how they are positioned with respect to alternatives. The enterprise must also understand the possible combinations of products or services that will provide better value to the customer. Without these, it is not possible to project how things might be done differently.

As was discussed in the definition of exchanges in Chapter 3, "The New Language of Relationships," exchange not only includes product and service but also information, advice, recommendations, and so on. So when an enterprise makes an assessment of the value of its contribution to its customers or to the value chain, it should not forget the value that customers can obtain from the less measurable parts of their offer. This could mean that there are opportunities to do things differently while providing exactly the same product or service. The value of the conversation between Call-Us-Painters and Ladders-R-Us changed when the signs at either end of the bridge entered the conversation.

Once it is clear how the enterprise fits into the value chain, then and only then can it proceed with the following questions:

- Does the organization present a consistent point of view to customers?
- How can the organization enhance the customer's buying experience?

- How can the organization create a learning environment?
- Does the organization have natural alliances forming?
- How can the organization leverage and understand customer surveys?
- How can customers be segmented to help define opportunities?
- Are customers aligned to the organization in a stovepipe manner?
- What potential is there for cross-selling?
- What changes can be made to information systems to assist customers?
- Is it important to focus exchanges through a single channel? Can the organization use portal technologies to help focus existing and future customers?
- How can the organization personalize the buying experience?

Focusing on How to Do Things Better

Given the results of both assessment and projection, it is time to focus and forge ahead. The critical question is "What can the organization do better?" In most cases organizations can make a series of small changes to the way that they handle the exchanges with their customers to provide significant and quick results. The largest risk is to do nothing.

Today's businesses can tolerate mistakes—but they cannot afford to waste time. There continues to be a pressing need to make adjustments to the business model that most businesses operate under. The Relationship-Based Enterprise focuses on learning through quick hits, then builds on that learning with initiatives that allow it to move forward and stay ahead. The new reality demands initiatives that enable "ready—fire—aim."

The following concepts can help organizations focus and figure out how to do things better:

- Doing nothing has cost and risk.
- Customers are critical—leverage the value chain.
- Select a course of action and get going—the learning exercise will help in selecting the next course of action.
- Reflect on how information from your suppliers is beneficial. Think how your information might be useful to customers.
- Act immediately on simple items—work towards the more complex ones.
- Communicate the plan—then communicate it again.
- Treat each opportunity as a challenge and each failure as a learning event.

What Tools and Techniques are Available?

Over the past few years, there has been an explosion in the number of tools that can support CRM. There are more channels and channel options than ever before: e-mail, phone, VoIP (voice over IP) calls, on-line chat groups, faxing, postal mail, and even face-to-face communications over the Web. This increased complexity affects the efficiency and effectiveness of the customer services role. To enable a continued conversation, the enterprise must have a single view of all exchanges—enabled by the right tools.

The following summarizes the main tool categories.

- **Product catalog tools** manage the configuration and features offered by different products, assist in matching customer requirements to product features, provide the capability to present standard products or highly customized combinations of product components.
- **Portal management tools** integrate a common view of products and services and offer this view to customers. They allow for tailoring or customization of these offerings based on customer type or interest, assist in presenting a

tailored view of the business, and can offer store-front
options for selling products and/or providing support
services over the Internet.

- **Contact software tools** provide detailed information on
  the contacts and interests for a customer. These are very
  helpful for managing new or existing buyer-producer
  relationships.
- **Multi-channel technology integration tools** assist in
  presenting a common interface to the customer for
  service-related questions no matter what the medium;
  e-mail, Web interaction, telephone, and fax are all
  channeled into a single view of the customer.
- **Campaign management tools** allow products and services to be packaged and offered to target customers. They
  provide evaluation services on the achievement of goals
  of the campaign.
- **Application service provider/full service provider tools**
  enable outsourcing or "out-tasking" of CRM applications
  to third-party vendors. A full service provider would
  assume responsibility for all the applications required
  to operate the front office of your business.

Other tools that need to be considered include middleware
products. Middleware can be used to make the connections
between existing applications and CRM tools. These are the off-
the-shelf products that can capture transactions from a CRM tool
and existing applications systems. The power that these middleware tools provide reduces risks around implementing CRM
tools. Generally, middleware is broken down into three categories:
messaging, data manipulation, and process translation.

Given the variety of the tools that are available, choosing a
CRM tool or set of tools must be approached with caution. There
is direct relationship between the functionality a tool provides and
the cost of that tool. Start slow and make sure every step is justified.

Systematic approaches to evaluating performance of the
enterprise can be quite challenging. The complexities of the com-

pany's value chain and the potential different stages of a product in its lifecycle are just a couple of the major issues that need addressing. Adopting proven methods from other companies can reduce these challenges. The methods discussed in this section are a sample of the many that are available. They provide information on the enterprise from a holistic perspective. Of course, the ideal measurement method for a Relationship-Based Enterprise would provide insight on the enterprise as seen by the customer and the efficiencies associated with delivering value. However, until this ideal method is developed and proven, the methods presented should prove helpful.

As with any approach, it is important to understand whether the results are driven by leading or lagging indicators. Leading indicators provide insight into the future behavior of other measures; they are the bridges between business strategy and business outcomes. Lag indicators provide insight into the past, as illustrated in Figure 14-3. In the story of Call-Us-Painters the financial results observed by both Ms. Smith and Mr. Black are lag indicators. The leading indicators were in the conversation that both had with Mr. Jones.

Leading indicators can provide a reliable mechanism to help an enterprise know its status with regard to profitability, employee morale, opportunities, customer expectations, and so on. Following are a few of the many possible measurement techniques:

- economic profit
- added value
- modified balanced scorecard
- benefits realization.

Economic Profit

Economic profit is a method that can be used to support decision-making by providing management with a line-of-sight between an investment and its value to shareholders. The method is fully described in the paper "Economic Value Added as a Management

Figure 14-3: *Lead and Lag Indicators*

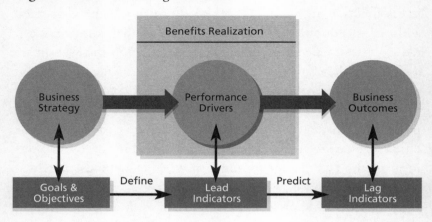

Tool" published on the Internet (www.Evanomics.com) by the Helsinki School of Economics and Business Administration. In the context of CRM, the method uses existing financial information from income statements and balance sheets as illustrated in Figure 14-4.

Figure 14-4: *Economic Profit*

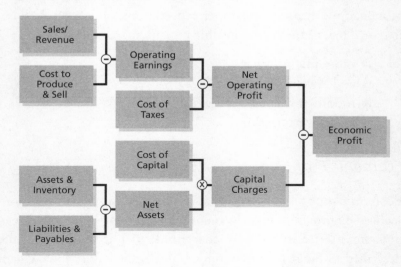

Added Value

The added-value approach is described by John Kay in his book *Foundations of Corporate Success: How Business Strategies Add Value.* Kay defines value as "the difference between the (comprehensively accounted) value of a firm's output and the (comprehensively accounted) cost of the firm's input." Added value is calculated as revenues less the sum of wages and salaries, capital costs, and materials. In this way added value embraces the relationships that exist with customers, suppliers, investors, and labor.

The Balanced Scorecard

The balanced scorecard, as described by Robert Kaplan and David Norton, is perhaps the most widely accepted framework for identifying performance measures. It provides a convenient way for executives to articulate and communicate a business strategy in a way that clearly links measurement and performance.

The balanced scorecard includes customers as one of its measurement domains, as illustrated in Figure 14-5. However,

Figure 14-5: *A Modified Balanced Scorecard*

Financial
To succeed financially, how should we appear to our shareholders?

Suppliers/Partners
To achieve our vision, how should we appear to our suppliers and partners?

Internal Processes
To satisfy our shareholders, customers, suppliers and partners what processes must we excell at?

Customers
To achieve our vision, how should we appear to our customers?

Leaning and Growth
To achieve our vision, how will we sustain our ability to change and improve?

successful conversations with customers are often contingent on successful conversations with suppliers and partners. For example, the on-time delivery of products and services to a customer may well depend on the on-time delivery of components, supplies, information, or other services by suppliers and partners. Because of this, the representation of the balanced scorecard has been modified to include an additional domain: suppliers and partners.

Benefits Realization

This method helps organizations realize the expected benefits from their investments in information technology and business transformation. This topic is fully developed in *The Information Paradox* by John Thorp and DMR's Center for Strategic Leadership. The approach helps organizations define the needed business outcomes and then details the initiatives, risks, plans, programs, and management processes that must be put in place to achieve those outcomes.

One of the keys to the success of benefits realization is the identification of intermediate outcomes or performance drivers. These are leading indicators that can be used to predict business outcomes. And since business outcomes or results are usually measures of historical fact, identification of the leading indicators is vital. Leading indicators provide insight into the future behavior of other measures; they are the bridge between business strategy and business outcomes. For those organizations that expect to undergo a major transformation, this type of mapping of performance drivers is essential. It is the ideal starting point for any transformation program.

The method, which was developed by DMR Consulting, has been used successfully for many clients to assist in developing and evaluating tactical business plans.

Selecting the Right Measures

Today's business environment is less predictable, and the possibility of an enterprise arriving at some steady state is a thing of the past. What people value today will most certainly shift. This is best characterized by Heraclitus's maxim, "You cannot step twice into the same river." The Relationship-Based Enterprise can't rely exclusively on the planning cycles and methods of the past. To good planning, it must add good sensing. It needs the ability and competency to recognize opportunities and unexpected outcomes, notice shifts in value, identify below-target service levels, and so on. Measurement enhances the dialogue and discovery processes and helps the enterprise understand how it has done, how it is doing, and, most importantly, gives it some clues to what is possible.

Finding the right measures is not possible without a complete understanding of the white space that exists between the enterprise and its customers. When it comes to CRM, the focus of these measures is that space. Turning back to the definition of a relationship described in Chapter 3, the right measures are those that deal with each aspect of that definition: conversations, exchanges, offers, value proposition, content, infrastructure, customer knowledge, context, management decisions, and business design. The most immediate in this list are those that deal with the value proposition, the content, and the infrastructure.

In the story about Call-Us-Painters, Amy Smith was able to change the value proposition from a high-quality product for money proposition to one that involved the joint success of both organizations. She converted a patron into a partner, changing the very nature of the measures associated with that and subsequent conversations.

The following actions can help organizations select the right measures:

- Ensure that more than just financially-related measures are used.
- Use quantitative *and* qualitative measures.
- Deploy a balanced set of indicators.
- Supplement historically focused lagging indicators with predictive/leading measures.
- Make measurement a shared corporate responsibility.
- Select measurements that reflect what is important to customers.

- Involve customers in the identification and development of measurements.
- Get employees involved in the design of measures.
- Constantly search for new measurement approaches.
- Create dialogues around measurement.
- Put in place the mechanisms to constantly govern the measurement system.

And the Right Approach Is...

The measurement system chosen must complement discovery and dialogue activities if it is to build the organization's competency to listen, sense, learn, predict, and anticipate its customers and business environment in the quest to add value. Measurement can be the catalyst for change. It can focus business resources on activities that need improvement. The discipline required is to design a sound measurement system, commit to the measurements, create dialogue around the measurements, and be organizationally prepared and ready to change behaviors and respond to unexpected outcomes.

Measurement of the relationship between an organization and its customers is an evolving science. There are few right or wrong answers. Selecting the right measurement approach will always remain an incremental, iterative process. Intuition about customers, or a hunch about their needs, can play a role, as can intuition or a hunch about the enterprise's performance. However, the right measures are the ones that are aligned with and support the results that a business expects to achieve, whether those results are related to increased revenue, increased profit, increased market share, and/or increased customer loyalty. The critical task is to find those measures that reflect the organization's business strategy and that drive the performance required to achieve the business outcomes that are being sought. Such measures must be implemented at the level of conversations and exchanges.

Window on the Real World:

At a major U.S. oil company, the biggest hurdle to overcome in the journey towards CRM was changing the roles, motivations, and skills of people who interface with customers. In the past, a typical role was to issue invoices to client. But in the new CRM environment, the role would be to focus on caring about the customer, with issuing invoices as a secondary task.

A mental shift needs to occur at all levels within the organization. Management sets the example by putting the customer at the center of their strategy, and involving customers during the planning stage.

Part of this mental shift was achieved through education, training, and technology. But this company also changed the way employees were measured (to determine their variable compensation). This change went a very long way towards making the desired transition happen. Instead of concentrating on having employees focus almost exclusively on satisfying their superiors, they introduced a corporate and individual scorecard with measures that involved customers—such as customer satisfaction and customer growth. Across the board, customer-facing personnel improved customer relationships.

Further Thoughts

For the Manager

- Is the organization prepared to take the measures that it selects as the cornerstone of management decision-making?
- Is the organization committed to deploying the measurement system and creating a sense of ownership?
- Is the organization committed to reward and recognize executives through a balanced measurement set that includes employee and customer measures as well as financial?

- Does the organization have the internal skill set to design the required measures?
- Does the organization have sufficient participation from customers?
- Do we have a system in place that ensures the continued relevancy of our measures?
- Do we have a balanced system of measures, both qualitative and quantitative, financial and other, leading and lagging?

15

How Do We Increase Our Capacity to Change?

Elements of an Answer

- **External issues**—Change in a customer-centric world
- **Change implications**—How change approaches must respond
- **The enterprise change space**—Understanding the organization's capacity for change
- **A practical approach**—The rules-based method.

Some organizations tend to be highly goal-directed, setting specific, measurable targets for change. Once a change target has been hit, the change is deemed to be complete, and everything reverts to the status quo. Employees and management both view change as a series of hurdles to be jumped so that things can "get back to normal." The problem is, in the period leading up to a major change, all meaningful work usually grinds to a halt. Like deer in the headlights, employees stop and wait to see what's going to happen. Then, after whatever happens, happens, there is a period of adjustment while things settle down. Eventually, everyone climbs back up the productivity curve—until the next major change appears on the horizon. Then it's deer-in-the-headlights time again. The capacity for change is very low.

In contrast, the Relationship-Based Enterprise, which emphasizes constant change in response to customer dialogue, needs to develop a very high capacity for change. One way of achieving this is to leverage its core competency—the ability to create conversations and exchanges. Conversations not only fill the white spaces between enterprises and customers, as discussed in Chapter 1, but they also fill an enterprise's internal white spaces. Inside the enterprise, people continually converse and exchange value with other people. Groups converse with other groups. And departments converse with other departments. The success of these conversations determines the enterprise's capacity for change. But how does one go about engineering these conversations and exchanges?

Standards such as the ISO900X series, the most popular quality standards in the world, ensure that an enterprise uses a rigorous, commonly accepted process for producing and delivering its products and services. However, when it comes to making changes to the enterprise, there are no such standards. Organizations rely on processes that are far less structured and rigorous than those that they use for the delivery of products and services. In some cases, these processes are re-invented with every new change to the enterprise. But if the Relationship-Based Enterprise is to be a change-capable enterprise, it must have rigorous, reliable, and repeatable processes for both production and change.

Change in a Customer-Centric World

To develop change processes for the Relationship-Based Enterprise, managers can once again apply the relationship management framework—discovery, dialogue, and discipline. The preoccupations of discovery and dialogue focus on understanding the main characteristics of the world in which all businesses now operate. By understanding these characteristics, managers can develop a set of principles for increasing the change capacity of the Relationship-Based Enterprise. These principles should inform the manager's approach to change—the discipline of change—and provide a way of achieving change successfully, based on the reality of the customer-driven world.

Consideration of the following characteristics of today's business world, which relate strongly to the Relationship-Based Enterprise and Customer Relationship Management (CRM), provide a useful starting place.

Customers are Connecting and Conversing as Never Before

Conversations with customers touch the organization at multiple points of contact, which means that everyone in the organization needs to understand how the conversation should go. This involvement must seem knowledgeable and natural from the customer's viewpoint. Prescribed, scripted dialogues are out; intelligent, natural, and knowledgeable dialogues are in.

Customers Demand to be Treated as Unique

"I'm different—understand me" is the customer's plea. Customers are demanding that the enterprise treat them as unique, and to put in place mechanisms that ensure that this occurs. The concept of customer segmentation, as we have seen in Chapter 6, needs to embrace much more detailed information based upon the customer's desire for dialogue and conversation, as long as this is not intrusive. And the notion of the "customer of one" is not new; indeed, many organizations have tried to become more capable in treating their customers this way. Such techniques all aim to treat customers uniquely, yet often only succeed in "force-fitting" a customer into a conveniently defined profile. In the same way, managers frequently adopt just such a "one size fits all" approach to the change approach itself, assuming that change is, itself, a generic process.

Customers are Grouping in Many New Ways

Customers are forming groups in many more ways than ever before. They are forming *alliances* to provide more effective ways of co-creating value as well as of delivering value to their customers. Both business and personal customers are forming *buying groups* to drive down prices from their suppliers. These trends are enabled and amplified by the power of the Net. Need insurance coverage for a party going to Nepal? A travel package for a party of sailors spending a month in a remote off-shore region of Peru? Until now, meeting the needs of such groups was virtually impossible or would have been prohibitively expensive. Today, it's business as (almost) usual.

Businesses are Creating Through Destroying

Today, enterprises are realizing that the only way to survive is to make many elements of their business forcibly obsolete on a periodic basis. If they don't do it, then the competition will. As a result, enterprises are giving their product divisions ultimatums. For example, when the Internet went mainstream, some banks were reluctant to start Web-based operations for fear of damaging the on-line banking approaches they had built, which were based on proprietary PC software. But many quickly realized that this was a risk they had to take and quickly dumped customized software solutions.

Turbulent Environments Will Remain for a Long Time

This age of creative destruction is not going to slow down any time soon. The global forces that are simultaneously driving business to the wall while allowing new ones to flourish will continue. The implication is that as soon as someone figures out a change process that is the correct, "final" destination, it's automatically flawed.

Trying to get a permanent, once-and-for-all fix in the turbulent business environment of today's customers is a doomed endeavor.

Change in the customer's world is complex and multifaceted. However, one pervasive theme emerges: customer demand, fueled by the possibilities of an expanding, technology-enabled environment, is an explosive mixture that will propel enterprises into the future. The enterprise that can harness that combustible force to its advantage will be a winner.

How Change Approaches Must Respond

Based on the foregoing characteristics of the business environment in which customers operate, what's the best approach for increasing an organization's capacity for change? Chapter 12, "Who are We?" and Chapter 13, "How Do We Organize to Move Value Closer to Our Customers?" discuss how to redefine the *raison d'être* for the organization, and how to rethink its scope and function. The following principles will help managers to bring about these suggested changes and to build a change-capable Relationship-Based Enterprise.

Approaches to Change should be Situational and Context-Specific

If the marketplace is characterized by companies driven by unique visions and radical new strategies for success, the approach to change must be similarly driven. Rebuilding a log home when the only construction tool available is a cement mixer will ensure that, while a new home may emerge, the process will be long, fraught with argument, and subject to interminable discussion—and there may not be much wood in the house that emerges!

Leadership for Change Can Occur Anywhere

Awareness of the changes needed to make dialogue and conversation effective can be found where those dialogues are taking place —in the exchange space. For example, the grocery-pickers in the on-line supermarket described in Chapter 3, "The New Language of Relationships," are the ones who may be best placed to change critical aspects of that operation. Pickers need to be empowered to assume the same stringent quality expectations as their customers, and they, not store managers or produce heads, need to be able to call time if they are not able to fulfill this expectation. Managers who guess what their teams need are likely to be outflanked and outpaced by market events.

People Demand to be Trusted to Bring About Change

Dialogue, and relationships, will only continue when both parties to the conversation are secure and confident that information revealed or discussed will not be used wrongly. This principle needs to apply equally to the enterprise side of the dialogue as well as to the customer side. Trust is at the heart of the relationship with the customer. If trust is important to the customer, but less important to the enterprise, then the disconnect will be bound to show. Empowerment only works if the empowered operate without fear.

Self-Organizing Subgroups Spearhead Change

Just as customer groups form dynamic and transient groupings to reflect loosely connected interests and affiliations, so the change process within organizations needs to embrace the idea that it can, itself, subdivide and reform to bring about change. Someone notices a rise in the number of customer groups reflecting, say, the over 60s age group. What better than to have a similar over-60s group within the organization decide to be first in serving the needs of this group? When both groups meet to discuss the needs of such a customer segment, problems, ideas, and solutions collide in a shared process of change. The organization begins, right there, to adopt approaches that both can understand and make happen.

Change, viewed this way, is something that needs to pulsate at the same frequency as the forces that are shaping the customer world. It needs to ebb and flow to the rhythm of customer change. Just as tectonic plates shift to accommodate massive subterranean forces, so change processes need to move in sympathy with both external forces and internal pressures.

One way of dealing with these pressures is to map change approaches against an enterprise change space. This helps the Relationship-Based Enterprise to choose methods and approaches that fit well with the customer's beliefs and practices.

Understanding the Organization's Capacity for Change

Organizations need to adopt an approach to change that is congruent with the organization's own situation. The enterprise change space, illustrated in Figure 15-1, provides a guide to the different kind of change methods that are appropriate to differing types of enterprise situations.

The vertical axis defines the organization's intent regarding change. The term "intent" poses the question, "What is the client's

Figure 15-1: *The Enterprise Change Space*

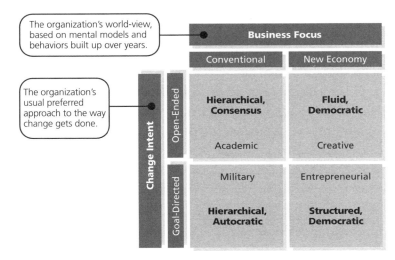

normal, preferred approach to the way change gets done in the organization?" An "open-ended" organization will look upon change as an organic process, will prefer to let change evolve, and will look for fundamental, long-term change. A "goal-directed" organization, on the other hand, will only be interested in specific, measurable targets. Once those are achieved, change will be deemed to be complete. Most organizations can be located somewhere in between these two extremes.

The horizontal axis defines the internal business focus of the enterprise in terms of structure, mindset, and organization. This axis reflects the deep and underlying "mental model"—much of which is tacit, or undocumented—that defines the culture or world-view. "Conventional" organizations have well-established forms of behavior built up over years, if not generations. They tend to be slow to adopt radical or untried ideas. By comparison, the "new economy" enterprise is just that: radical, innovative, openly embracing new technologies. As with the vertical axis, a typical organization might be classified somewhere in between the two extremes described.

Whereas the vertical axis looks specifically at the organization's view about how *change* should be conducted, the horizontal axis looks at the overall culture of the enterprise. In this sense, the vertical axis can be—and usually is—something articulated explicitly by the change program's sponsor. The horizontal axis, on the other hand, usually cannot be articulated explicitly. The vertical axis is the expression of a particular individual's approach; the horizontal axis is the embodiment of a way of thinking held by the organization as a whole, and evolved over many years.

Mapping an enterprise or organization onto the various quadrants of Enterprise Change Space, as described below, suggests the types of challenges managers will face when they seek to increase capacity for change, or to implement CRM initiatives.

Goal-Directed and Conventional

Organizations in this quadrant are usually hierarchical, and have strong or autocratic leadership styles. Their inherent culture tends to be traditional. People defer to authority, the line of command is fixed and rigid, and people do not challenge the status quo. Their preferred approach to change is to set explicit objectives through a rigorous process and drive hard to meet them, regardless of the human cost. Their application of technology may be slow and limited to operational areas. They do take risk, but tend to identify single owners as a way of managing this risk, and punish those who fail. They may find it hard to make a transition to becoming a Relationship-Based Enterprise.

From a CRM perspective:

- they are unlikely to think of themselves as a Relationship-Based Enterprise
- their relationships are likely to be formal and limited to contracts and agreements
- they find it hard to engage in open dialogue with customers, resorting to forms and procedures where this is done.

Typical organizations in this quadrant might include government departments and the military.

Open-Ended and Conventional

Organizations located here are hierarchical, traditional, and often slow-moving. They prefer to do things the way they always have. On the other hand, they accept it as a given that everyone should be consulted, but this process is often bureaucratic and tedious, and initiatives often flounder because agreement cannot be reached in time. There is little appetite for risk. The organization has a stoic acknowledgment that, in the event of failure, there will be a lengthy review that will take little action other than attempt to prevent the same mistake from happening again. People in the organization care deeply about their business, work long hours, and are often paid little. They tend to be unstructured, responsive, and caring. People in the organization do not think much about risk, but, if asked, would tend to be risk-averse. This type of organization will be willing to change, but will want to discuss and debate possible moves at length.

The CRM approach of these organizations is characterized as follows:

- they prefer traditional approaches such as surveys and feedback forms
- they are slow-moving in terms of acting on customer feedback
- they tend to favor analytical approaches and those based on customer-segmentation.

Charity or academic organizations fit naturally into this quadrant.

Goal-Directed and New Economy

Here, organizations are operating on the cutting edge of turbulence. They espouse modern technology, which they will apply to all areas of their business. Their culture is a blend of the Nike ("Just Do It") and the "Do It My Way" variety. Everyone knows who the boss is, but the atmosphere can be confrontational when people disagree. Objectives are set, but not in any structured fashion, and there is little or no analysis; the organization prefers to try solutions, see what works, discard what doesn't, and move on. There is a great appetite for risk, and a tolerance for failure, believing that "the same mistake doesn't happen twice." This type of organization will be very willing to change, but will not want a theoretical or detailed approach, preferring to see what works.

These organizations tend to favor approaches to CRM that are:
- active, but tending to talking rather than listening, or
- unsophisticated, preferring quick interventions rather than analysis,

or that require:
- limited patience with customers, preferring to extract what they need and move on.

Typical organizations in this quadrant are successful hi-tech start-ups and entrepreneurial ventures.

Open-Ended and New Economy

This quadrant describes organizations that are fluid, "new age" enterprises. They are run on very democratic lines, and there is a conscious desire for everyone to have fun and enjoy their work. Decisions tend to be taken in open forums with plenty of discussion. However, there is an absence of rigorous challenge, people preferring to "go with the flow" and see what happens. Many projects tend to fail, mainly because this style of decision-making places little value on analysis. This organization would use technology well. The culture encourages risk-taking, not deliberately, but rather from lack of basic awareness or consideration. This type of organization would openly espouse change, would want to experience and live through it, seeing the journey as much more important than the destination.

From a CRM perspective, organizations in this quadrant would have approaches characterized by:

- an emphasis on experiential, subjective techniques
- little regard for formal analysis of results
- willingness to dialogue at length, even at extreme cost to their organization.

In this quadrant belong creative organizations such as some advertising or market research companies.

The enterprise change space is a framework that operates on two principle levels. First, it provides a means for organizations to understand how they are positioned for a change effort. This positioning enables the enterprise to consider where it is now, and what it may see as a vision for what it needs to become. The framework lets people within the organization visualize quickly the kinds of transformation that may be required.

Secondly, it allows organizations to think about and discuss the "corridors of change"—the route maps between quadrants that might be taken as the enterprise undergoes change. One enterprise may realize that they need to find change agents that are more goal-oriented as a first step to change, but may have to settle for remaining "conventional" while the initial moves of change happen. Another organization may have to place reliance on goal-directed approaches to make the rapid moves to become more "New Economy" oriented. These are the corridors down which the thrust of the organization must be pursued.

An approach to change that makes most sense for one organization is likely to differ significantly from that of an organization in another quadrant. So, for example, an enterprise located in the bottom left (conventional and goal-directed) would look for a rigorous, step-by-step process, with measurable outcomes. Conversely, an organization at the top right (open-ended—new economy) would champion the use of an evolutionary, experiential approach, where the precise nature of the outcome was fluid but where the organization learned from the process.

However, any organization embarking on significant change in the context of CRM needs a more detailed understanding of the methods, tools, and techniques that are best suited to its situation. Two key factors should be considered:

- What are the **obstacles and challenges** (including those specific to CRM) that it can expect to face when seeking to bring about change in those quadrants?
- What change **approaches and techniques** are best suited for each quadrant or as organizations migrate between quadrants?

Of course, no organization is a perfect fit to any particular quadrant of the model. So the following obstacles and challenges, and the approaches and techniques, should be viewed as a checklist rather than a definitive and final list.

Goal-Directed and Conventional

Obstacles and Challenges

- A high degree of fear and a lack of participation
- A reluctance to take risks for fear of failure and historical consequences
- Hierarchies, and a "command and control" culture, constitute barriers to new ideas/creativity
- A high degree of skepticism about the motives and rationale for change
- A "them" and "us" culture
- A reluctance on the part of senior/middle management to change for fear of losing control—"Turkeys voting for Thanksgiving."

Approaches to CRM are likely to be traditional and focused on satisfying specific interest groups such as regulators. CRM may be seen a means of controlling their dealings with customers, rather than using them as a way of building new business.

Change Approach and Techniques Most Suited

This quadrant is best suited to classic organizational design approaches, tools and techniques focusing at the individual, function, and enterprise level. The emphasis (initially at least) has to be on proven approaches, guaranteed delivery and prototyping as a prelude to rollout. However, the conventional organization is unlikely in the first instance to welcome open dialogue. Change concepts need to be introduced to senior management in one-to-one, unthreatening interventions. Other tools, techniques, and approaches can be successfully deployed to assist in effecting change in this quadrant such as, for example:

- change history surveys
- change landscape surveys

- communication planning
- sponsorship
- pain and remedy management
- resilience assessment
- mentoring and coaching of senior management
- cultural change assessment (Burke-Lewin Method, for example)
- personal change capability (Myers-Briggs Type Indicator Assessment, for example).

Organizations in this quadrant need to focus their attention on the key issues that need to be addressed by the organization as a whole to enable acceptance and adoption of change. It has been suggested that focus on five key questions is essential to success:

1. Why change? How is change relevant to what I do?
2. What do you want me to do differently? What's the priority?
3. How will you measure me and what are the consequences?
4. What tools and support will I get?
5. What's in it for me? What's in it for us?

This is especially true in dealing with an organization found within this conventional economy, goal-oriented quadrant.

Open-Ended and Conventional

Obstacles and Challenges

- Reliance on data and logic as a prerequisite to decision-making
- Endless desire to debate issues without reaching agreement or consensus
- Pace and speed of response may increasingly impact this organization.

Obstacles specific to effective CRM include a reluctance to explore less traditional aspects of dialogue and a tendency to discuss and debate the meaning of conversational outcomes at length.

Change Approach and Techniques Most Suited

The most appropriate change approach in this quadrant is one that focuses on "agreement management"—essentially assisting the organization to reach decisions much more crisply. In addition, focus and attention must be given to the following:

- classic communication management
- politics management
- clear and crisp recommendations
- good understanding of issues and agendas
- broad outreach
- negotiation/problem-solving/conflict resolution.

Organizations in this quadrant must emphasize the "overwhelming case for change." Equal emphasis must also be placed upon a process for reaching agreement and closure on what to do, by when and by whom. As before, the organization must employ excellent facilitation skills to achieve successful change.

Goal-Directed and New Economy

Obstacles and Challenges

- It is hard to maintain focus and scope within these organizations. The desire to move to something new is a powerful force.
- High stress levels permeate this organization and burn-out is a concern.
- These organizations are performance driven —"You're only as good as your last project."
- These enterprises experience high turnover/strong competition for resources.
- These types of companies have some difficulty in forming cross-functional teams—people will go it alone when they have to, in order to achieve a breakthrough or fail miserably.

Organizations in this quadrant will tend to treat CRM as a peripheral activity or assume that it is already being done effectively.

Change Approach and Techniques Most Suited

The most appropriate change approach in this quadrant is one that focuses on:

- short steps that can be achieved quickly—it's about deliverables
- constant reviews with sponsors, agents, targets of change
- modularity—bite-sized chunks
- quick hits
- sensitivity to goals of individuals/reward mechanisms
- keeping the organization challenged and rewarded.

The techniques and approaches applicable here are not dissimilar from those found in the goal-directed conventional economy quadrant. What changes is the manner in which they must be delivered, recognizing that organizations living within the new economy have adapted and adopted new operating rules, the most important of which is that it must be fast.

Open-Ended New Economy

Obstacles and Challenges

- Fuzzy focus—a degree of resistance to get to a tight specification or statement of detail
- A lack of readiness to be accountable
- Financial control is erratic—the "concept" is what is important.

Organizations located in this quadrant will view CRM as something to be enjoyed and experienced, rather than something from which to reap benefit. Their approaches are likely to be varied, extensive, unfocused, and unconcerned about outcomes and results.

Change Approach and Techniques Most Suited

An approach which harnesses the innate creativity and spontaneity of this group is essential when working within this quadrant. The focus must be on:

- idea management/harvesting ideas
- triage system for ideas/initiatives
- alignment of ideas to strategic goals
- transparent business support systems—ones that support, but don't get in the way
- boundary management.

Expert facilitation skills are essential to success in this quadrant. It would be a mistake to use the word "change" or to introduce any notion that a "change program or initiative" was to be implemented. The ability to tap into existing efforts, harness these, and align them to new goals and benefits is the most appropriate approach. This will be undertaken through mentoring, coaching, workshops, and individual assistance to help the organization make better use of what is already in existence.

To sum up, the Enterprise Change Space demonstrates that a "one change method fits all" approach to change does not work. Building a Relationship-Based Enterprise, increasing capacity for change, and implementing CRM effectively will require taking risks and being willing to experiment. Above all, it will require staff and customers involved in conversations to be at the heart of the change process. Change is likely to happen organically rather than through top-down command. However, the manager is still responsible for making change happen. One technique that is becoming increasingly useful as a means to understanding resistance and effecting long-lasting change, is the rules-based change method. It is an approach worthy of a slightly more detailed explanation as one of many complementary approaches and has particular relevance to organizations of the conventional-economy and goal-oriented quadrant of the enterprise change space.

The Rules-Based Method

The rules-based method offers a unique solution to the question "How do we increase our capacity to change?" It is based on the notion that the organization is a complex adaptive system. The rules-based method is specifically designed to evaluate and modify the vast network of exchanges—defined in this book as the building blocks of conversations—that make up that system. Managers can apply this approach to continually reshape the enterprise.

In *The Complexity Advantage*, authors Susanne Kelly and Mary Ann Allison describe how Citicorp has already applied the ideas that come from this same field of research. Kelly and Allison maintain that organizations that can successfully apply management frameworks based on an understanding of complex adaptive systems will have "enthusiastic employee contributions, better information, dramatic increases in both productivity and creativity, lower costs, and the ability to respond rapidly to changes in direction."

So how is this achieved? As described below, the rules-based method concentrates on changing the rules that govern behavior.

The Relationship-Based Enterprise and the Rules Space

Unlike conversations with customers, which are consciously designed and developed, and conscientiously maintained, the enterprise tends to constantly "mumble" to itself. Information flows continually over an internal network. Heard and half-heard conversations are everywhere: on the shop floor, in the halls, on the Net, and over dividers. Hundreds of conversations tie people and groups of people together through a series of exchanges that convey information, solidify relationships, and transfer value between groups and members of groups.

Each conversation consists of a layered, constantly changing set of exchanges. Exchanges that are perceived to offer value are sustained and strengthened while those without value atrophy, resulting in consistent patterns of behavior. These patterns can be loosely defined as "culture"—or more rigorously as the interactions in a complex, adaptive system of employees and managers. People join the company, change jobs, or leave, but the enterprise network lives on—as does the protocol governing the exchanges that occur over the network.

The value of each exchange is rarely tangible and typically cannot be measured in visible rewards or immediate economic incentives. But a payoff (real or potential) is always present behind any long-standing conversation. These exchanges occur according to precise rules—rules that dictate which exchanges are allowable, who can participate, and what payoffs can be expected. These rules, or behavior routines, are rigorously enforced by the organization itself.

The context of these exchanges is as varied as the exchanges themselves. People share jokes over the intranet, tell stories of their children at the coffee machine, and in many other ways build alliances. These alliances form the contextual web for the data flowing through the organization. Individual exchanges—the molecules of interaction—are the basic building blocks of an organization and fill the white spaces *within* the organization.

Just as people within an organization cannot escape being part of the organization network, neither can they escape from the rules that control information flow over the network. The best that individuals within the company can do is adapt to the rules that the enterprise imposes on them or leave the organization. People come and people go, but the rules remain. Because of this, companies like Cosmos have a hard time in a deregulated world when there is a sudden need to change the personality of the corporation. This is true even when those who have built the organization for that regulated environment have long since left.

Types of Rules

So what is the exact nature of enterprise rules? As is illustrated in Figure 15-2 there are three kinds of rules operating within any organization: common rules, custom rules, and core rules.

Figure 15-2: *Rules: The Fundamental Algorithms*

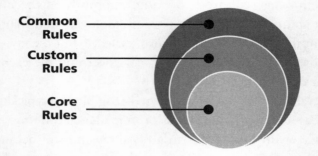

Common Rules

Some enterprise rules are shared by everyone within a society. Common rules determine in large part how people dress, how they talk to each other (the jargon, colloquialisms, dialect, inflection, and mannerisms they use), and the etiquette with which they treat one another. Common rules distinguish people by nation, state, and community. As people move from company to company within their community or even across the country, they may find little variation in common rules. Stereotypes exaggerating characteristics of people from a particular country, region, or company arise out of an innate recognition of the effect of common rules on people's behavior.

Common rules often remain unchallenged until a person travels to another country. That first trip abroad may bring with it serious culture shock. Culture shock is one way of saying that a person's common rules have been violated—that following "common sense" rules of behavior resulted in unexpected consequences.

Custom Rules

A second type of enterprise rule is the set of custom rules an enterprise develops over time. Custom rules are the subset of common rules that have evolved within a company or a business unit. Custom rules vary by organization. These rules grease the wheels of corporate exchange. Some of them can be found in the company handbook.

Here they describe expected behavior related to ethical conduct, corporate security, or employee safety. However, documented rules represent only a small portion of the total set of custom rules. Many custom rules are never voiced, much less documented. Some of these unspoken rules determine who holds the strings of power, who goes to lunch with whom, how problems get resolved, or who gets patted on the back. They also define the opposite.

The role of custom rules is to keep the organization stable over time, especially when the organization is under stress. Everyone is expected to play by the rules, even if some rules don't make sense from a business perspective. And every behavior that persistently happens within an organization—even crazy behavior—happens because it is rewarded in some way.

Core Rules

Core rules are the rules that individuals live by. These rules provide guidelines for personal behavior, personal goals attainment, and motivation, as well as individual ethics and values. Core rules are unique to each individual and are as unique as fingerprints. This, in part, is the reason why no two individuals can be motivated in precisely the same way. For example, putting one person in the limelight is a reward, but another goes into shock when asked to take a bow.

As illustrated in Figure 15-3, the degree to which all three types of rules are in alignment shapes corporate culture. Rules

Figure 15-3: *Rules Alignment*

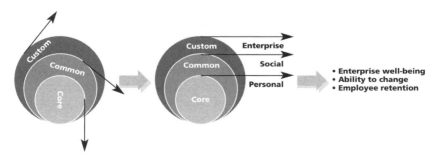

alignment is a measure of the overall well-being of the company, reflecting the degree to which everyone is "on the same page"—a critical factor in developing the ability to change. And the degree to which each employee's core value set is aligned with common and custom rules contributes significantly to employee retention, determining the kinds of employees that stay or go.

People whose core rules largely overlap the custom rules of the organization feel comfortable working in the organization. Because they are comfortable, they tend to stay with the company, unless forced to leave. Conversely, people whose core rules conflict with custom rules feel uncomfortable in the organization and with those tenured by the organization. Individuals who cannot adapt to the custom rules of the organization face mounting frustration and invariably leave without significantly impacting the custom rules of the organization. This filtering mechanism ensures that custom rules, and the corporate culture that reflects them, survive.

How Rules Work

Rules have structure, they are dynamic, they compete for use, and they are contextual.

Rule Structure

Regardless of type, each rule has a common anatomy. In the same way that exchanges have context, offers, and a value proposition, a rule has three components: a behavior (action), the exchange (or context), and a payoff. For example, one person can send a joke by e-mail to a colleague on another project (action). An exchange provides the context for a rule and a value proposition. The person who sends the joke over e-mail (context) is acknowledging a colleague (reward given). Payoff is the *expected reward* to be received for following the rule. Sending the joke builds the relationship (value received) with the colleague who will, in turn, acknowledge the sender—perhaps by laughing, sending the joke to others, or merely sending a reply. In any case, the exchange has a value proposition.

Rule Dynamics

The set of actively followed custom rules are dynamic in that they will change over time. Changes in the expected rewards will influence rule use in a dramatic way. When the expected reward is occasionally not delivered (for example, the recipient of the joke fails to acknowledge it) the jokester may find another way to deliver the joke (change in context), or may send the joke to another recipient who responds enthusiastically (change in context and payoff). When the expected reward is never received (the recipient has been promoted to manager and cannot reply), or if the payoff is resoundingly negative (HR sends a warning) the rule—that it is okay to send jokes via company e-mail—may be abandoned entirely.

Rule Competition

The third characteristic of rules is that they compete for use. When given a choice between any two rules, individuals and groups will always choose to follow the rule that offers greatest personal payoff in the form of comfort, security, and belonging.

Rule Context

The fourth characteristic of rules is that they are contextual. A payoff that may be interpreted as positive in one situation may be considered negative in another. For example, an employee may be delighted with a two-percent raise if two percent is the maximum raise allowed by the organization. That two-percent raise may appear insulting to the same individual when he or she learns that industry peers consistently receive much higher increases.

To summarize, each rule is an object that encapsulates action, exchange, and payoff functions. Rule objects compete for dominance, based on the amount of comfort, security, and belonging each rule offers to the employee or organization. Rules that offer the most comfort, security, and belonging (value) become established as offering the most enterprise stability, often becoming exempt from the change cycle, which involves increasing risk. It therefore becomes extremely difficult to change an established enterprise. Attempts to do so can be seen by the participants in the system as destabilizing, risky, and even subversive—since by definition, a new rule lacks comfort, security, and a sense of belonging until it has competed with other rules for dominance and is accepted.

Like individuals, enterprises too continually weigh the value of competing rules, but enterprises have a different set of motivators than individuals. Individuals follow rules that pay off in safety, security, belonging, and comfort. People want to be liked, respected, included, and praised. Enterprises, on the other hand, will always choose to follow rules that offer greatest corporate stability. In other words, organization rules compensate for destabilizing change. *It is part of the dynamics of the system.* This means that organizations and individuals within them could operate according to value propositions that are at odds with the economic success of the organization. Not only that, but the process by which individuals and organizations achieving payoff differs significantly from that required for the economic success of the enterprise.

Changing the Rules

The premise of the rules-centered approach to change management is that if the rules are changed then behavior will change. This implies that performance will also change. So the natural question is, "How does one change the rules?" To answer this question, let's start by looking again at the various types of rules.

Changing Common Rules

Given the definition of common rules, it is obvious that no enterprise would undertake an initiative to change such rules. Common rules are the rules of society—nation, region, or community. However, it is still important to understand the implications of common rules for corporate transformation programs. An enterprise that has offices around the globe may well need to pay close attention to the common rules that are at play in each of its office locations prior to the approval of a transformation program. These rules may support the transformation at one location and work against it in another.

Changing Core Rules

The core rules—those that guide personal behavior, attainment of personal goals, and motivation, as well as individual ethics and values—are the result of a lifetime and cannot be changed easily. The rules-centered approach makes no attempt to change these rules per se. This is where change management in its truest form is required. Through coaching, training, and facilitation, change managers serve a critical role in the "soft" side of change. Employees need confidence and a sense of control to take the risks represented by change.

Changing Custom Rules

Custom rules—those evolved within an enterprise or organization—are the focus of the rules-centered approach to change management (Figure 15-4). Rapid change and growth in the ability to change depends on changing these rules in two ways. The first is to increase the number of alternative behaviors that are rewarded under the old rules. In other words, the current set of custom rules is modified to increase behavior diversity. This is referred to as *system learning*. The second is to modify the rules incrementally to reward new behaviors; that is, incrementally evolve old rules into new rules. This is referred to as *adaptation*.

System learning and adaptation are both characteristics of the whole organizational system. The operating routines of this

Figure 15-4*: *Rules-Centered Approach and the Organizational System*

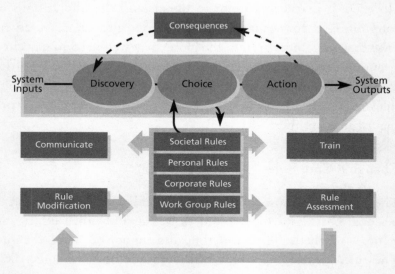

*This figure is adapted from the model Feed-Back in Human Networks described by Ralph D. Stacey on page 29 of his book, *Complexity and Creativity in Organizations* (Berrett-Koehler Publishers, 1996).

organizational system consist of its organizational processes—based on the rules that drive them. It makes sense, then, that the rules-centered approach is in fact a special form of system engineering that uses a customized set of tools, techniques, "engineering language," and processes.

When the organization is system-engineered by designing-in new rules, and all employees are engaged by communication (conversation), new behaviors start to emerge and the system begins to change. This happens because communication creates a common language; common language activates networks of exchanges and relationships; and building networks generates change through new types of value exchange.

The primary role of the change agent in system-engineering new rules for the organization is to act as an interpreter, bridging the many dialects within the organization. As employees learn to speak a common language under the guidance of a trained change facilitator, rules for success change, teams and individuals adapt to diversity, barriers to change fall, and subcultures merge. Process engineering is a well-understood technique, and developing processes has never been the problem in organization change. Engineering the rule systems that govern the use of processes is the dilemma.

Rules systems must be engineered like any other system. The context and reward portion of dysfunctional rules must be redesigned to specification, tested against requirements, delivered per plan, monitored, and debugged. They must then be placed under change control.

Putting All the Components Together

Like any other system engineering approach, the rules-centered approach to organizational change requires a library of documents, tools, measurements, and other artifacts to assure that all engineers involved are following the same methodology. And like any engineered process, it follows a defined life cycle where deliverables are defined, roles and responsibilities are clear, every step generates tangible and measurable results, and every result contributes purposefully to organizational change. When all change agents are following this methodology, under the management of a steering committee and a trained transformation manager, results can be mapped to predefined milestones. Deviations can be corrected. Target dates can be met.

The successful Relationship-Based Enterprise recognizes that internal conversations between employees are just as dynamic and fluid as external conversations with customers. Understanding how organization rules work to build internal exchanges and conversations creates an effective process for changing the organization. The same management preoccupation with discovery, dialogue, and discipline must be applied to these internal conversations. The main difference is that, unlike conversations with customers, the enterprise gets to make the rules.

In an increasingly perceptive world, customers are attuned to those organizations that "walk the talk"; where the processes and practices they observe in their supplier reflect the actual experience of the products and services being delivered. And, in an increasingly open, relationship-driven world, these internal practices are undoubtedly in full-view. Organizations must therefore strive for open and inclusive *internal* dialogues. The Relationship-Based Enterprise must *be* what it seeks to offer its customers.

Window on the Real World:

Alabama Power

Alabama Power, a Southern Company, provides electric service to nearly 1.3 million homes, businesses, and industries in the southern two-thirds of Alabama. It is one of five U.S. utilities operated by Southern Company, the nation's No. 1 producer of electricity.

Regulated utilities, such as Alabama Power, are becoming more market-driven enterprises. To achieve continued success, it has undertaken a major CRM integration effort. Its goal is to achieve a 360-degree view of its customers enterprise-wide.

According to Marsha Sampson Johnson, vice-president of customer services, "CRM is time-consuming and difficult, particularly when it came to adapting various business processes. However, CRM is well worth every bit of investment, energy, and effort."

"The number-one critical success factor we found is *people*. Managing the people factor includes encouraging subject matter experts from different silos (disciplines) to work together on the re-engineering effort; re-training everyone involved in CRM properly; getting customer service agents to deliver quality services consistently over time; building an environment and culture of excellence; hiring the right people (i.e., customer service agents who want 'the' job as opposed to agents who simply look for 'a' job)."

To address the people factor, Alabama Power undertook (1) comprehensive, multi-functional training, and (2) ongoing coaching with all those involved in CRM. Training and coaching, a form of internal conversation, dramatically increased Alabama Power's capacity to change—and to implement CRM.

"CRM is not a technology-driven program," adds Johnson. "Organizations lacking a customer-oriented cultural mindset should be careful. Investing in CRM requires this cultural mindset to be inherited hierarchically throughout the enterprise, from the CEO down. CRM requires a clear vision, strong leadership, and corporate commitment."

Further Thoughts

For Change Programs

- Where in the organization can we expect the most resistance to change?
- How will this resistance manifest itself?
- What are the current patterns of pushback?
- What can we do to counter pushback?
- What plans do we have in place to get the change back on track if things should start to slip backward?

V PART

Customer Relationship Management and Customer Relationship Futures

16

Relationship Futures and External Issues

Key Considerations

- **Privacy Protection**—Company standards for protecting customer privacy
- **Security**—Degrees of anonymity and digital cash
- **Information Ownership**—Profiles as assets
- **Consumer Protection**—Making sure CRM practices are fair
- **The Digital Divide**—Access rights in a knowledge-based economy

The successful Relationship-Based Enterprise will accumulate personal information about an unprecedented number of its customers. And its business strategies will often require sharing personal and family information with other companies over long periods of time. How will this privileged information be treated?

To a significant degree, the future of business relationships and the Relationship-Based Enterprise depend on external issues such as privacy protection, security, information ownership, and the burgeoning "digital divide." Companies cannot control these external issues, but awareness and foresight can help lessen the impact and prevent obvious missteps with Customer Relationship Management (CRM) programs.

Practically speaking, managers involved in implementing CRM programs and building a Relationship-Based Enterprise need to develop a "radar screen"—one that picks up external issues that *may* (or may not) have an impact on CRM programs and technologies. First the issues must be made *visible* and then they need to be *understood and assessed* to determine their effect on a CRM program. The assessment needs to be systematic and applied across the relationship management framework—which is to say, during discovery, dialogue, and discipline. And finally, CRM program managers need to be prepared to *take action* to limit exposure to risk.

Company Standards for Protecting Customer Privacy

Before the computer age, only doctors, priests, and lawyers had privileged access to personal information, usually about a very small segment of society, the very rich. Now, CRM solutions promise (or threaten?) to make intimate details of everyone's lives—or at least everyone with Internet access—widely available. The promise is one of great economic progress through improved personal service. The threat is loss of privacy—and much more. The Internet and e-business explosion represents a major shift in the privacy debate and is even drawing attention from world leaders:

> I hope that the Internet will be more secure and reliable,
> and allow people to use it while maintaining control over
> their personally identifiable information.
> —*U.S. President Bill Clinton, June 25, 2000*

Company CRM initiatives are at the very center of this debate because so many CRM initiatives involve the creation of personal and family profiles. These profiles provide the information needed for customizing services, products, and relationships. In many cases, the profiles are quite sensitive, especially when they cover finance, health, education, reading/viewing preferences, weekly shopping patterns, travel, daily habits, and major purchases. Building profiles may also involve "mining" detailed personal transaction records to develop purchase-pattern and lifestyle analyses. Accurate profiles are key to effective CRM. Companies and customers need to manage these profiles and personal files jointly, in ways acceptable to both. Some questions that should be asked as part of any CRM initiative include:

- What are the ground rules and standards of privacy protection? For example, when is consumer purchase and lifestyle tracking authorized or unauthorized?
- How do these rules limit the company's ability to collect, disclose, share, and use profiles? For example, when should customer representatives ask for customer consent and when not? And what is the underlying rationale?
- Is there a point at which "privacy protection" threatens effective CRM (and vice versa)?
- What are the main regulatory options, for example, industry self-regulation, legislation, mixed models, that governments will employ? What is considered legal or illegal, and ethical or unethical?
- What are the impacts on CRM methods and strategies?

The answers involve international considerations, technologies for physical tracking and surveillance, and developing technology checklists.

International Privacy

Global companies like airlines and communications companies may wish to use CRM to offer customized products and services to customers in many countries. They encounter varying standards and regulatory regimes. In this regard, the United States and the European Union have radically different approaches to privacy protection. The United States tends towards industry self-regulation combined with legislation by sector (cable TV, telephony, credit, and so on) and a national policy of laissez-faire for Internet commerce. The European Union tends towards centralized data-protection legislation covering the private sector as a whole. These laws are being harmonized by a European Union Data Protection Directive designed to ensure equivalent and/or adequate protection of the personal data of all Europeans. The direction taken in Europe may be used to judge the adequacy of privacy protection in the other parts of the world and could create a barrier to international e-commerce using CRM and similar software. The following questions arise:

- How will differing privacy protection standards and the possibility of a trade dispute affect businesses using CRM to manage personal data flows across both continents? Businesses likely to be affected include private banks, e-brokers, airlines, medical experts delivering diagnoses via the Web, insurance services, auto manufacturers, and so on.
- What is the prospect of global standards based on European and/or the more general standards of the Organization for Economic Cooperation and Development (OECD) Guidelines on privacy?
- Will standards help?

Physical Tracking and Surveillance

A number of new technologies can be used to track individuals in their daily movements and trips. While originally used for military and scientific purposes, these technologies are now used to create services which have tracking at their core. Examples include "plain old" cellular telephony, Global Positioning Systems (GPS), communication of real-time street video footage via the Web, and 24-hour video-surveillance. Certain types of services may combine 24 x 7 tracking with customization and CRM software.

A well-known example is the General Motors OnStar driver assistance service, which tracks vehicles on electronic maps second-by-second 24 hours a day using GPS and cellular telephony. OnStar could create detailed customer profiles. Similar services track hikers, parolees, and mountain climbers. It is also easy to envisage packages of mobile communications services that combine physical tracking with single-number voice, e-mail, and Web browsing services.

In most cases, customers will actually pay to be tracked—and therefore give their consent. They will also want the molded services that come with profiling their movements and habits. So far, so good. But then a number of questions can be posed:

- Who else (inside the company and outside) should be able to track people and get access to their customer records?
- How long should such records be retained?
- Are special privacy safeguards needed?
- What conditions should the following parties need to satisfy to gain access to tracking data: police, former spouses, current spouses, employers, revenue authorities, creditors, and so on?
- What should be the position of those companies that are custodians of customer information, when asked (or ordered) to disclose customer-tracking records?

Technology Checklists

Privacy experts have identified a number of technologies for surveillance that they argue must be strictly controlled. Some of these are clipper chips, which enable legal surveillance of telephone and e-mail systems, caller identification systems, government identification cards, biometric identification systems, geographic information systems, GPS systems, and intelligent highways and air transport systems. Privacy experts have also identified privacy-enhancing technologies: personal encryption, digital and blind signatures, anonymous re-mailers, caller identification blocking, information trustees, and key holders.

Such checklists can be used as the basis for these questions:

- To what extent do CRM systems depend on any of these technologies?
- What are the impacts?
- What privacy safeguards are needed?

Degrees of Anonymity and Digital Cash

Encryption is often viewed as a technical subject. At its core, however, are controversial legal and political questions. Does the individual have a right to remain invisible and anonymous in an electronic society? Can reasonable limits be placed on that right? How can the state exercise its powers of electronic search-and-seizure and surveillance? These questions do not appear to involve business directly. However, it is clear that companies can be caught in the middle. In particular, they may find themselves trying to balance conflicting duties—to guarantee anonymity to customers, on the one hand, and to help police investigate crime, on the other.

Encryption can be viewed as conferring "keys" to people, who can use them to open and bar access to digital information. The core question is, who should own the keys required to gain access to the digital objects such as personal messages (voice and written), business messages, personal profiles, transaction records, bank accounts, digital cash and digital cash transfers, requests for emergency assistance, credit files, legal files, and medical files?

The question of the ownership of these keys is of vital concern to companies using CRM. Managers will be responsible, legally and morally, for using encryption to protect customer information. They must answer the corollary questions: To whom do we give keys? And when, under which conditions, for which categories of customer information?

Some libertarians claim that any adult should own the keys to virtually all his or her information, and thus have the absolute right to remain invisible and anonymous. (Each individual should also have the right to publish messages to any audience of his choosing and the right to screen out messages coming from others.) In contrast, police and other agencies (public health, fire department, emergency response, national security) claim they need keys to gain access to certain types of information, in certain circumstances. "Certain" remains to be clearly defined (perhaps reasonable and probable grounds to believe a crime has been committed, that a person may hurt himself, or that a terrorist act will be committed next week). Companies, for their part, will need keys to the information that they require to operate their businesses.

The debate on who holds the keys and when they can use such keys will not be resolved overnight. It is part of a larger public policy debate on encryption standards that includes whether governments should allow, or prohibit, strong encryption technologies, which may even prevent governments from holding the keys. The outcome of this debate is of particular interest to managers of CRM initiatives in two areas: cash as information, and risk versus customer security.

Cash as Information

In the digital world, cash is a special category of information. Consequently, the debate on encryption takes a special form in discussions of digital cash, e-cash, cyber-cash, and the like. Digital cash will be used to pay for goods and services using the Web and similar networks, including many transactions generated by CRM-based systems. Secure digital cash is regarded as a cornerstone of public trust and widespread use of the Web.

Some public policy questions in this field are:

- Should encryption standards guarantee the complete anonymity of digital cash transactions, just as paper money does today?
- Should there be an "electronic tender" system in which only the individual cash carrier holds the keys—making cash transactions untraceable?

Today, the banking system and governments can trace any form of payment except cash (this includes deposit accounts, credit cards, debit cards, and money orders). Some privacy advocates argue that the cash avenue should remain open in the electronic world, offering equivalent privacy to that of the paper-money world. Some law enforcement agencies and central bankers argue that digital money is truly a new world, a world where huge amounts of money can be transferred out of a country via the Web, at the click of a mouse—much different than a planeload of paper drug-money. No encryption system, they say, should prevent governments from being able to trace such large transfers. These opposing views bring up some tough questions for businesses:

- How can CRM initiatives be framed to accommodate different treatments of digital money, depending on which argument prevails? Is there a tenable middle position?
- What position should companies take with regard to encryption used to protect sensitive personal financial profiles and transaction records required to operate CRM systems?
- What standard of anonymity will clients demand?
- Is a major encryption battle on the horizon?

Risk Versus Customer Security for CRM

A host of technical issues, in addition to encryption, surround the safeguarding of the personal information and profiles that lie at the heart of CRM systems. Clearly, most customers will demand a high standard of security as one pillar of the trust they will place in companies whose computer systems serve as "information vaults." The widespread concern and media coverage of attacks on commercial Web sites is a clear indication of the importance of this matter.

Companies will need to determine acceptable levels of risk and determine the costs. The issue could become increasingly important because customer profiles will gain economic value over time and the potential rewards of theft and fraud will grow. A particularly chilling prospect is that of identity fraud (see next section). The questions are:

- What are the top three security issues from three distinct standpoints: (1) technical, (2) customer trust, and (3) business loss?
- What is the overlap?
- What are the risks and costs?

Profiles as Assets

Personal and family profiles, especially in areas such as finance, health, education, reading/viewing preferences, weekly shopping patterns, and major purchases, become valuable economic assets. As these profiles are built over time, they produce revenue streams for companies, which give individuals the option of selling/trading their personal information in return for price discounts, better service, and the soft benefits of personalization. A number of questions need to be answered about how these assets will be managed:

- Who owns and controls an individual or family profile? Is it the individual, the companies that use/hold the profile, or trusted third parties (infomediaries, information trustees)?
- Should ownership and control rights be shared among these parties, and if so, how?

- At the extreme, should individuals have personal Web pages with which companies transact business?
- Should individuals own and control their personal databases?
- What are the main scenarios and the business implications?

The answers to these questions will obviously have a major effect on how e-business is conducted and eventually on how *all* business is conducted. CRM strategies will be affected in many ways, as follows.

Identity Theft and Fraud

As individual and family profiles gain economic value, the rewards of profile theft and fraud will grow. The problem could make 20th century credit-card fraud look like a small-time operation. And it could wreck relationship-based business models. For example, state regulators recently fined a telecommunications company $1.5 million after a customer claimed that the company's failure to deal with identity theft kept her from getting a job. In this case a false account was opened in her name without her knowledge. After the false account had been discovered and the matter apparently resolved, she discovered that she had been denied credit and employment because the telecommunications company had failed to notify its collection company that her record should be cleared.

The top three questions with regard to identify theft are:

- What is the risk exposure of a company's CRM systems to identity theft?
- Who would assume liability for the losses of its customers?
- What measures need to be taken (security, privacy, insurance, liability for loss)?

Intellectual Property

CRM strategies may well involve the joint creation of information-based products and services—especially in the lucrative and growing small-business marketplace. Consider the example of an entrepreneur who purchases personalized news services from 10 to 15 electronic news services (Dow Jones, Reuters, economist.com, industry news services) with which she has cordial business relationships. She then combines these into 30 packages of information for expert audiences that the "biggies" (her information suppliers) have missed. She does all this with three business students working on a new "super-news" workstation located in her home. It becomes a million-dollar business. The large news organization decides to enter one of the specialty segments that she serves and decides to sue her for unauthorized use of its copyrighted material. This suit means that the courts will have to answer questions like these:

- To whom do all these information packages belong?
- How much should the entrepreneur pay?
- What should the law say?
- How does all this affect customer relationships along the information value-chain?

Making Sure CRM Practices are Fair

Relationship-based pricing is complex and may lead to results that could be questioned. For example, different prices could be charged for the same product and different prices could be charged for the same service package in different geographic or cyber-markets. And companies could increase prices once customers become locked in and face high switching costs. Examples of this include such offers as zero percent interest for the first six months. The questions that may be asked by politicians and consumer advocates are:

- How will prices for complex service packages and customized product/service suites be compared?
- Will predatory pricing be defined in the case of loyalty schemes that move from deep price discounts (Year 1) to full pricing later (Year 5)?

- What common sense standards of fairness will emerge?
- What legislation, regulation, and court action may be required?

The Risks of Lock-In

Related to the issue of unfair pricing is the broader question of whether companies can lock in customers to relationships in which they may be treated unfairly. While this question may seem far-fetched to managers in today's competitive marketplace, it has become a major issue in the personal computer software industry. There is a possibility that successful relationship-building business strategies, using CRM, will lock in groups of consumers and create monopolies in narrow market segments. Many e-businesses are trying to build dominant brands and customer relationships that will last for a lifetime. The questions are:

- If they are successful, will they be applauded or accused of predatory pricing, abuse of market power, and monopolistic practices?
- What rules will regulate cross-sector alliances and co-branding arrangements that may be used to create complex service packages?

Discriminatory Practices

One of the primary principles of loyalty-based marketing is learning to turn away or discourage "unprofitable customers," meaning those who do not match the optimal profile of a profitable long-term customer. This can lead to accusations of discrimination and unfairness, especially when: (1) individuals discouraged from continuing the relationship are lower-income or live in a certain district; (2) the process used to turn down requests for service is arbitrary or insulting; and (3) when services declined are deemed "essential" (banking, telecommunications, e-mail, air transportation). Incidents of unfairness could lead to these public policy questions:

- What standards of fairness should apply?
- Should a business be limited in its right to turn down customers?
- What is the definition of "essential services" in the current context?

International Consumer Protection

When products and services are sold, via the Internet and CRM systems, and are delivered across national borders, what consumer protections apply? When consumers use the Internet to purchase goods from suppliers in other countries, it becomes unclear which legislation applies when the consumer wants to file a complaint, return defective products, obtain financial compensation, and so on. The world consumer movement has claimed that it is the legislation of the consumer's home jurisdiction that should apply. Businesses have been hesitant. Some of the major questions are:

- What standards should apply and how will they be enforced?
- If standards are developed to protect consumers for worldwide Internet sales, will the same standards apply to bricks-and-mortar worldwide sales?
- What will be the impact on businesses building relationships with consumers in many national jurisdictions (travel, tourism)?

Access Rights in a Knowledge-Based Economy

Early CRM programs focused on high-value customers in upper income and wealth brackets, and were conducted through more traditional media, such as telephone and personal contact. But as loyalty-based schemes and CRM applications have become increasingly Web-oriented, the *potential* market has expanded to middle-class Internet users—a growing segment. Those without Web access, the so-called "information have-nots," and particularly those in low-income groups, are likely to be excluded. As a result, it is possible that CRM programs will be perceived as limited to the wealthy or computer literate, and that CRM will reinforce the so-called "digital divide."

At the moment, CRM is a small part of a very big debate about the digital divide. That debate focuses mainly on the use of the Web in business and education, not on CRM. The problem is symbolized by the contrast between Palo Alto, Silicon Valley, and the nearby community of East Palo Alto, which not long ago registered the highest murder rate in the United States.

According to the journal *The Economist*, "Government and the Internet Survey," Page 27, June 24, 2000: "Palo Alto's Web site has 251 sections and is a paragon of e-government. Among many other things, it allows users to send forms to the planning department and search the city's library catalogue. During storms, it even provides live video footage of flood-prone Fancisquito Creek. East Palo Alto's site, by contrast, has only three pages, containing little more than outdated population figures and the address of City Hall."

The digital divide was debated in the recent U.S. presidential campaign. It is closely related to concerns about the public education system and the fact that educationally advantaged children are far more Web-literate than children in less advantaged families. Computer makers have developed inexpensive computers and begun working with government to address the issue of giving all schools easy access to the resources of the Internet.

The digital divide is also a global phenomenon, with the World Bank and development experts concerned about the contrast between rich countries and developing countries in terms of telecommunications infrastructure, Internet access, and access to computers. It is also perceived as a divide between the young and the elderly.

It is hard to forecast where the debate on the digital divide is headed. It could take many directions. It is even harder to predict its effects on the worlds of e-commerce and CRM. Companies should keep this item on their radar screens. They need to be prepared for questions such as:

- Does a CRM program unfairly exclude people without Internet access?
- How can a company justify this exclusion?
- What steps is the company taking to broaden access to the e-marketplace?

A Risky Business?

So, is becoming a Relationship-Based Enterprise a risky endeavor? An obvious exposure is government intervention. Formal regulation and legislation could ban certain types of CRM activity or make them too costly. However, legislation may be the *least* risky scenario.

Legislation is usually slow to come. It usually comes in response to problems and incidents. A greater risk to CRM is that problems and incidents arising from the external issues identified in this chapter will erode the highly sensitive link between customer confidence and the success of CRM. CRM is not like bulk oil transportation. It is like the story of Tylenol—highly dependent on consumer confidence and trust. Without trust, it is dead as a business strategy.

Here is a short list of the many types of risk that could affect CRM-based business strategies:

- negative word of mouth among clients and potential clients that affects corporate, product, or brand reputation
- negative "viral word of mouth" transmitted via e-mail and chat rooms that affects corporate, product, or brand reputation
- media controversy and consumer group action that affect corporate, product, or brand reputation
- court cases and threats of court cases

- political controversy—legislative committee hearings, question period, etc.
- publicized efforts at "moral suasion" from government
- regulation (actions by the executive branch or agencies)
- legislation.

Given the number and variety of issues—and the variety of potential risks—it seems clear that CRM strategies need to be pursued with full knowledge of "external issues." Many of these issues may be hidden by cloud cover from time to time but they will not disappear. They represent areas of focus that are outside the control of the enterprise and generally are in the domain of governments, politicians, and advocacy groups. It will be hard to predict how a controversy might arise from one of these external issues and how it would affect the CRM program of an individual organization.

In view of these difficulties, several warnings are in order. Solutions to these issues will *not* be easy to find. Most solutions will *not* be one-time fixes, but rather one of many steps towards a solution. Solutions will be developed through public sector or through cooperative public-private action. Certainly, a single company will *not* be able to develop solutions to the kind of issues identified in this chapter.

After All the Nots ...

After all the "nots," what *can* managers do? What practical actions can they take to influence relationship futures and limit the risks of external issues? One approach is to incorporate the following safeguards into the organization's relationship management framework.

Discovery

- Build **radar screens** to track and monitor external issues. The goal is visibility. Managers can't decide whether an issue is important or not until they can see and understand it. Promoting visibility minimizes the risk of surprises, maximizes preparedness, and builds executive awareness of the issue. This makes a fast, appropriate response more likely if there is a problem.

- Develop **assessment filters** for identifying probable impacts on the CRM program and CRM in general. The goal is to *deepen practical understanding*. Once an issue is visible and understood, it may take time and effort to assess how it might—and might not—affect customer relationships and how they are managed.

Dialogue

- Learn when to **engage "the outside world"** in conversations about external issues. The goal is to promote *openness and flexibility*. There are several groups that might be consulted or involved in the CRM program, including external experts such as privacy consultants, encryption experts, and government officials. Consumer groups and advocacy groups are not always the enemy when asked for an opinion.
- Ask the **tough questions**. The goal is a to get a *realistic assessment* of the situation and the risks. Examples of these questions have been given throughout this chapter. Like the ten critical questions identified in this book, these questions too need to be asked not once, but continuously.

Discipline

- Develop **management frameworks** for taking specific actions in response to the external issues identified, tracked, and monitored through the radar screens and assessment filters implemented for discovery. The goal is to limit *risk* and develop *opportunities* to build the confidence and trust of customers and other external players. Possible areas for action are the design of CRM programs, choices of technology, and customer involvement in solutions development.

Integrating these safeguards into the relationship management framework will help managers predict and control the effects of external issues on customer relationships and their CRM program. The assessment and management of external issues is an important competency of the Relationship-Based Enterprise.

17

Testing Customer Relationship Futures

Take Action By ...

- **Playing Tough Customer**—Stepping outside the enterprise for a different view
- **Discovery Testing**—Testing the enterprise's knowledge about its customers
- **Dialogue Testing**—Testing how customers react to conversations
- **Discipline Testing**—Testing the approaches, mechanisms, systems and procedures for delivering value
- **Playing Tough Program Manager**—Stepping back inside the enterprise

Because relationships with customers change constantly, Customer Relationship Management (CRM) initiatives are difficult to manage. As a result, one of the most important tasks in the Relationship-Based Enterprise is testing CRM operations, programs, and initiatives to ensure that they are and remain relevant to the needs of customers. It's a lesson even fast-moving dotcoms have had to learn.

Amazon.com's approach towards its customers uncovered a huge pent-up demand for personalized conversations via the Internet. In terms of discovering new sources of economic value, this is similar to Henry Ford's discovery that ordinary middle-class Americans would buy plain black cars if they were affordable. Amazon's challenge will be to continue to evolve these conversations and to keep its approach to CRM relevant to all its customers as it adds electronics, toys, health and beauty products, software, computer and video games, kitchen tools and hardware, lawn and patio items, and even new cars to its ever-growing list of products. In making the decision to extend its product lines, Amazon or any other company can't afford to be surprised by changes in what customers value or in the way they want to interact.

The process of testing customer relationship futures, the subject of this chapter, offers a way to avoid being surprised by such changes. It is a form of stress testing in which a CRM approach is confronted with a series of independently generated customer perspectives. The working assumption is that, in today's marketplace, CRM programs *must* change to remain relevant. To change, they must be challenged—by the market or by managers who anticipate the market. This is not because CRM software packages are changing, but because the very heart of CRM—relationships with customers—can be expected to change quickly and unexpectedly. CRM technologies and programs that are narrowly managed risk becoming irrelevant, at which point customers will terminate conversations with an enterprise, and the relationship will die. The testing process involves *stepping outside the corporate CRM program*. Stepping outside involves adopting the perspective of a tough customer. Having understood this perspective, the trick is to shift gears and adopt another perspective—that of a tough program manager—by *stepping back inside the corporate CRM program* to assess whether it is being managed effectively.

The stress-testing process involves five clearly defined activities:

- Playing Tough Customer—Stepping outside the enterprise for a look at trends, issues and solutions through the eyes of a tough customer, one that is not easily impressed.
- Discovery Testing—Testing the enterprise's knowledge about its customers. How much does your organization really know?
- Dialogue Testing—Testing how customers react to conversations. Do they feel their conversations with the company are adding value?
- Discipline Testing—Testing whether approaches, mechanisms, systems, and procedures are organized for delivering value. Do the solutions make sense and provide value, from the point of view of both the customer and the enterprise?
- Playing Tough Program Manager—Stepping back inside the enterprise. Assess multiple CRM initiatives through the eyes of a tough program manager.

These activities, particularly discovery testing, dialogue testing, and discipline testing, should not be undertaken without reading Chapter 5, "The Relationship Management Framework," which explains the need for management's preoccupation with the three Ds—discovery, dialogue, and discipline.

Playing Tough Customer

The purpose of focusing on relationship futures is to shock the enterprise and challenge existing patterns of thought and behavior. The most direct route to achieving this is talking with tough customers—members of consumer groups, chat rooms, and affinity groups. Especially those who question whether they are getting value from their relationships with their suppliers.

Tough customers have these characteristics:

- They expect a degree of conflict between buyer and seller.
- They do not assume that intimate relationships are in the customer's interest.
- They have sharp eyes for value in its many forms.
- They participate in the emerging, on-line, information-rich markets of today.
- They have visions of the future and opinions about where the market is heading.

The following four scenarios illustrate the value of tough customers. Imagine the customers described in these scenarios are the ones providing your organization with perspectives on the deluge of choice in the economy, the battle for their attention, and above all, the impact of the Internet and its vast array of information.

Deluge of Choice

Tough Customer Insights—Scenario One: Customers today face too much information, too much advice, and too many offers. In short, they face too much choice. The little time each has to make intelligent decisions is a poor match for this abundance of choice.

The deluge of choice is obvious from the contents of door-mats and mailboxes, which yield stacks of unsolicited junk mail. It is obvious from the glut of advertising. And it is obvious from an unguided tour of the Web—a truly bewildering experience for those not familiar with search engines. Customers may have access to a vast pool of advice and information, but the problem is efficient use of this vast resource and making informed choices without feeling overwhelmed. The refrain of the tough customer may well be, "Decisions, decisions bear down on us unremittingly."

This proliferation of choice makes everyone anxious and uncertain about whether they are getting the best deal, the best advice, or the best service. The evidence for this can be seen when people turn to friends and family for advice about products they wish to purchase. They simply want some assurance that the product *matches* what they are looking for. And it takes someone who knows them to help make that judgment. For example, when someone asks about a new movie, they are likely to ask, "Would I like it?" They are not just asking for their friend's opinion, but also for a judgment on their behalf.

Businesses can't do this. They have endless sources to draw upon, but they cannot provide the needed judgment as easily—they are not their customer's friend.

What are the solutions? One possibility is personal referral systems—the electronically enabled equivalent of "ask your neighbor." Amazon has shown the way, with its reader review facility. What other customers think about a particular book is often more important than the officially endorsed review.

The effect of this on individual corporate CRM programs may not always be clear. But the implications are very clear—to remain credible, companies may have to avoid positioning themselves as the sole provider of advice. A better position may well be to become co-participants in referral networks or to enable such networks.

The Battle for Attention

Tough Customer Insights—Scenario Two: With product manufacturing times and costs shortening and product content becoming "soft" rather than "hard," customers are deluged by products and multiple product lines. And new products are becoming obsolete faster than ever before. The shift to a more transitory world of products and services can have an effect on a customer's view of his relationship with the producers of these products and services and create a battle for customer attention.

The drivers of this trend are many and varied. Product manufacturing cycle times are shortening and costs are dropping. A much greater percentage of product content depends on software, which can be easily replaced or reprogrammed. As a result, products are easier to customize and modify. This is conditioning customer behavior, especially in the pre- and early teen segments. In addition, products that were once paid for are becoming free, and so even the very idea of a product is changing.

The shift towards a more transitory world of products and services is driving important changes in the consumer's view of the relationship with the producers of these products and services. Businesses have lost any sense of treating a particular product as anything other than temporary. They hop from product to product. In such an environment, customers have a different view of customer loyalty than many enterprises. Customers used to make simple links between the product, the brand, and the company. Those links are being eroded and even broken.

Customers can also become confused about whom they are dealing with. The commercial environment, with its shifting landscape of alliances, networked ownership structures, and multiple distribution networks presents a very different picture to the one faced by the average consumer less than a generation ago. "Is that the same as... ." is a common refrain when faced, for example, with a new branded Internet bank that is, in fact, a subsidiary of an established bricks-and-mortar enterprise. Customers still make simple product-to-producer equations, such as "a Dell computer," "a Nokia phone," "an Amazon book." Yet Amazon sells patio furniture, and that phone will soon deliver branded digital services such as stock purchases, ticket reservations, and traffic reports. Who stands behind these services?

In this rapidly changing environment we have lost, for the most part, any sense of treating a particular product as anything other than temporary. In such an environment customers have a much different view of customer loyalty than do enterprises. So product evolution itself is both an opportunity for building and sustaining customer relationships as well as a potential impediment to progress. The tough customer might say that the days when he or she was comfortable with long-term relationships with a few key suppliers are quickly fading.

One approach to this dilemma that is being attempted by producers is to offer complete "solutions" rather than products. A simple example might be mortgage producers that also offer house-moving and relocation services. But such solutions may even further confound the problem by blurring the notion of the relationship in the mind of the customer. Does the customer feel warm towards the mortgage provider or the relocation service, or both? And if one lets the customer down, does that infer a quality judgment on the other?

The effect of this on individual corporate CRM programs is not always clear. However, the implications are clear—loyalty to one producer or brand is becoming harder to deliver and organizations will have to find ways of getting their customers' attention. Ideally they will eliminate any element of confusion and uncertainty about who they are, while using the evolution of their products and services as an opportunity to sustain their relationships with customers.

The Effect of the Internet

Tough Customer Insights—Scenario Three: One catalyst of the deluge of choice is the ability of the Web to deliver anything, anywhere, anytime, anyhow. But how do people find what they want, and how do they decide?

This challenge is getting bigger because of the continued expansion of the Internet into something that some call the *pervasive Web*. It flows from the ongoing transition from PC-based access to mobile, personalized connections with the Web. The car is already being talked about as a mobile hub. The mobile phone is set to become the portable portal where much of the day-to-day transactions of life—booking tickets, trading stocks, checking bank balances—will be conducted. More than that, domestic appliances such as refrigerators, microwave ovens, and many others will be connected to the Web—and advanced communications networks. All of this will come together in the wired homes and wireless offices that are now being tested.

Early in the 21st century, customers will reach a transition point where the presence of the Web becomes as essential to modern life as the telephone; Microsoft's idea of the "webtone" may well become a reality. The Web will just be there, no more connecting, disconnecting, and the associated paraphernalia and inconvenience. When customers want to say something to someone or something, or when they need to access some information, music, or video, it will simply be there—wherever they are.

The pervasive Web is not an unmitigated blessing. It makes possible so many conversations and interactions at any one time that customers could start to lose track. In a typical day, customers will interact with many forms of electronically enabled objects (people, music, companies). Each interaction represents some event—important or trivial—in the customer's life or business. Events may have close connections to other events, or may have no connection at all. Collectively, however, these events are evidence of lives that are increasingly complex, hurried, and fragmented.

The tough customer, at all stages of his or her life, is therefore looking for ways to simplify the business of living so that more time can be left free for the things that matter: family, friends, holidays, study, entertainment. Tough customers may well say that they need products, services, and connections that simplify life, not complicate it.

Again, the effect on individual corporate CRM programs may not always be clear. But the implications are clear—the pervasiveness of the Web means that the individual interactions between the customer and the producer will grow in volume and become shorter and shorter. Customers will "dip in and out" of the Web for many concurrent purposes. Take the example of an on-line mortgage application. The customer first looks at options, then goes away to reflect. Later the customer comes back to examine alternatives, and after a period of time comes back again to enter some personal details to refine the query. Then still later to look at projections. And even much later making a formal application. In and out, of this conversation and then that one.

Each of these conversations is likely to utilize an increasingly varied set of devices, including some that are totally transparent to the customer. Many exchanges will be performed in real time. The result is that customers will need help keeping track of their progress. They will look for solid navigational systems that support conversations with a variety of suppliers, systems similar to the ones that are seen in video games—"stop playing," "remember the score," "remember the last exchange," and then "restart."

Companies will need systems that track the entire conversation. The services and facilities that surround the product will become as important as the product itself. Systems that enable a producer to assist the customer, to stop and restart during an extended purchase or product research activity, will attract customers. Customers will need the help of trusted database managers and suppliers to handle all the data so that they can make better use of it. This would represent a major shift for many CRM applications. For example, personal and household information—rather than products and services—would be at the core of a conversation and relationship. The customer will need trusted partners. But how will enterprises win that trust?

Deluge of Information

Tough Customer Insights, Scenario Four: Too much information is a key aspect of the pervasive Web. Unlike telephones and TV, which are also "just there," Web applications, especially e-business applications, need personal information about people in order to serve them and deliver value.

Each touch with the pervasive Web will generate information that consumers may need to retain, store, and process, or that companies need to be able to deliver their services. Today, such information is manually entered into portable information repositories: diaries, electronic organizers, mobile phones, account books, palmtops, laptop computers, calendars, and the like. In a world where the importance of knowledge and information is rising, a new paradox is emerging: it would seem that the absolute value of any particular piece of information declines more rapidly than before. That research report requested on the latest advances in cancer therapy, that bank statement, or that financial report of a possible acquisition: how valuable are they after one day, one week, or one month? Information now has a perishable quality, just like the groceries in the weekly grocery cart.

The tough customer may well feel overloaded with information and at the same time have few guidelines about what is useful and what should be disposed of. The tough customer may leave this for an annual or semi-annual trawl through his or her files—a dismal exercise that is postponed for as long as possible!

The effect on individual corporate CRM programs may not always be clear. But the fact remains that corporate information about customers is perishable, whether the customer is a consumer or a business. Each enterprise must have the required mechanisms to identify the "best before" date on all its customer information. Some enterprises will provide their customers with such labeling.

The insights revealed by tough customers in these scenarios provide a picture of their mindset. This picture has implications for CRM programs. However, it was developed *without reference* to CRM. This separation enables managers to test whether the concerns of customers intersect with the solutions offered by their CRM program. This kind of testing is essential because while the picture presented by tough customers has implications for CRM, the exact nature of the effect on individual corporate CRM programs is not.

The next activity is to get specific by relating this general perspective to the three main facets of the relationship management framework—discovery, dialogue, and discipline. The CEO or, even better, a senior executive team, should lead this activity. It is similar to the market research study, described in Part II, which was conducted to prepare the launch of E-Hearth home-management services. The idea, once again, is to step outside the enterprise of today, wipe the slate clean—and assume that little is really known about the customer. The focus is on the future—specifically relationship futures.

Discovery Testing

The core question for discovery testing is, "Are relationship futures unfolding in ways that are different from those that are expected?" To answer this question accurately and completely, the enterprise needs to challenge its own established patterns of thought. Participants must be prepared for critical self-questioning. Most likely customers are moving faster than the enterprise, which means that discovery testing is likely to become a groundbreaking exercise. The CEO will have to pose basic questions that will challenge established thinking to release any inhibitions. Many possibilities need to be discussed, and no possibility should become "undiscussible," to use the language of Chris Argyris in *Overcoming Organizational Defenses* (Simon & Shuster, 1990).

This is not a time for improving on what is already being done; it's a time for challenging the fundamentals. Controversial statements, such as the ones that follow, can be used to shake up established thinking:

■ We don't know who our customers are.

Businesses may think they do, but they don't. They can segment them and classify them, but what does that really tell them? Ask, "Can anyone name a real customer from one of those segments? Would those customers recognize themselves as, for example, a 'rootless renter' or a 'nest-making family'?"

■ Customers expect us to know them by name. Do we?

The truth is that customers have multiple personalities, and companies have to learn to deal with a richly varied expression of need and of affiliation.

- We know nothing about what customers really think about us.

With CRM, businesses spend so much time thinking about managing the relationship that no time is spent asking what customers think about them—or if their customers think of them at all. And if customers do give the subject any thought, how, when, and where?

- We don't all agree on what we mean when we say customer.

Is a customer someone who has bought something? Is it someone who might buy something? What about people who may never buy? Should they be treated as customers? What about people who may eventually own a product that was purchased second-hand? Is a customer a person, a family, a company, the purchasing agent, or the design engineer? And what if Internet auctions become such a big business that customers become resellers?

- We know nothing about how the Internet will change what we understand about customers.

Customers deal with the company predominantly over electronic channels and have become more remote than before. And they like it! This is going to have a major impact on the meaning of CRM and the way it operates. How does the customer want to use the Web site in conjunction with other channels of communication?

- We have not thought about how demographics will change CRM.

A company may think it has this covered through its customer segmentation programs. It will have to think again. New generations of consumer are entering the marketplace with very different attitudes and behavior patterns. Each will choose to interact with a business differently. Companies are not prepared for this. These are also the people who may be running the businesses that an enterprise must deal with on a daily basis.

Discussion of these points, from the perspective of the tough customer, will begin to give the CRM management team an idea of customer futures.

Dialogue Testing

Dialogue testing means asking, from the perspective of a tough customer, "Are conversations with customers making any sense? Are there any worrying silences? Do these conversations deliver value?"

As with earlier activities in the testing process, it is important to set aside the current CRM program, and only later explore whether customer concerns intersect with the solutions offered. Try to find the five best reasons why customers might find the conversations boring and of no value. The following controversial statements may help shake up established thinking about these conversations:

- We aren't managing relationships. The smart customers are managing their relationship with us and our competitors. They are getting tired of the time and effort—the sacrifice—involved.

How can businesses make it easy for customers to deal with them—manage them, in fact? Going down this thought path may lead businesses to some interesting, perhaps surprising, conclusions. For example, an organization may have enabled its customers by supporting self-service, when in fact the customer wants the enterprise to provide the service or vice versa.

- Customers are coming to our Web site and phoning the call center. But they are not getting much value and are getting tired of the conversation.

Customers may experience irritating technical problems that are the equivalent of white paint on a storefront window, an aging TV tube, or static on a cell phone. Businesses need to find out.

Or perhaps customers are tired of the content, style, and flow of the conversation. Are companies *listening* and *solving* these problems? Or is the Web site running like a cable TV channel—*pushing* stuff out at the customer?

- Our customers are ganging up on us in Web-based communities and consumer groups. We are not in the clubhouses and chat rooms where these conversations are happening. In a word, we are absent.

The Web is beginning to facilitate dynamic and powerful customer groups. Businesses have to get comfortable with this. From common-interest groups looking for medical advice, to customers forming travel clubs, to automobile purchase groups, customers are affiliating themselves with all kinds of groups and in a typical day may participate in many of them. Such groups engender loyalty, camaraderie, and clan spirit.

- We are kidding ourselves when we talk about giving customers truly individual treatment.

The "segment of one" concept focuses on personalizing service to meet individual needs. How close are companies? Do they recognize customers at first sight and remember them as individuals? Do they really personalize and customize?

- All we do is manage customer relationships.

Businesses don't sell products (although that's how they make their revenue); they may not even make products. What they do, at the core of their business, is totally satisfy their customers, and they do that by understanding them and their needs better than anyone. This is a core competence that they need to develop and nurture.

If enterprises really believe that all they do is manage customer relationships, all the activities that are a part of their business may be up for grabs. Products that businesses may not have thought of as being "theirs" may have to become part of their complement of products (though that doesn't mean they should make them). And products they now hold dear may, on analysis, have to be discarded as being irrelevant.

- Look around—the inputs to, and outputs from our businesses and industries are being restructured and reshaped.

Supply chains are becoming consolidated by realizing economies of scale, and deconstructed by emerging new sources of supply. In the former case, businesses should consider disbanding their capabilities in these areas and handing them to someone who can perform them effectively. In the latter, perhaps there are opportunities for devising new products, or at least for regrouping suppliers.

- Let's take a look at our distribution chains. Have we talked to our customer's customer lately? How are we perceived? Are we perceived at all?

Distribution chains are breaking up and reforming by being disintermediated and re-intermediated. Let's look at these in turn. What does this mean? If their business is CRM, they may effectively want to *become* the distributor. But there may be complementary outlets that can help deal with the myriad of ways in which customers want to interact.

Discussion of these points, from the perspective of the tough customer, will begin to give the CRM management team an idea of the relationship futures that could impact their CRM program.

Discipline Testing

Discipline testing means asking if the CRM solutions developed by an enterprise make sense and deliver value to customers—from the perspective of a tough customer. Referring back to the scenarios presented earlier, this could mean asking questions like, "How do current Web-based CRM systems and procedures match the need of a tough customer for personal referral? For help managing personal information? For navigational support?"

This approach allows managers to critically examine whether their CRM systems and procedures offer solutions that, when taken together, address customer concerns. If there is a mismatch, then these CRM systems and procedures or the programs that deliver them may need revision.

The following are controversial statements that may help shake up established thinking about the decisions and choices made concerning CRM:

- Our brand has nothing to do with what "tough customers" want.

A large, century-old bank, for example, may be using its Web site to publish its extensive menu of products or it may simply put its existing paper-based credit-card application process on-line. Customers may want to have conversations about financial planning, travel plans, or home ownership before deciding which products they may need. If the brand represents an extensive line of products while customers are seeking extensive conversations—advice, information, and help—then what should be done?

- We don't have the right strategic goals.

If the bank wants to move to the forefront in an area such as navigational systems, this cannot be done overnight. It will take significant resource commitments. For a goal such as this, businesses need to establish a competency and begin to build initial releases of the required software. This may, in turn, require a significant overhaul of the whole customer-facing capability within the organization. Customer-facing systems would need to enable customers to start and stop conversations about potential financial purchases without loss of comprehension.

- We do not have the right business partners and allies to deliver what customers want.

In this connected world, all of a company's actions, initiatives, and programs depend, more than ever, on others for their success. Organizations no longer have exclusive control of all of the elements of production and distribution. More than ever, businesses have chosen to achieve their goals through collaborations, partnerships, and alliances. And in some cases collaborators are competitors. Defining and managing this complex interplay of resources is critical to the success of CRM programs.

- The way we are organized does not allow us to get to know our customers.
- We have hundreds of measures but none that clearly describes the value we provide to customers.
- We are not changing as quickly as is needed to satisfy our customers.

These are only a few of the many topics, from the perspective of the tough customer, that begin to give a CRM management team an idea of the relationship futures. Each of these can affect a CRM program.

Playing Tough Program Manager

Having fully explored the "tough customer" mindset, it is time to take the insights of this outside perspective and transform them into actions—starting tomorrow morning.

It is often said that, leaving the big ideas aside, management is the art and science of "getting from here to there." This is especially true of large, complex CRM programs that touch many parts of the enterprise. The process of testing relationship futures up to this point has transported managers outside the enterprise to "there"—giving them a clear idea of where CRM programs need to be heading. Developing CRM program guidelines brings managers back inside the enterprise to "here"—the starting point. And this helps answer the question: "How do we get from here to there?"

CRM program management guidelines offer a sound approach to program and project management. Most large organizations have more than one CRM project. And these projects are being managed by many different players, some in call centers, Web sites, sales forces, and different business groups. Pulling all this activity together into an enterprise-wide program or into a consolidated approach is a major challenge.

The following guidelines suggest a practical set of steps that can be taken to ensure that the program (or programs) will work at all levels, from strategy articulation to software installation and training. The goal of these program management guidelines is to improve the success rate of CRM programs. With these an enterprise can measure success through a clear linkage between program initiatives to desired business results.

CRM Program Management Guidelines

Each of the following steps matches a phase of CRM program design and implementation:

1. Program Diagnosis
2. Strategy Review
3. Enterprise Architecture
4. Enterprise Application Integration Services
5. Package Selection and Implementation
6. Application Outsourcing Assessment
7. Implementation Review
8. Program and Project Management.

Each step and its associated activities have been proven in previous large-scale change and improvement programs, such as business process re-engineering and implementation of Enterprise Resource Planning (ERP) initiatives. The hard lessons learned in those programs can be applied to CRM programs today with the aim of improving their success rates—as measured by clear linkage to desired business results.

The steps in the program management guide include the following.

1. **CRM Diagnosis.** The place to start is with a diagnosis of the current status of CRM and its related programs. An organization needs to assess its business objectives against current CRM programs in order to highlight the areas for improvement. The aim should be to identify where it can get the biggest bang for its investment. The diagnosis can cover CRM approaches, conversation

design, relationship styles, organizational structure, and IT infrastructure. Understanding how these compare with other organizations, with best practices, and how they fit into the enterprise's business strategy, will help identify areas for improvement. (CRM maturity models can also be used to assess customer information, customer interaction channels, customer experience, people, processes, metric and organizational structure.) The aim of the diagnosis is to articulate recommendations for improvements and highlight the critical conditions necessary for CRM program success and optimal benefits realization.

2. **Strategy Review.** An organization needs to assess its CRM strategies against the answers to the ten most critical questions in this book, as listed in Chapter 5 and explored in parts II, III, and IV. Current strategies can also be challenged using the approach to relationship futures testing described earlier. The aim of this review is to paint a vivid picture of the conversation designs and spaces that make its customer relationships profitable. This forms the basis for the right CRM game plan for an organization and the joint development of business and IT strategies.

3. **CRM Enterprise Architecture.** The CRM Diagnosis and Strategy Review will highlight the benefits of pulling all the CRM-related initiatives that may be scattered across the company into a comprehensive, enterprise-wide strategy. To do this, an organization needs answers to the ten most critical questions, combined with a dynamic, robust model of its CRM architecture. A CRM architecture will help create new conversation spaces (dialogue); transform the customer information into a strategic tool to profile, segment, target, and retain valuable customers (discovery), organize sales, marketing, and customer care in a consistent way

(discipline), and integrate back-office and front-office processes (also discipline). The architecture should integrate all elements of a CRM solution—people, processes, technologies, and organization. The aim is to ensure that CRM improvement programs are designed company-wide, in a balanced way—and with clear links to business results.

4. **Enterprise Application Integration**. One key to success in enterprise architecture development, and in CRM overall, is the seamless integration of channels, people, and technologies into conversation spaces that deliver value to customers. Seamless customer experiences, in turn, depend on the seamless integration of enterprise-wide CRM application packages, legacy applications, and Web-enabled systems. The integration challenge continues to vex even the most sophisticated organizations. Meeting this challenge is the purpose of an Enterprise Application Integration (EAI) game plan. The aim is to develop enterprise-wide solutions using a variety of processes, techniques, and, where relevant, software alliances.

5. **CRM Package Selection and Implementation**. An organization needs a system for navigating through the crowded marketplace of CRM packages and assessing the effect of changes on its business. Expert assistance is often required both for package assessment and for implementation. Packages must be integrated into the IT environment, with attention paid to process design and change management. The aim is to develop a game plan for managing package selection, implementation, and testing through multi-year life cycles. Going beyond technical installation, the transformation of business processes must be managed so that new software packages deliver maximum value.

6. **CRM Application Outsourcing Assessment.** Like other software packages, CRM applications require support, maintenance, and enhancement over a period of years. An organization needs to assess whether it would benefit by outsourcing responsibility for this technology-intensive side of the CRM program. This may help it evolve and maintain its CRM application portfolio—call centers, e-commerce, and so on—in a logically phased, cost-effective manner. All such contracts need to define clear service-level agreements. The aim of this activity is to allow the enterprise to focus on customer relationships and not the supporting technology.

7. **CRM Implementation Review.** An organization may need to get an overview of all implementation activities. The focus is on the game plan for building the complete set of business and technical solutions—whether in one area of the company or enterprise-wide. The aim is to ensure a coordinated approach to the design, redesign, or consolidation of CRM programs—from e-commerce initiatives to call-center operations to integrated customer information systems to campaign management.

8. **Program and Project Management.** CRM involves a multiplicity of initiatives across the enterprise. Each initiative needs to be well managed. Just as importantly, all need to fit into coherent CRM programs. Advanced program and project management methods are often required. Program or project management offices (PMOs) can be created to ensure that CRM-related projects deliver value and fully support strategic business initiatives. This activity can be undertaken in phases:

   ■ PMO Establishment—Creates an effective PMO structure that defines roles and responsibilities and reporting relationships, and provides a start-up plan.

- PMO Assessment—Confirms the readiness and capabilities of the PMO by examining the existing program organization, along with the plans and activities conducted to date. Measures need to be identified that reduce risk and increase the potential for success.
- PMO Operation—Outsourcing the PMO for a particular project or program allows an organization to concentrate on other areas more suitable for internal resources.

There are methods for linking programs and projects to the achievement of business benefits. For example, a value management office (VMO) provides greater understanding of program interdependencies, resource limitations, progressive resource commitment, risk management, and capital budgeting. The VMO helps an organization to group, organize, and sequence projects into high-value investment programs and to select those programs that represent an optimal portfolio of business and IT investments. A VMO applies the Benefits Realization Approach, developed by DMR Consulting, to track, measure, and deliver business value, while adjusting the portfolio composition to take advantage of new knowledge, new opportunities, and innovation.

No Surprises—but Machiavelli?

No one knows for sure what surprises CRM initiatives may bring. Future relationships are, after all, in the future—and constantly changing. But, as Niccolo Machiavelli wrote in *The Prince* (1532), the future can be contained by taking the right actions now—like shoring up the banks of a levee so the river will be channeled down the right course when the rainy season comes. Good management, after all, is largely about foresight and taking the actions required to leverage opportunities and to prevent future problems. At the same time, managers must leave room for improvisation because the dynamics of business are a fast-flowing current. Testing customer relationships can prepare an organization for the uncertain future.

Machiavelli offers the following warning to the "manager" of his day: "There is nothing more difficult to take in hand, more perilous to conduct, or more uncertain in its success, than to take the lead in the introduction of a new order of things."

For the managers in a Relationship-Based Enterprise, or any manager in need of CRM success, this warning still rings true. The approach described in this chapter—of stepping mentally outside the enterprise to understand the "tough customer" and then stepping back inside the enterprise with equally tough program management guidelines—is one way to reduce the risk inherent in introducing a "new order of things."

The end result should be a *climate and direction-setting process* that will create simple pictures of where relationships are headed and what CRM needs to become. This vision should be one that the organization has worked through and understands. As with all visioning exercises, this "working through" is essential to creating a company's own explicit and implicit language with which to talk about CRM.

BIBLIOGRAPHY

Books

Anderson, Paul, and Art Rosenberg. *The Executive's Guide to Customer Relationship Management.* Houston: Doyle Publishing Company, Houston, 2000.

Anton, Jon. *Customer Relationship Management: Making Hard Decisions with Soft Numbers.* New Jersey: Prentice Hall, 1996.

Brandenburger, Adam M., and Barry J. Nalebuff. *Co-opetition.* New York: Doubleday, 1998.

Brown, Stanley A. *Strategic Customer Care, An Evolutionary Approach to Increasing Customer Value and Profitability.* Toronto: John Wiley & Sons Canada Limited, 1999.

Curry, Jay. *The Customer Marketing Method : How to Implement and Profit from Customer Relationship Management.* New York: Free Press, 2000.

Cusack, Michael. *Online Customer Care: Strategies for Call Center Excellence.* Milwaukee: ASQ Quality Press, 1998.

Forsyth, Patrick. *Communicating With Customers.* London: Orion Business Tollkit, 1999.

Gallagher, Roger W., and Raymond E. Kordupleski. *Customer Value Management.* New Zealand: The CVA Collection, 1999.

Hagel, John, and Arthur G. Armstrong. *Net Gain: Expanding Markets Through Virtual Communities.* New York: McGraw-Hill, 1997.

Hagel, John, and Marc Singer. *Net Worth: Shaping Markets When Customers Make the Rules.* New York: Harvard Business School Publishing, 1999.

Hanan, Mack, and Peter Karp. *Competing on Value.* New York: AMACOM, 1991.

Heskett, James L., and Earl W. Sasser. *The Service Profit Chain: How Leading Companies Link Profit and Growth to Loyalty, Satisfaction, and Value.* New York: Free Press, 1997.

Isaacs, William. *Dialogue and the Art of Thinking Together: A Pioneering Approach to Communicating in Business and in Life.* New York: Doubleday, 1999.

Johnson, Thomas H. *Relevance Regained: From Top-Down Control to Bottom-Up Empowerment.* New York: Free Press, 1992.

Johnson, Thomas H., and Robert S. Kaplan. *Relevance Lost: The Rise and Fall of Management Accounting.* New York: Harvard Business School Press, 1987.

Kaplan, Robert S., and David P. Norton. *The Balanced Scorecard: Translating Strategy into Action.* Boston: Harvard Business School Press, 1996.

Kawasaki, Guy. *Rules for Revolutionaries.* New York: HarperBusiness, 1999.

Kay, John. *The Foundation of Corporate Success: How Business Strategies Add Value.* Oxford (U.K.): Oxford University Press, 1993.

Kelly, Suzanne, and Mary Ann Allison. *The Complexity Advantage.* New York: McGraw-Hill, 1998.

Lessig, Lawrence. *Code: And Other Laws of Cyberspace.* New York: Basic Books, 1999.

Levine, Rick, Christopher Locke, *et al. The Cluetrain Manifesto: The End of Business as Usual.* Cambridge, Massachusetts: Perseus Books, 1999.

Martin, Chuck. *Net Future: The 7 Cybertrends That Will Drive Your Business, Create Wealth, and Define Your Future.* New York: McGraw-Hill, 1998.

Mintzberg, Henry. *Structure in Fives: Designing Effective Orgainzations.* Englewood Cliffs, NJ: Prentice-Hall, 1993.

Newell, Frederick. *Loyalty.com: Customer Relationship Management in the New Era of Internet Marketing.* New York: McGraw-Hill, 2000.

Papows, Jeff, and David Moschella. *Enterprise.Com: Market Leadership in the Information Age.* New York: Perseus Books, 1998.

Pine II, Joseph B. *Mass Customization, The New Frontier in Business Competition.* New York: Harvard Business School Press, 1999.

Pine II, Joseph B., and James H. Gilmore. James H. *The Experience Economy: Work Is Theatre and Every Business a Stage.* New York: Harvard Business School, 1999.

Ries, Al, and Laura Ries. *The 22 Immutable Laws of Branding: How to Build a Product or Service into a World-Class Brand.* New York: Harper Business, 1998.

Rogers, Martha, and Don Peppers. *Enterprise One to One: Tools for Competing in the Interactive Age.* New York: Doubleday, 1999.

Seybold, Patricia B. *Customers.com: How to Create a Profitable Business Strategy for the Internet and Beyond.* New York: Random House, 1998.

Shapiro, Andrew L. *The Control Revolution, How the Internet is Putting Individuals in Charge and Changing the World We Know.* New York: A Century Foundation Book, 1999.

Sherman, Howard, and Ron Scultz. *Open Boundaries, Creating Business Innovation Through Complexity.* New York: Harper Collins, 1998.

Siebel, Thomas M., and Pat House. *Cyber Rules: Strategies for Excelling at E-Business.* New York: Currency Doubleday, 1999.

Slywotzky, Adrian J., David J. Morrison, *et al. Profit Patterns: 30 Ways to Anticipate and Profit from Strategic Forces Reshaping Your Business.* New York: Random House, 1999.

Sterne, Jim. *Customer Service on the Internet: Building Relationships Increasing Loyalty and Staying Competitive.* New York: John Wiley & Sons, Inc, 1996.

Tapscott, Don. *Blueprint to the Digital Economy: Creating Wealth in the Era of e-business.* New York: McGraw-Hill, 1999.

Tapscott, Don. *Creating Value in the Network Economy.* Boston: Harvard Business Review, 1999.

Tapscott, Don, Alex Lowy, *et al. Blueprint to the Digital Economy, Creating Wealth in the Era of E-Business.* New York: McGraw-Hill, 1999.

Thorp, John. *The Information Paradox: Realizing the Business Benefits of Information Technology.* Toronto: McGraw-Hill Ryerson, 1999.

Wellemin, John. *Successful Customer Care.* New York: Barron's Educational Series, 1997.

Periodicals

Albert, Bill. "Software Hardball," *Barron's*, August 23, 1999, 18.

Anderson, James C., and James A. Narus. "Business Marketing: Understand What Customers Value," *Harvard Business Review*, November–December 1998, 69-76.

Anthony J. Rucci, Stephen P. Kirn, and Richard T. Quinn. "The Employee-Customer-Profit Chain at Sears," *Harvard Business Review*, January–February 1998, 1-16.

Beckett-Camarata, Elizabeth Jane, Martin R. Camarata, Randolphe T. Barker. "Integrating Internal and External Customer Relationships through Relationship Management: A Strategic a Changing Global Environment," *Journal of Business Research*, January 1998, 71-81.

Beer, Michael. "Organizational Fitness: The Context for Successful Balanced Scorecard Programs," *Harvard Business Review Report*, September 15, 1999, 1-5.

"Business and the Internet, the Net Imperative," *The Economist*, June 1999, 199-208, 5-40.

Cooper, Robin, and Bruce W. Chew. "Control Tomorrow's Costs Through Today's Designs," *Harvard Business Review*, January–February, 1996, 79-86.

Craig, Robert. "The Evolution of CRM Applications," *ENT*, February 17, 1999, 32.

Cross, Kim. "B-to-B, By the Numbers," *Business 2.0*, September, 1999, 40-41.

Evans, Philip, and Thomas S. Wurster. "The Strategy and The New Economics of Information," *Harvard Business Review*, September 1997, 78-85.

Fournier, Susan, Susan Dobscha, *et al.* "Preventing the Premature Death of Relationship Marketing," *Harvard Business Review*, January–February 1998, 1-8.

Gemmer, Art. "Risk Management: Moving Beyond Process," *IEEE Software*, May 1997, 33-43.

Geyskens, Inge, Jan-Benedict E.M. Steenkamp, *et al.* "A Meta Analysis of Satisfaction in Marketing Channel Relationships," *Journal of Marketing Research*, Vol. 36, May 1999, 223-38.

Gilmore, James H., and Joseph B. Pine. "The Four Faces of Mass Customization," *Harvard Business Review*, January–February, 1997, 91-101.

Haeckel, Stephan H., and Thomas S. Nolan. "Managing by Wire," *Harvard Business Review*, September 1993, 65-72.

Hall, Richard. "Rearranging Risks and Rewards in a Supply Chain," *Journal of General Management*, Vol. 24, No. 3 (1999), 22-32.

Hamel, Gary, and C. K. Prahalad. "Competing for the future," *Harvard Business Review*, July 1994, 60-81.

Hoffman, Thomas. "Bank System Keeps Heavy-Hitters Happy: Customer Relationship Management Tailors Info Delivery to Client," *Computerworld*, February 22, 1999, 22-25.

Kaplan, Robert S. "Can Bad Things Happen to Good Scorecards?" *Harvard Business Review Report*, September 15, 1999, 1-4.

Kaplan, Robert S., and David P. Norton. "Building a Strategy-Focused Organization," *Harvard Business Review Report*, September 15, 1999, 1-7.

Kaplan, Robert S., and David P. Norton. "Using the Balanced Scorecard as a Strategic Management System," *Harvard Business Review*, January–February, 1996, 75-78.

Kaplan, Robert S., and Mohanbir Sawhney. "E-Hubs: The New B2B Marketplaces," *Harvard Business Review*, May–June 2000, 97-103.

Kim, Chan W., and Renee A. Mauborgne, "Value Innovation: The Strategic Logic of High Growth," *Harvard Business Review*, January–February, 1997, 66-79.

Kolesar, Peter, Garret Van Ryzin, *et al.* "Creating Customer Value Through Industrialized Intimacy," *Strategy and Business*, Third Quarter, 1998, 33-43.

Lapierre, Jozee, Filiatrault, *et al.* "Value Strategy Rather than Quality Strategy: A Case of Business-to-Business Professional Services," *Journal of Business Research*, 45, 1999, 235-46.

Magretta, Joan. "The Power of Virtual Integration: An Interview with Dell Computer's Michael Dell," *Harvard Business Review*, March–April 1998, 90-106.

Mingail, Sandra. "Fishing for Surfers," *Financial Post*, September 20, 1999, E2.

Mintzberg, Henry, "The Fall and Rise of Strategic Planning," *Harvard Business Journal*, January–February 1994, 107-114.

Ostermeyer, David C. "Great Expectations: What Customer Access and Convenience Mean Today," *Mutual Fund Service Guides*, No. 01, 1999, 10-11.

Peppers, Don, and Martha Rogers. "Staying in Touch with Customers," *CIO Enterprise Magazine*, September, 1998, 18-21.

Prahalad, C. K., and M. S. Krishman. "The New Meaning of Quality in the Information Age," *Harvard Business Review*, September–October, 1999, 109-18.

Prahalad, C. K., Venkatram Ramaswamy. "Co-opting Customer Competence," *Harvard Business Review*, January–February, 2000, 79-82.

Prahalad, C. K., Venkatram Ramaswamy, *et al.* "Consumer Centricity," *InformationWeek*, April 10, 2000, 67-76.

Rayport, Jeffrey E., and John J. Svokla. "Managing in the Marketplace," *Harvard Business Review*, November–December 1994, 73-81.

Seybold, Patricia B. "Niches Bring Riches," *Business 2.0*, June 13, 135-36.

Spekman, Robert E., John W. Kamauff, Jr., *et al.* "An Empirical Investigation into Supply Chain Management: A Perspective on Partnerships," *Supply Chain Management*, Vol. 3, No. 2, 53-67.

Stuart, Linda. "Is CRM a High Priority?" *CIO Canada*, May 2000, 50-56.

Sweat, Jeff. "Fast Focus on Web CRM," *InformationWeek*, May 15, 2000, 22-24.

Sweat, Jeff. "The Well-Rounded Consumer," *InformationWeek*, April 10, 2000, 44-52.

Sweat, Jeff. "Front-Office Shake-Up," *InformationWeek*, October 18, 1999, 22-24.

Tapscott, Don, David Ticoll, *et al.* "Relationship Rule," *Business 2.0*, May 2000, 300-319.

Tapscott, Don, David Ticoll, *et al.* "The Rise of the Business Web," *Business 2.0*, November 1999, 199-208.

Ward, Scott, Larry Light, *et al.* "What High-Tech Managers Need to Know about Brands," *Harvard Business Review*, July–August 1999, 81-90.

Werbach, Kevin. "Syndication: The Emerging Model for Business in the Internet Era," *Harvard Business Review*, May–June, 2000, 85-93.

Wise, Richard, and Peter Baumgartner. "Go: Downstreams: The New Profit Imperative in Manufacturing," *Harvard Business Review*, September–October 1999, 75-89.

Woodside, Arch G., Daniel P. Sullivan, *et al.* "Assessing Relationships among Strategic Types, Distinctive Marketing Competencies, and Organizational Performance," *Journal of Business Research*, 45, 1999, 135-46.

Internet

Abell, Derek F. *Competing Today While Preparing for Tomorrow*, Spring 1999, Volume 40, No. 3.
[On-line: http://mitsloan.mit.edu/smr/past/1999/smr4037.html]

AT&T, *AT&T to Create Family of Four New Companies; Company to Offer to Exchange AT&T Common Stock for AT&T Wireless Stock*. News Release from AT&T Press Room, New York, October 25, 2000.
[Online: http://www.att.com/press/item/0,1354,3420,00.html]

Banco Central Hispano: Implementing Customer Relationship Management in Retail Financial
[On-line: http://www.crm-forum.com/crm_forum_case_studies/bch.htm]

Bennett, Jeffery W. *Constrained Change — Unconstrained Results*, Third Quarter, 1998. [On-line: http://www.strategy-business.com/strategy/98303/page1.html]

Caufield, Simon. *Does Customer Relationship Management Really Pay?* [On-line: http://www.crm-forum.com/crm_forum_white_papers/dpay/ppr.htm]

Collins, Steve, and Mike Byrne. *Implementing CRM at a European Telco*, 1999. [On-line: http://www.crm-forum.com/crm_forum_case_studies/sca/ppr.htm]

Cooper, Robin, and Regine Slagmulder. *Develop Profitable New Products with Target Costing*, Spring 1999, Volume 40, No. 4. [On-line: http://mitsloan.mit.edu/smr/past/1999/smr4042.html]

Cross, Richard, and Janet Smith. *The Customer Value Chain*, January, February 1997. [On-line: http://www.demographics.com/publications/mt/97_mt/9701m14.htm]

Goldenberg, Barton. *Customer Relationship Management: What Is It All About?* 1999 [On-line: http://www.crm-forum.com/crm_forum_white_papers/wiiaa/ppr.htm]

Goth, Nikki Itoi. *Syndicating the Web*, Red Herring, 1999. [On-line: http://www.redherring.com/mag.issue63/news-syndication.html]

Heygate, Richard. *Harnessing Technology to Win Customer Loyalty*, November 1997. [On-line: http://www.crm-forum.com/crm_forum_white_papers/htcl/ppr.htm]

Kim, Chan W., and Renee Mauborgne. *Strategy, Value Innovation, and the Knowledge Economy*, Spring 1999, Volume 40, No. 3. [On-line: http://mitsloan.mit.edu/smr/past/1999/smr4034.html]

Kirsner, Scott. *The Customer Experience*, Net Company, Fall 1999 [On-line: http://www.fastcompany.com]

Makelainen, Esa. Helsinki School of Economics and Business Administration, *Economic Value Added as a Management Tool*, 1998. [On-line: http://www.evanomics.com]

Meltzer, Michael. *What Consumers Value* [On-line: http://www.crm-forum.com/crm_forum_white_papers/wcv/ppr.htm]

Puckey, David. *Modelling Customer Relationships* [On-line: http://www.crm-forum.com/crm_forum_white_papers/mcr/ppr.htm]

Sproul, Bill. *CRM, Customer Service and Workflow in the Call Centre*, 1999 [On-line: http://www.crm-forum.com/crm_forum_white_papers/ccsw/ppr.htm]

Thearling, Kurt. *Increasing Customer Value by Integrating Data Mining and Campaign* [On-line: http://www.crm-forum.com/crm_forum_white_papers/icv/ppr.htm]

The Associated Press and Knight Ridder Newspapers. "Still Undecided? Read Up," *The Seattle Times*, November 5, 2000. [On-line: http://www.archives. seattletimes.nwsouce.com/cgi-bin/texas/web/vortex/display?slug=stand 05+date=20001105+query=Bush+and+Gore+positions+on+technology]

INDEX